PRIMARY SOURCES IN POLITICAL THOUGHT

THOEMMES

RESPONSE TO THE PARADOXES OF MALESTROIT

Jean Bodin

Translated and edited by
Henry Tudor and R. W. Dyson

Introduction by D. P. O'Brien

Notes by J. C. M. Starkey

UNIVERSITY OF DURHAM

THOEMMES PRESS

Published by Thoemmes Press, 1997

Thoemmes Press
11 Great George Street
Bristol BS1 5RR, England

US office: Distribution and Marketing
22883 Quicksilver Drive
Dulles, Virginia 20166, USA

Hardback : ISBN 1 85506 532 0
Paperback : ISBN 1 85506 533 9

© the estate of Henry Tudor, and R. W. Dyson, 1997
Introduction © D. P. O'Brien, 1997

All rights reserved. No part of this publication may be
reproduced, stored in a retrieval system, or
transmitted in any way or by any means, electronic,
mechanical, photocopying, recording or otherwise, without
the written permission of the copyright holder.
Enquiries should be addressed to the publisher.

CONTENTS

Preface	7
Introduction	
Jean Bodin	11
The Monetary Background	14
Price Inflation	15
The Scholastic Background	17
Navarrus	18
The Emergence of Quantity Theory	20
Malestroit's Paradoxes	22
Bodin's Response	23
Bodin and the Causes of Inflation	24
The Gains From Trade	27
Gresham's Law	28
The Demand for Money	30
The Effects of Inflation	30
Remedies for Debasement	31
Bodin's Legacy	33
Bibliography	35
The Paradoxes of the Seigneur de Malestroit on the Subject of Money	39–48
First Paradox	41
Second Paradox	44
The Response of Jean Bodin, Advocate, to the Paradox of Monsieur de Malestroit Concerning the Increase in the Cost of All Things and the Means of Remedying It	49–127
For the Book on Money	49
To Monsieur Prevost, Seigneur of Morsan, President for the King in His Court of Parlement	51
Notes	129–166
Index	167–177

To the memory of Henry Tudor
(1937–1997).

PREFACE

The short pamphlet, *Les Paradoxes du Seigneur de Malestroict, Conseiller du Roy, & Maistre ordinaire de ses comptes, sur le faict des Monnoyes*, appeared in 1566. Bodin's reply, *La Response de Maistre Jean Bodin Advocat en la cour au paradoxe de Monsieur de Malestroict, touchant l'encherissement de toutes choses, & le moyen d'y remedier*, was published two years later, in 1568, by Martin le Jeune in Paris. It is commonly, and more briefly, known as his *Response to Malestroit*, and that is how we will refer to it in what follows. Bodin published a second edition in 1578 under the title, *Discours de Jean Bodin sur le rehausement et diminution des monnoyes, tant d'or que d'argent, & le moyen d'y remedier: & response aux Paradoxes de Monsieur de Malestroict*. The publisher this time was Jacques du Puys, also in Paris.

In the second edition, Bodin made a number of stylistic amendments and corrected a few factual errors. But he also made a large number of additions, the most significant of which was to incorporate in his treatise the bulk of bk. 6, chap. 3, of his *Les Six Livres de la Republique*, which had been published two years earlier. To make room for this major addition, Bodin struck out a shorter, but still substantial, passage from his first edition. He also made a number of other, less significant deletions.

The present volume is based on the first edition, but it also gives the amendments, additions and deletions which Bodin made to his second edition. We have not drawn attention to all of Bodin's stylistic amendments, most of which are trivial and virtually none of which make any difference to the sense; but we have indicated his corrections of factual errors. More importantly, we have tried to make as clear as possible the major changes that occurred between the first and second editions. The passages struck out of the first edition are therefore included but are indicated by curly brackets. The additions made to the second edition are also included but are distinguished by being enclosed in square brackets. In one or two places, this makes for discontinuity, but we hope that the reader will not find our method too confusing. Occasional editorial interventions are indicated thus < >.

The publisher, Jacques du Puy, prefaced the second edition with a letter to the reader in which he claimed that the first edition had been translated into English 'by the command of the Archbishop of Canterbury, Chancellor of England'. This is a bit odd. Elizabeth's Chancellor at the time in question was Nicholas Bacon, and he was not Archbishop of Canterbury. The Archbishop was Matthew Parker. It may be that one or other of them commanded Bodin's Treatise to be translated, but, if so, the translation was never published. Certainly no-one has managed to trace it. There is, however, an excellent translation of Bodin's treatise by G. A. Moore under the title *Response of Jean Bodin to the Paradoxes of Malestroit and the Paradoxes* (Chevy Chase, Md: Country Dollar Press, 1946). It was a 'collector's edition...limited to signed and numbered copies' and is now extremely scarce. Extensive efforts to trace the supposed sixteenth century English translation were made by Moore, who reports the results (Moore, 1948, pp. vii–ix). It must be concluded that no such translation existed. We have also been greatly helped by A. E. Monroe's translation of extracts from Bodin's treatise in his *Early Economic Thought, Selections from Economic Literature prior to Adam Smith*, (Cambridge, Mass: Harvard University Press, 1951). Finally, we should mention that there is a translation of the chapter on money which Bodin incorporated into the second edition of his treatise. It is in Richard Knolles's translation of *Les Six Livres de la Republique* published as *The Six Bookes of a Commonweale* by G. Bishop in London, 1606.

In 1932, Henri Hauser published a critical edition of Bodin's work under the title, *La Response de Jean Bodin a M. de Malestroit* (Librairie Armand Colin, Paris). It was based upon Bodin's first edition but, in addition to notes on the text and other useful apparatus, Hauser included, in appendix 2, 'Variantes et additions de l'edition de 1578'. Unfortunately, the variations and additions given by Hauser are incomplete and could possibly give a misleading impression of the contents of Bodin's second edition. The present volume includes further variations.

Bodin was writing at a time when Middle French was being transformed into what we now know as modern French. The rules of grammar and syntax had not yet been fixed, spelling had not yet been standardised, and punctuation was still devoid of any rationale. Unlike some of his distinguished contemporaries (*e.g.* Montaigne, du Bellay and Etienne Pasquier), Bodin was not interested in bringing order into this linguistic chaos. He wrote directly as he thought. His spelling is inconsistent, and he did not always feel it necessary to write in whole sentences. This, needless to say, presents the translator with certain problems. In order to convey Bodin's meaning accurately, we have sometimes had to paraphrase; and we have often had to impose an alien sentence structure on his otherwise unstructured prose. We have not followed G. A. Moore in dividing the text into headed sections, but we have tried to make the text digestible by introducing paragraph breaks, a stylistic device which Bodin despised or, at least, ignored.

In his treatise, Bodin uses a great deal of technical terminology, and this also creates problems of translation. For the most part, the terminology of, say, chemical processes or financial transactions can be translated into acceptable English. However, in the cases of weights, measures, monetary denominations, legal and political institutions, personal names and titles we have thought it best to keep the original French, except where there is a clear and generally accepted English equivalent. Thus, Monsieur de Malestroit remains as such, but Philippe le Bel becomes Philip the Fair; and '*livre*' becomes 'pound' when it indicates a weight, but is retained as '*livre*' when it is a monetary denomination. It would be tempting but misleading to translate, for instance, '*parlement*' as 'parliament' or '*denier*' as 'penny'. They and their like have therefore been left in the original French.

Henry Tudor

The initial translation of Bodin's *Response* was prepared by Henry Tudor. Unfortunately Henry died before the translation was in a final state. Dr R. W. Dyson heroically took over the task of translating, and the translation in this volume owes its present polished state to his work.

The decline in Henry's health in the months before his death also made it impossible for him to start work on the notes which, it was intended, should accompany the text. In these circumstances, Mrs Janet Starkey promised to prepare notes for him, to which he would then apply his immense knowledge of early modern France. Although he was never able to work on the notes which she completed, it was decided to include them as useful information for students, and as a pointer to the vast amount of research still required on this interesting tract. Indeed, we are indebted to Mrs Starkey for the high standards of scholarship she has brought to the work, a task that was made especially difficult by the limited time and resources available.

Apart from the crucial interventions of Dr Dyson and Mrs Starkey which enabled the project to be brought to fruition, we must extend gratitude to the interlibrary loans service of the University of Durham, without which this project could never have been undertaken. An acknowledgement is also due to Ms Lisa Harris, who worked effectively in conjunction with all concerned and set the text from its rude beginnings. Finally, two generous Chairmen of the Department of Politics – Dr Peter Stirk and Mr R. J. Williams – agreed to meet the unexpected costs entailed by the production of this book.

The dedication of this volume reflects the shared sense of loss experienced by those who knew Henry Tudor as a fine scholar and much loved teacher. It is also a tribute to his drive and initiative which not only conceived, and partially carried through, the work on this volume but also launched the series of which this volume constitutes a part.

D. P. O'Brien

INTRODUCTION

Jean Bodin

The life of Jean Bodin (1530–1596), whose seminal work is reprinted in this volume, seems to have been a turbulent one. In part this reflected the turbulence of the age in which he lived, characterised by violent and bloody conflicts over religion; but to these external forces Bodin added characteristics of his own which on at least two occasions placed his life in considerable danger.

According to the standard accounts, Jean Bodin was born at Angers in 1530 and died of the plague at Laôn in 1596. His origins are not clear, although there is a persistent – and credible – story that he was in fact the son of a Jewish mother, a circumstance which may well have bearing on the dangerous ambiguities in Bodin's later attitudes towards the competing Catholic and Protestant factions in France. At all events it now seems clear, despite the doubts expressed in the early authoritative study by Baudrillart,[1] that Bodin entered the Carmelite Order as a young man – the house of Notre Dame at Angers. He entered at about fifteen or sixteen and seems to have left at about the age of eighteen or nineteen in circumstances which suggest he narrowly escaped being burned for heresy – others were not so lucky.[2] Between 1550 and 1560 he was apparently in Toulouse, where he studied law and attempted to establish a school of classical culture attached to the legal faculty. From there he seems to have gone to Paris but to have lacked skill both as a court intriguer and as a lawyer. But he enjoyed official positions from 1568 onwards, though – once again – narrowly escaping death in the St. Bartholomew's Day Massacre. He was a magistrate at Laôn from 1576 and took part in the Assembly of the Third Estate at Blois where he argued for toleration, at no little personal risk. There is a vivid account, drawn from material written by Bodin himself, of his

---

[1] Baudrillart, H., *Jean Bodin et son temps* (Paris: Guillaumin, 1853).
[2] Tooley, J., introduction and translation of J. Bodin, *Six Books of the Commonwealth* (Oxford: Blackwell, 1955), pp. vii–viii.

proceedings at Blois.³ As a result of this episode he incurred royal displeasure; the issue was partly money, but behind this lay Bodin's opposition to the forcible resolution of religious strife.

Royal disgrace sent Bodin back to his studies, and he became attached to the Duke D'Alençon, with whom he travelled abroad – to England in about 1580, and to the Low Countries in 1583. But the Duke died in 1584 and Bodin returned to Laôn to act as a magistrate, succeeding his father-in-law Nicholas Trouillard in the legal office of Procureur Général in 1587. From regard to his own safety rather than his religious beliefs, he joined the Catholic League, and remained in it for about four years, an episode which has attracted subsequent criticism although, given the pressures and dangers which he faced, it seems entirely understandable at this distance. At all events he died within the Catholic fold and was buried in consecrated ground.

Nonetheless, it is apparent that Bodin's attitude towards religion was relativist rather than absolute. This is very clear from his philosophy of history – for him, periods of history are dominated by races rather than religions and, as MacIver⁴ has pointed out, in attacking the universalism of the Middle Ages, he adopted a relativist attitude towards religion. This also shows in his treatment of religious institutions in which he stresses the influence of climate on human behaviour. Such relativism is reflected in uncertainty about Bodin's own religious beliefs⁵ and in the spectacular evidence provided by a comparative work on religion which Bodin compiled and which would, had it ever been published in his lifetime, have cost him his life. Its existence was known by later scholars⁶ but it did not appear in any form at all until three and a half centuries after his death.

Bodin's possibly enforced departure from the religious life deprived the Catholic Church of an outstanding intellectual. But at least the abandonment of celibacy enabled France to profit from the continuation of his line, the family being ennobled in

---

³ Baudrillart, H., *op. cit.*, pp. 118–28.
⁴ MacIver, R. M., 'Bodin, Jean' in E. R. A. Seligman with Alvin Johnson (eds.), *Encyclopedia of the Social Sciences* (New York: Macmillan, 1930), vol. 2, pp. 614–16.
⁵ Reynolds, B., introduction and translation of J. Bodin, *Method for the Easy Comprehension of History* (New York: Columbia University Press, 1945), p. xxvi.
⁶ Baudrillart, H., *op. cit.*, chap. 5, pt. 2.

1654 and one of his descendants publishing an excellent book about him.⁷

Bodin's name is far more widely known to writers on history and political philosophy than it is to economists. Although the work translated in this volume is of very considerable significance in the history, of monetary thought, it is other works by which Bodin is much better known in a wider world.

The work by which he first came to public attention was his study of history, which is known in its English translation as *Method for the Easy Comprehension of History*; it was published in 1566 and became a best seller.⁸ In this work Bodin not only discusses types of historians but attempts to explain stages of history and institutions in terms of races and climates, the driving force being that history is seen as a way of understanding modern politics. Even more famous is his *Republic* which was early translated into English⁹ and which is regarded as his masterpiece. This deals with the key issue of sovereignty, as well as social justice (Bodin was a proponent of proportional taxation) and – again – climate. These works are discussed extensively and informatively in Baudrillart's nineteenth-century study. But later commentators have pointed to serious difficulties in key parts of Bodin's political philosophy. As Sabine has pointed out, Bodin had no clear theory of what it was the state was supposed to achieve, and he tried to combine an inalienable right in the family with absolute power in the state (though the Sovereign was constrained by the law of God and of nature).¹⁰

One element in all this, which was picked up by his descendant Bodin de Saint Laurent, is the importance of the concept of natural law in such diverse aspects of Bodin's work as the references to climate, the idea that differences in resource endowment give rise to trade, and community of interests among nations. In turn it is arguable that this reflects the Scholastic background, both in Bodin's time as a religious novice and in his

---

[7] Bodin de Saint. Laurent, J., *Les Ideés Monétaires et Commerciales de Jean Bodin* (Bordeaux: Cadoret, 1907; reprinted New York: Burt Franklin, 1970).
[8] Reynolds, B., *op. cit.*, p. x.
[9] Knolles, R., *Six Books of a Commonweale* (a translation of Bodin's *Republic*) (London: Bishop,1606).
[10] Sabine, G. H., *A History of Political Theory*, 3rd ed. (London: Harrap, 1951), pp. 340–53.

The Monetary Background

The background to Bodin's seminal essay the *Response to Malestroit* is the extraordinary increase in the supply of precious metals in Europe following the discovery of the New World and the exploitation of its gold and silver resources. The flood of silver from Potosi[11] ensured that silver became the predominant monetary metal and Europe effectively switched for about 200 years from a gold to a silver standard[12] as the silver spread out from Spain across Europe. In this it is important to stress the remarkable efficiency of the market mechanisms in distributing the silver and, in particular, the importance of unofficial silver channels,[13] not least because piracy was used as an official policy by Britain, France and Holland.[14]

The interpretation of the impact of this is however made difficult by a distinction which has to be drawn between the unit of account and the money in circulation. The unit of account in France, which is the subject of our concern, was the *livre tournois*. This was divided into twenty *sols* and each of the latter was divided into twelve *deniers*. France thus had a unit of account similar to that enjoyed by Britain before the introduction of decimal currency in 1973.[15] (After 1803 the *livre tournois* became the franc).[16] The *livre tournois* did not correspond to an invariable quantity of fine silver; rather, its value was fixed by royal decree in relation to the *marc* a unit of 245 grams of silver. According to calculations by the French economist Levasseur, the ratio was eleven *livre* thirteen *sol* in 1511, falling to twenty-

---

[11] Davies, G., *A History of Money* (Cardiff: University of Wales Press, 1994), pp. 187–9.
[12] Spooner, F. C., *The International Economy and Monetary Movements* (Cambridge, Mass: Harvard University Press, 1972), chap. 1.
[13] Davies, G., *op. cit.*, p. 185.
[14] See also Peronnet, M., 'De L'Or Splendeur Immortelle...' in A. Tournon and G.-A. Pérouse, *Or, Monnaie, Échange dans la Culture de la Renaissance* (St. Etienne: University of St. Etienne, 1994), p. 48.
[15] Hauser, H., ed., *La Response de Jean Bodin* (Paris: Librairie Armand Colin, 1932), p. xxvii. See also Vilar, P., *A History of Gold and Money, 1450–1920*, trans. J. White (London: NLB, 1976), pp. 178–9.
[16] Spooner, F. C., *op. cit.*, p. 90.

Introduction 15

one *livre* to the *marc* at the end of the century.[17] The unit of account was thus subject to a continual process of down-grading.

At the same time the purchasing power of silver was itself falling in relation to commodities. Although there was a bewildering variety of different kinds of money in circulation,[18] with that circulation, which included foreign money, evaluated by its metallic content, the main circulatory medium was the *écu*. This itself fell in value against the *marc* as a result of debasement. The combination of a reduction in its precious metal content and of variations in the official value of the unit of account in turn produced variations in the rate of exchange between currency and accounting money. The *écu* was worth one *livre* thirteen *sol* in 1487; by 1575 it was worth three *livre*.

At the end of the nineteenth century the course of debasement was tabulated by D'Avenel[19] and the data he provided shows that the reduction in the precious metal content of the coinage was not trivial. Detailed information later calculated by Spooner[20] showed the *écu* at around twenty-three carat going from a face value of thirty *sol* three *denier* to fifty *sol* between 1488 and 1561 and then to 200 *sol* by 1640.

However, although these variations were those on which Malestroit sought to focus, they were of subsidiary importance in relation to the change in the relative values of the precious metals and of commodities produced by the New World Discoveries.

Price Inflation

Detailed work on price inflation in France was carried out before the First and Second World Wars, notably by Hauser[21] and D'Avenel.[22] Perhaps the single most striking fact to emerge from this work is the three-fold increase in the value of land in terms

---

[17] Hauser, H., 1932, ed., *op. cit.*, p. xxviii.
[18] Bodin de Saint Laurent, J., *op. cit.*, pp. 77–8.
[19] D'Avenel, G., *Histoire Economique de la Propriété, des Salaires, des Denreés et de Tous les Prix en Général depuis l'an 1200 jusq'en l'an 1800* (Paris: Imprimerie Nationale, 1894), p. 481.
[20] Spooner, F. C., *op. cit.*, p. 330.
[21] Hauser, H., *Recherches et Documents sur l'Histoire des Prix en France de 1500 à 1800* (Paris: Les Presses Modernes, 1936).
[22] D'Avenel, G., *op. cit.*

of silver between 1526 and 1600 which D'Avenel reports.[23] The French inflation was discussed specifically within the context of Bodin's work by Hauser[24] and, drawing on the work of Levasseur, he found the price of wheat to have risen by two and a half times between 1520 and 1580. This figure came from Paris data; but, because of the system of internal barriers to trade, the French market was distinctly imperfect and price experiences in other regions differed from those of Paris. In particular, prices seem to have risen to a greater degree in some other regions. The nineteenth-century English statistician William Jacob calculated that the prices of some commodities in France rose by as much as six times during the sixteenth century, starting from the low at the end of the previous century.[25] Comparison of the estimates of inflation produced by different statisticians indicates a rise in price by a factor of around three[26] during the sixteenth century. More recent research by Phelps-Brown and Hopkins[27] has the disadvantage of being stated only in *livre tournois*, and thus only taking account of official devaluations. However this shows a huge rise in land prices (the index – 1451–75=100 – rises from 175 to 1062 between 1500 and 1600) while, with wages typically lagging behind prices, building wages rose by a factor of two and a half.

The price rise in the sixteenth century was modest by modern standards. (British prices rose nearly twenty-fold between the late 1940s and the early 1990s.) But it came after a period of falling prices at the end of the fifteenth century and followed a period, as Bodin graphically explains, in which the precious metals were in such short supply that it was difficult to raise the money to pay ransoms. This may be because successive bouts of debasement had succeeded in driving out first gold and then

---

[23] D'Avenel, G., *op. cit.*, p. 338.
[24] Hauser, H., 1932, ed., *op. cit.*, pp. xix–xxiv.
[25] Jacob, W., *op. cit.*, *An Historical Enquiry into the Production and Consumption of the Precious Metals*, 2 vols. (London: Murray, 1831), vol. 2, p. 83.
[26] Bodin de Saint Laurent, J., *op. cit.*, p. 4.
[27] Phelps-Brown, E. H. and Hopkins, S. V., 'Builders' Wage-rates, Prices and Population: some further evidence' *Economica* 27 (1959), p. 26.

silver via the operation of Gresham's Law. At all events the change in the stock of money produced a significant alteration in the trend of general prices, even though the upward climb which followed was indeed relatively modest.

It was this climb which, however, Bodin brilliantly analysed in his *Response*. But before we come to the details of his analysis we need to examine his intellectual background in rather more detail.

The Scholastic Background

As already indicated, Bodin had a considerable background in the scholastic writings, both from his novitiate and also from his time at Toulouse where the influence of the Spanish scholastic writers, the leaders in Europe at that time, was particularly in evidence. This is important because, as Schumpeter recognised in his great *History of Economic Analysis* [28] the roots of what was to become the quantity theory of money lay in the writings of the scholastic philosophers – essentially those building on the work of Thomas Aquinas (1225–1274). But it is as the pioneer, in his *Response*, of the first full statement and application of the quantity theory of money that Bodin has been seen as an important figure by later economists.

By 'the quantity theory of money' we mean, in this context, the following related propositions. First, that there is a demand for money, dependent primarily on the existing price and (national) income level. Secondly, there is a supply of money, represented in this historical context by (coined) precious metals. Thirdly, the money market clears, so that the demand for money is equal to its supply. Fourthly a disturbance to either demand or supply – in this context, an addition to the money supply is of central interest – requires an adjustment in the price level (and possibly in the level of output) to enable the money market to clear. Fifthly, and following from this, causality runs from (changes in) the money supply to (changes in) the price level.

Clearly we do not expect to find, in the earlier writers, the theory formulated in such a way that all these issues are clear.[29]

---

[28] Schumpeter, J. A., *History of Economic Analysis* (London: Allen and Unwin, 1954), p. 101.

[29] Unfortunately, Hegeland attempts to deprive Bodin of credit for the development of the quantity theory precisely on the grounds that in 1568 it

But the foundation of the whole approach is the fundamental recognition that an increase in the money supply, from whatever cause, is likely to raise the price level; and it is this recognition which we find developing amongst the later Scholastics and which was to be first fully explored by Bodin.

Amongst the scholastic writers, particular mention should be made of Nicholas Oresme, whose analysis of debasement, written about 1360,[30] paved the way for treating the value of metallic money like that of other commodities, and thus making it subject to the analysis of the Just Price.[31]

But this was a contribution which was to provide a basis for further important developments. For the scholastic analysis of the Just Price had, largely under the influence of Aquinas, developed into a form of subjective value theory in which the Just Price was one reflecting competitive market valuation (the qualification 'competitive' is important, since both fraud and monopoly were ruled out). The Just Price thus reflected relative scarcity. So an analysis of value in which relative scarcity was the key became established in the universities of late medieval and Renaissance Europe, especially in the seventeenth-century Spanish writers whose influence on Bodin is more or less direct.[32] The writer who is most important in this story and to whom we now turn actually taught at Toulouse.

Navarrus

Martín de Azpilcueta Navarro (1493–1586) taught Canon law at Toulouse and Cahors before becoming a leading member of the

---

was not as fully worked out as it was in later centuries. Hegeland also makes the baseless claim that Bodin believed 'that the price level was solely a function of the quantity of money', Hegeland, H., *The Quantity Theory of Money* (Göteborg: Elanders Boktryckeri, 1951), p. 37n. See also *ibid.* p. 153.

[30] Extracted in Monroe, A. E., ed., *Early Economic Thought. Selections from Economic Literature prior to Adam Smith* (Cambridge, Mass: Harvard University Press, 1951), pp. 81–102.

[31] O'Brien, G., *An Essay on Mediaeval Economic Teaching* (London: Longman, 1920), pp. 145–55; Gordon, B., *Economic Analysis before Adam Smith* (London: Macmillan, 1975), pp. 188–95. See also Monroe, A. E., *Monetary Theory before Adam Smith* (1924; reprinted New York: A. M. Kelley, 1966), p. 26, on Antonine.

[32] Dempsey, B. W., 'The Historical Emergence of Quantity Theory', *Quarterly Journal of Economics* 50 (1935), pp. 174–84.

School of Salamanca.[33] Marjorie Grice-Hutchinson has claimed that the first clear statement of the quantity theory of money is to be found in the work by Navarrus *Comentario Resolutorio de Usuras* dated 1556.[34] After explaining that relative scarcity determines the value of money, which he says is a well established opinion 'common to all men, good and evil, throughout Christendom', and that money is a commodity subject to the same analysis of relative scarcity as other commodities, Navarrus goes on:

> Third, that (other things being equal) in countries where there is a great scarcity of money all other saleable goods, and even the hands and labour of men, are given for less money than where it is abundant. Thus we see by experience that in France, where money is scarcer than in Spain, bread, wine, cloth, and labour are worth much less. And even in Spain, in times when money was scarcer, saleable goods and labour were given for very much less than after the discovery of the Indies, which flooded the country with gold and silver. The reason for this is that money is worth more where and when it is scarce than where and when it is abundant.[35]

Thus Navarrus recognised that the value of money varies, and, correspondingly, its purchasing power is inversely related to its available supply. Note also, however, that – as a writer experienced in both France and Spain – Navarrus does *not* claim that Purchasing Power Parity exists; the slow spread of the precious metals throughout the European economies ensured that this could only be a very long run equilibrium proposition.

There is no doubt that Jean Bodin was exposed to the influence of these ideas. As already noted, Bodin indeed studied for the priesthood, and was thus exposed to Scholastic

---

[33] Grice-Hutchinson, M., *The School of Salamanca: Readings in Spanish monetary theory 1544–1605* (Oxford: Clarendon Press, 1952), p. 45; Gordon, B., *op. cit.*, p. 203.

[34] Grice-Hutchinson, M., *op. cit.*, pp. 52, 95; Grice-Hutchinson, M., *Early Economic Thought in Spain, 1177–1740* (London: Allen and Unwin, 1978), p. 95.

[35] Extracted in Grice-Hutchinson, M., 1952, *op. cit.*, pp. 94–5.

philosophy, although he abandoned his training. He also studied civil law at Toulouse, where Navarrus had taught.[36] Indeed, according to one source, Bodin actually lectured at Toulouse.[37] However, it was established in the 1960s by H. W. Spiegel that there was a twenty-five year gap between Navarrus leaving Toulouse and Bodin arriving.[38] There is thus no question of Bodin having been directly taught by Navarrus. At the same time it is inconceivable that he would not have been aware of the contribution of a major thinker who had taught at the institution only slightly earlier, at a time when the corpus of academic ideas was evolving only slowly.

The Emergence of the Quantity Theory

It is generally recognised that the quantity theory of money emerged in the second half of the sixteenth century. The objective priority of Copernicus – not merely an immortal astronomer but a currency adviser to governments who explained, in 1522, the basic idea of a quantity theory – is widely recognised.[39] But it really was nothing more than the basic idea that 'money usually depreciates when it becomes too abundant'[40] and it is highly unlikely, as Hauser has pointed out, that Bodin owed anything to Copernicus. While he clearly knew the name of Copernicus, and while he does indeed refer elsewhere in his writings to Copernicus's astronomical theories, it is most improbable that he was familiar with the monetary writings of an author whose astronomical writings were themselves strongly contested.[41] Moreover, there was no need for Bodin to have read Copernicus; everything which he required was either in, or could have been developed from, the scholastic writings with which he was certainly familiar.

Nonetheless, Copernicus can claim objective priority. Mention should also be made of Nöel du Fail who drew attention to the

---

[36] Franklin, J. H., 'Bodin, Jean' in D. L. Sills (ed.), *International Encyclopedia of the Social Sciences* (New York: Macmillan, 1968), vol. 3, pp. 110–12; Hauser, H., 1932, ed., pp. xxxvi–xliii.

[37] MacIver, *op. cit.*

[38] Spiegel, H. W., *The Growth of Economic Thought*, 3rd ed. (Durham, N. C: Duke University Press, 1991), pp. 90, 702.

[39] *Ibid.*, pp. 86–8.

[40] Grice-Hutchinson, M., 1952, *op. cit.*, p. 34.

[41] Hauser, H., ed., 1932, *op. cit.*, p. xlvi.

effects of the inflow of treasure rather earlier than Bodin.[42] His work is dated 1548, which would also give him some priority over Bodin.[43] Again, however, there is no evidence that Bodin owed anything to du Fail; rather his own comprehensive treatment was developed from the Scholastic intellectual background *combined with* an exemplary concern with the available data.

In general, Bodin's achievement, albeit on a Scholastic foundation, is recognised by leading commentators in the field such as Monroe.[44] Yet, for the most part his important development of these ideas, while recognised, has not been the subject of much research by English speaking authors. There has, however, been significant research effort both in France and in Germany; the French contribution to an evaluation of Bodin's work itself has been notable, including the work of Baudrillart,[45] Bodin de Saint-Laurent,[46] and Hauser.[47] The German contribution has focused more upon the precious metal inflation experienced and on the economic background against which Bodin was writing. Comprehensive references will be found in Spiegel[48] and in Hauser's introduction to Bodin's *Response*.[49]

Bodin's analysis was developed, initially at least, as a critique of two 'paradoxes' put forward by a M. Malestroit of whom not a great deal was known,[50] although later research has identified him as Jean Cherruies (or Cherruier, the signature is not clear), lord of Mallestoit, amongst the *conseillers-maîtres des comptes* 1562–1568, who from 1569 held an important financial office in

---

[42] Bodin de Saint-Laurent, J., *op. cit.*, pp. 34–5.
[43] As Bodin de Saint Laurent points out, what du Fail offered was a perception, not a developed argument (*ibid*, p. 35). There is in any case some doubt over the dating of the relevant material in du Fail – see Harsin, P., *Les Doctrines Monétaires et Financières en France du XVIe au XVIIIe Siècle* (Paris: Félix Alcan, 1928), p. 40, n. 1.
[44] Monroe, A. E., 1924, *op. cit.*, pp. 46–7.
[45] Baudrillart, H., *op. cit.*.
[46] Bodin de Saint-Laurent, J., *op. cit.*.
[47] Hauser, H., 1932, ed., *op. cit.*.
[48] Spiegel, H. W., *op. cit.*, pp. 700–703.
[49] Hauser, H., 1932, ed., *op. cit.*, pp. vii–lxxvii.
[50] *Ibid*, pp. xxiv–xxv.

Brittany, dying by 1578.[51] To understand Bodin's starting point, it is thus necessary to examine the 'paradoxes', with which he prefaces his *Response* to them.

Malestroit's Paradoxes

The essence of Malestroit's first paradox is that although prices have risen in terms of the debased currency, they have not risen at all in terms of the precious metals. Thus, while Malestroit concedes that there appears to have been a remarkable rise in prices, he claims that this is simply because the unit of account has changed through debasement. No prices have gone up *in terms of the precious metals* in the last 300 years (p. 41). He bases this claim primarily upon another claim concerning the steadiness of the price of velvet in terms of precious metal, after allowing for changes in the precious metal content of the currency, although he extends the claim to perishable commodities such as corn and wine.

His second 'paradox' – 'That a significant loss can be made on an *écu* or other gold and silver money, although it is paid out at the same price as that at which it was received' (p.44) – seems incomprehensible; but the essence of the argument turns out to be that rents *specified in silver* now exchange for less gold than they used to. This is because the rents are specified in silver *coinage* which has become debased.

Exactly what Malestroit was hoping to achieve by the publication of these 'paradoxes' is not clear. It is, however, apparent that, in advancing them, he was employing a rhetorical technique which has much in common with that which was later employed by the English economist Sir William Petty and, in turn, satirised by Swift.[52] In essence this technique involves describing in words a simple algebraic relationship involving ratios and then employing, as if by sleight of verbal hand, a ratio implied but not specified by the verbal exposition. Thus, let s/v be the silver price of velvet and s/g the silver price of gold. Then the ratio

---

[51] Servet, J.-M., 'Les Paradoxes des *Paradoxes* de Malestroit' in A. Tournon and G.-A. Pérouse, *Or, Monnaie, Échange dans la Culture de la Renaissance* (St. Etienne: University of St. Etienne, 1994), pp. 73–4.

[52] Letwin, W. O., *The Origins of Scientific Economics* (London: Methuen, 1963), pp. 128–40.

$\dfrac{s/v}{s/g}$ yields $\dfrac{g}{v}$, the gold price of velvet, without this being specified directly. It is easy to imagine the impression of expertise which this must have produced in the minds of those unfamiliar with such calculations in mid sixteenth-century France.

Bodin's Response

Bodin was able to dismiss this performance without much difficulty. Despite Malestroit's confident use of what he claimed to be the price of velvet, Bodin advanced cogent reasons for doubting whether velvet was even known in fourteenth-century France (pp. 53–4). Aware as he was that inflation had spread throughout Europe (p. 57), he pointed to a rise in prices in terms of the debased silver currency by a factor of twenty, basing this upon records to which he had access. This was far in excess of the five-fold depreciation which Malestroit had recorded. In terms of gold currency, the price of corn had risen by a factor of two (p. 55).

Despite the employment of data from price records, it is clear that Bodin had immediately encountered a problem which continued to dog economists until the popularisation of index numbers by William Stanley Jevons in the late nineteenth century.[53] Like a number of economists, he decided that the price of land – as reflecting the price of a range of commodities – would provide a good measure of depreciation. It was fixed in amount and of constant fertility in France (p. 55). The price of land had trebled in the last fifty years, in terms of gold coin; the gold content of the *écu* had only fallen by ten per cent, and thus the implied inflation was around 2.7 times (p. 56).

However, Bodin is not obviously consistent in his measures of depreciation. At a later stage we find him referring to a rise in the price of property, after correction for debasement, of 3.5 times (this was in terms of gold) (pp. 79–83), and at one point we even find the extraordinary claim that Crown lands are now worth as much in rental as they were once worth in outright

---

[53] Jevons, W. S., *A Serious Fall in the Value of Gold Ascertained and its Social Effects Set Forth* (London: Stanford, 1863).

purchase price. On the face of it this, employing the standard mathematics of the value of a perpetual flow, and assuming that the French Crown could borrow at four per cent, implies a twenty-five-fold rise in price.[54] The argument, however, becomes comprehensible when one recognises that rents were specified in silver coinage, and that Bodin's calculation allows *both* for the debasement of the silver coinage *and* the fall in the value of silver itself. (Confusingly, this claim is embedded in a discussion most of which centres around a three-fold rise in the price of land in terms of *gold* currency).

Once clarified in this way it becomes apparent that Bodin's basic estimate of inflation was somewhere in excess of 2.5 times. This was not unreasonable, and we find support for his interpretation of the data by later, and much more systematic, researches, as reported by Hauser.[55]

Bodin had thus established that there was more to the problem of inflation than simple debasement of the silver currency, as Malestroit claimed. In itself this is interesting, and a tribute to his grasp of the data which, as becomes apparent in his later discussion of coinage and exchange rates, was quite remarkable.[56] But the key interest lies in his analysis of the causes of this inflation.

Bodin and the Causes of Inflation

Bodin lists five main causes of inflation (p. 59). These are:
1. 'the abundance of gold and silver, which is greater in this kingdom today than it has been in the last 400 years.'
2. Monopolies.
3. 'scarcity which is caused both by the export trade and by waste'.
4. Fashionable demand for luxuries.
5. Debasement.

In Bodin's expressed view, the first cause was by far the most important. The lessons of history – and Bodin was prodigiously

---

[54] Chiang, A. C., *Fundamental Methods of Mathematical Economics*, 3rd ed. (London: Mc Graw Hill, 1984), pp. 462–64.
[55] Hauser, H., 1932, ed., *op. cit.*, p. xx.
[56] Bodin's methodology is discussed in detail by Baudrillart, H., *op. cit.*, pp. 145–68.

well read – demonstrated this clearly (pp. 59–60). The value of the precious metals depended (as in the Scholastic analysis) on relative scarcity, and the relative scarcity of both gold and silver had changed significantly, as evidenced by the fact that in past centuries it had not even been possible to raise royal ransoms in precious metals, whereas precious metals could now be obtained without difficulty. The difficulties of raising revenue experienced by the French Crown had now disappeared.

> If Monsieur de Malestroit consults the records of the *Chambre*, he will agree with me that more gold and silver has been found in France to meet the needs of the king and the commonwealth between 1515 and 1568 than could be found in the previous 200 years. (p. 63)

The reason for this extraordinary turn around lay in a dramatic improvement in the French balance of payments. In part this arose because of an improvement in the terms of trade, resulting from the Portuguese expansion eastwards, which enabled France to buy the products of the East on much better terms than those at which trade with the Italians, who previously monopolised this trade, were conducted. In addition to this the Spaniards were paying for French agricultural output in gold and silver. Furthermore, there was a flow of precious metal from northern Europe in exchange for French agricultural output and, in particular, for salt. The increase in agricultural output because of peace had enabled the French agricultural sector to thrive and to find export markets. The New World treasure flowing in from Peru to Europe since 1533 had thus found its way into France (pp. 62–5).

The improvement in the current account was matched by an inflow on capital account to service the French public sector deficit – the French Crown offered high interest rates and the City of Paris granted annuities at very favourable implied interest rates. This seemed to Bodin a healthy development, and he believed that there was scope for further development of banking which would strengthen this capital inflow.

Compared with the influx of gold and silver (and Bodin was quite clear that commodity arbitrage was incomplete, so that one country could experience significant inflation at a rate different from that experienced by its trading partners), the other causes which he lists he clearly regarded as being of minor importance. Goods and labour monopolies were already restricted by law (p. 68). It was true that exports both reduced aggregate supply and increased aggregate demand (because corn was paid for in precious metal); but Bodin who, as we shall see, had a very advanced view of the benefits of trade, clearly did not attach much importance to this, at least as a long run cause of inflation. Nor did he attach much importance to the fashions for luxury goods, at least as a cause of inflation. (What is however extremely interesting is that, in the analysis of this aspect (pp. 69–72), he consistently employed the analysis of relative scarcity, which underlay both his development of the quantity theory and the preceding Scholastic analysis of the Just Price.)

Coupled with the analysis of luxuries was a discussion of the role of fashion and of extravagance in the use of materials. While Bodin clearly regarded this as distasteful, he did not believe that it offered an explanation for sustained inflation.

Bodin pays some attention to his fifth cause, debasement. Not only was this a significant feature of monetary history, but, as we have already seen, Malestroit himself had attributed all the price rises to debasement. However, Bodin did not accept either that debasement was the fundamental problem (if it were, it would have left the relative values of commodities and of the precious metals unchanged) or that Malestroit's account of debasement was correct. Displaying a remarkable command of the complexities of the history of French currency,[57] Bodin was able to demonstrate both that Malestroit was not well informed and also that he had used his data very selectively, choosing particular years in order to establish his case.

> It is, therefore, a mistake to take as the basis of our calculations a year when money was strongest and to set aside the years when money was weakest, which were incomparably more frequent than the good years. (p. 79).

---

[57] These complexities are discussed in Bodin de Saint Laurent, J., *op. cit.*, pp. 74–93.

Bodin's estimate of depreciation was ten, twelve, or even twenty-fold (pp. 80–81), rather than the five-fold conceded by Malestroit as resulting from debasement. But debasement was not the end of the story; the precious metals themselves had, through trade, become relatively less scarce.

The Gains From Trade

An interesting aspect of this argument – and one which undoubtedly led Bodin to play down the importance of exports (his third cause) in raising prices, at least in the short term, was his appreciation – during an era of mercantilism in the most mercantilist country in Europe – of the benefits of trade. Indeed, it was this which was later to occasion the plaudits of the nineteenth-century economist J. R. McCulloch, who had apparently been alerted to Bodin's liberal views on trade by the 1853 work of Baudrillart.[58]

The Doctors of the early church were rather uneasy about trade; but from Aquinas onwards there was an acceptance that trade was a legitimate form of economic activity.[59] Given his background in the Scholastic writings, Bodin would have been well aware of this. It is still remarkable, however, to find his emphasis on the wealth-creating effects of trade. He believed that because France was now able to trade with the Near East directly, this had increased the wealth of France (p. 66); and he argued, as economists were to do in the 1950s,[60] that trade made available goods which would not otherwise be obtainable.

> God has with admirable foresight made provision, for He has distributed His favours in such a way that there is no country in the world so well provided for as not to lack many things. (p. 86)

Indeed trade had the great advantage that it bound nations together in mutual benefit. Trade need not raise the price level at all since imports could reduce shortages (though this would not,

---

[58] McCulloch, J. R., *A Catalogue of Books, The Property of a Political Economist* (London: privately printed, 1862), p. 37.
[59] O'Brien, G., *op. cit.*, pp. 145–150.
[60] Kravis, I., 'Availibility and Other Influences on the Commodity Composition of Trade', *Journal of Political Economy* 64 (1956), pp.143–55.

of course, happen where a country was running a balance of payments surplus as was the case with France at the time of writing). Bodin is not entirely consistent in his treatment of trade and, in particular, in his recognition of its benefits. While his suggestion of export duties (pp. 88–89) is also to be found amongst nineteenth-century English economists,[61] he was still capable of decrying imports from Italy as unnecessary, especially given French natural resources (p. 69) and as involving luxurious trivia. But then Bodin had a somewhat low opinion of Italians; while expounding the benefits of trade, and arguing that foreigners should be treated with kindness, he made an exception for rogues from Italy (p. 86).

Gresham's Law

The proposition which is known as Gresham's Law owes its name to the late nineteenth-century British economist H. D. MacLeod. In fact the idea is not to be found in the passage of Gresham which he quotes[62] and one commentator has stated the matter bluntly, 'MacLeod was endowed with a marvelous ability for reading into a text what is not there'.[63] The idea in fact goes back to Aristophenes's play *The Frogs*. Given the familiarity of the Scholastic writers with Greek literature, it is hardly surprising that the same proposition is to be found not merely in the work of Oresme but well before him.[64]

The proposition itself is fundamental to a currency containing more than one precious metal. It is that, *given a fixed ratio of value between the two metals* (usually in the form of a Mint par), whichever metal is less valuable in terms of the *world* price, when compared with the official value, will drive out the more valuable metal which, being obtained at the Mint Par more cheaply in exchange for the other metal than it could be obtained in the world market, will be exported to take account of its

---

[61] O'Brien, D. P., *The Classical Economists* (Oxford: Clarendon Press, 1975), p. 190.
[62] Monroe, A. E., 1924, *op. cit.*, p. 66.
[63] De Roover, R., *Gresham on Foreign Exchange* (Cambridge, Mass: Harvard University Press, 1949), p. 91.
[64] Seligman, E. R. A., 'Bullionists', in E. R. A. Seligman with Alvin Johnson (eds.), *Encyclopaedia of the Social Sciences* (New York: Macmillan, 1930) vol. 3, pp. 61–2.

greater purchasing power abroad. The proposition however is usually cited in the context of debasement – 'bad money drives out good' – under which the coinage with a lower precious metal content will circulate while the coinage with a higher precious metal content will be withdrawn in order to make purchases abroad.

It is in this latter form that Bodin recognised the Law, understanding that full-weight coin would be exported (pp. 114–15). He does not seem to have understood the Law in terms of the difficulties faced by a bi-metallic currency in which the Mint Par, being fixed, perpetually diverged from a fluctuating world price. Indeed it seems clear that he favoured a ratio of 12:1 as the standard silver/gold ratio, on the grounds that this had been the world price for more than 2,500 years (pp. 109–10). In fact of course the world price was constantly changing; Navarrus himself was aware that the 12:1 ratio could change because the relative values were determined by relative scarcity like other relative values:

> if there is a shortage of gold coins their value may well increase, so that more coins of silver or other metal are given in exchange for them. Thus we now see that because of the great scarcity of gold money some people will give 23 and even 24 and 25 *reales* for a doubloon, which according to the law and price of the kingdom is worth only 22. Similarly, if silver money becomes scarce its value may rise, so that more gold or metal money is given in exchange for it.[65]

If pressed, Bodin would undoubtedly have conceded this point, since he understood the analysis of value in terms of relative scarcity. But he does not make the issue clear here, preferring to cite the historical evidence in support of the ratio 12:1.

Although he uses the analysis of relative scarcity, as the basis for developing the quantity theory, he does not cite the Scholastic analysis of demand directly. This then raises the question of his treatment of the demand for money.

---

[65] Extract in Grice-Hutchinson, M., 1952, *op. cit.*, p. 95.

The Demand for Money

The quantity theory does not, of course, except in its most naively mechanical form, imply that the price level must rise *in proportion* to an increase in the money supply. An explanation of non-proportionality, however, involves an analysis of the demand for money. Some writers have taken the view that Bodin neglected this issue.[66] In fact, however, a careful reading would indicate that Bodin understood well enough that the demand for money – and thus the velocity of circulation – varied according to the stage of economic development, and that there would be greater demand for transactions balances in countries with a greater degree of commercial development than in others (p. 67), so that the effect of an increase in the money supply could be damped if increased economic activity, and increased demand for balances in proportion to the price and output level, resulted. But this is hardly surprising, because Bodin showed a consistent understanding of the importance of relative scarcity throughout at least most of his treatment, and indeed distinguished clearly between general and relative price effects precisely on this basis. Once again we come back to the proposition that the analysis of the value of money was subject, since we are talking about commodity money, to the general treatment of value.

The Effects of Inflation

From Aquinas onwards it had been recognised that inflation causes confusion and thus injures trade, and this insight was reinforced by Copernicus.[67] Bodin then followed in this tradition, emphasising the harmful effects of inflation in his *Response*. The economic uncertainty introduced by the lack of a stable standard of value was harmful to both the public and private sector.

> For if money, which ought to govern the price of everything, is changeable and uncertain no one can truly know what he has: contracts will be uncertain, charges, taxes, wages, pensions and fees will be uncertain, fines and penalties fixed by laws and customs will also be changeable and uncertain; in short, the whole state of

---

[66] Monroe, A. E., 1924, *op. cit.*, p. 198.
[67] Monroe, A. E., 1924, *op. cit.*, p. 69.

finances and of many public and private matters will be in suspense. (p. 102).

Bodin is here talking about price changes brought about by debasement; but the arguments apply equally well to inflation engendered by precious metal inflows.

Given the difficulties caused by inflation, it is hardly surprising that Bodin devoted some attention to possible remedies for inflation. In the event, the only inflationary force which he felt could be tamed was debasement. It was certainly not desirable to try to drive out the precious metals; there was no will to enforce measures against monopoly and extravagance; there was no point in prohibiting exports (and losing the benefit of trade). Thus the only area in which Bodin seems to have considered action to be both necessary and practical was that in relation to his fifth cause of inflation – debasement.

Remedies for Debasement

Bodin emphasised that debasement was endemic with rulers. It made price stabilisation impossible (pp. 110–14). It also introduced uncertainty into foreign exchange markets and trade, because it made equilibrium exchange rates difficult to determine (pp. 112–13), even though, ultimately, the rate of exchange would have to be on a metallic basis – the nominal exchange would adjust fully to take account of debasement (p. 117).

In order to avoid such uncertainty it was necessary, Bodin argued, to embark on a coinage reform to prevent debasement in future. In his discussion of this proposal, Bodin showed an astonishing command of European coinage, in a situation in which the factual background concerning debasement was exceptionally complicated.[68] It was complicated further by the fact that, though governments were mainly responsible for the debasement that had occurred, there was also a problem of free enterprise (and illegal) debasement. Bodin's remedy for this latter problem (which was subject to severe but ineffective penalties)[69] anticipates the nineteenth-century English economist

---

[68] Hauser, H., 1932, ed., *op. cit.*, pp. xxvii–xxxi.
[69] Bodin de Saint Laurent, J., *op. cit.*, p. 77.

Thomas Joplin[70] – the aim was not to make forgery impossible but to make it unprofitable, as a result of which it would be reduced to a tiny fraction of its existing level (pp. 94–7, 118–19).

Private debasement was, however, a minor problem compared with debasement undertaken by government (just as in a modern economy private forgeries pale into insignificance when compared with government inflation of the money supply). Government undertook debasement for a variety of reasons and, though it was almost never unavoidable, it was urged on kings by courtiers (pp. 98–99). Driven on by the supposed needs of the public revenues, kings had embarked on debasement on a huge scale (pp. 110–14).[71] But in so far as debasement did in fact increase royal command over resources, what was involved was a zero sum game, with the private sector losing a corresponding amount of resource command (pp. 120, 124–125). There was no communal benefit.

Monarchs were enabled to engage in debasement because the very confusion engendered by it destroyed public awareness of the integrity of the coinage. The remedy – for both public and private debasement – was a reformed, full weight, coinage which would be without alloy and at the 12:1 ratio between silver and gold (pp. 99–108). Once established in this way, public awareness of what constituted a valid coin would make it difficult for future debasement to occur, since debased coins would be rejected.

> We will also, by these means, prevent all falsification of the coinage; and even the most stupid and ignorant will know the worth of any coin by the sight, the sound, and the weight, without fire, graving-tool, or touchstone. (p. 107)

The coinage should be milled, to prevent clipping, and cast rather than hammered (pp. 121–3).

---

[70] O'Brien, D. P., *Thomas Joplin and Classical Macroeconomics*, (Aldershot: Edward Elgar, 1993), p. 24.
[71] As Bodin de Saint Laurent points out, debasement (at least as practised by monarchs) was widely approved both before and after Bodin, Bodin de Saint Laurent, J., *op. cit.*, pp. 78–84.

Introduction   33

This still left to be resolved the question of the supply of the small coins used by the poor. A full weight gold and silver coinage would not contain coins of a sufficiently small denomination for retail transactions by the lower income groups. On this issue it is apparent that Bodin had not developed a position which was fully thought through – indeed there are inconsistencies sufficient to suggest that his *Response* was not written all at once but was added to and tinkered with over some lengthy period. At one point he says that small value coinage should be phased out (pp. 102–3) while elsewhere he recommends copper coins for the poor (or very small silver ones) (pp. 107–108). Yet, he believes that copper is not suitable for coinage and not even of a uniform value across either time or space, varying historically in relation to silver (pp. 108–9). Towards the end of the essay he says that no 'base money' should be issued (p. 120).

But this is a minor issue, however pressing for the poor, compared with the need to stabilise the standard of value and to rid the system of avoidable, government induced, inflation. Moreover, as English experience showed (pp. 97–98), there was no easy solution to the problem of a suitable denominator for retail transactions in an economy with large amounts of subsistence agriculture and barter.

Bodin's Legacy

Bodin probably exercised more influence in England than in any other country – this is certainly the judgement of his French editor.[72] There is supposed to have been a contemporary English translation of Bodin's *Response*, though no trace of it has been found by any scholar in modern times. But Bodin did go to England in 1581, and he may have been there in 1579.[73] As early as 1581 his ideas were appropriated by the anonymous editor of John Hales's *Discourse of the Commonweal of this Realm of England*. Schumpeter noted the borrowing by the editor of Hales[74] as had Monroe earlier.[75] But this was to be only the start of the process of appropriating – usually without

---

[72] Hauser, H., 1932, ed., *op. cit.*, p. lxvi.
[73] Bodin de Saint Laurent, J., *op. cit.*, p. 44; Baudrillart, H., *op. cit.*, pp. 128–9.
[74] Schumpeter, J. A., *op. cit.*, p. 166.
[75] Monroe, A. E., 1924, *op. cit.*, p. 59.

acknowledgement – his ideas. According to De Roover,[76] Malynes, one of the leading seventeenth-century mercantilist writers in England, also borrowed from Bodin. His French editor in this century noted, with nice irony, the extent of the plagiarisation which he has suffered in France[77] and Monroe has documented extensively the more widespread early seventeenth-century influence of Bodin's work.[78]

Bodin's achievement was an important one. He not only provided, in the mid sixteenth century, the first clear analysis and documentation of the inflation which was taking place around him; in so doing he drew on the Scholastic analysis of the Just Price (transmuted into a relative scarcity theory of value), showed himself master (at least as far as its application to debasement goes) of Gresham's Law, related the demand for money to the degree of economic development, and showed a degree of perception, remarkable for the time in which he lived, concerning the nature and benefits of trade. Though he was a lawyer by training, and although he is chiefly famous in a wider context for his legal and political writings, he certainly deserves recognition from economists as well.

D. P. O'Brien

---

[76] De Roover, *op. cit.*, p. 84.
[77] Hauser, H., 1932, ed., *op. cit.*, pp. lxix–lxxv.
[78] Monroe, A. E., 1924, *op. cit.*, pp. 90, 93–5, 99, 101, 113, 117, 120, 144. Bodin's influence is also discussed by Bodin de Saint Laurent, J. *op. cit.*, pp. 40–51.

BIBLIOGRAPHY

Baudrillart, H., *Jean Bodin et son temps* (Paris: Guillaumin, 1853).

Bodin de Saint Laurent, J., *Les Idées Monétaires et Commerciales de Jean Bodin* (Bordeaux: Cadoret, 1907; reprinted New York: Burt Franklin, 1970).

Chiang, A. C., *Fundamental Methods of Mathematical Economics*, 3rd ed. (London: McGraw Hill, 1984).

D'Avenel, G., *Histoire Economique de la Propriété, des Salaires, des Denreés et de Tous les Prix en Général depuis l'an 1200 jusqu'en l'an 1800* (Paris: Imprimerie Nationale, 1894).

Davies, G., *A History of Money* (Cardiff: University of Wales Press, 1994).

Dempsey, B. W., 'The Historical Emergence of Quantity Theory', *Quarterly Journal of Economics* 50 (1935), pp. 174–84.

De Roover, R., *Gresham on Foreign Exchange* (Cambridge, Mass: Harvard University Press, 1949).

Fix, A. C., 'Bodin, Jean', in J. Eatwell, M. Milgate and P. Newman, *The New Palgrave Dictionary of Economics* (London: Macmillan, 1987) vol. 1, p. 254.

Franklin, J. H., 'Bodin, Jean' in D. L. Sills (ed.), *International Encyclopaedia of the Social Sciences* (New York: Macmillan, 1968) vol. 3, pp. 110–12.

Gordon, B., *Economic Analysis before Adam Smith* (London: Macmillan, 1975).

Grice-Hutchinson, M., *The School of Salamanca: Readings in Spanish monetary theory 1544–1605* (Oxford: Clarendon Press, 1952).

———, *Early Economic Thought in Spain, 1177–1740* (London: Allen and Unwin, 1978).

Hamilton, E. J., *American Treasure and the Price Revolution in Spain* (Cambridge, Mass: Harvard University Press, 1934).

Harsin, P., *Les Doctrines Monétaires et Financières en France du XVIe au XVIIIe Siècle* (Paris: Félix Alcan, 1928).

Hauser, H., ed., *La Response de Jean Bodin* (Paris: Librairie Armand Colin, 1932).

Hauser, H., *Recherches et Documents sur l'Histoire des Prix en France de 1500 à 1800* (Paris: Les Presses Modernes, 1936).

Heaton, H., *Economic History of Europe* (rev. ed. New York: Harper, 1948).

Hegeland, H., *The Quantity Theory of Money* (Göteborg: Elanders Boktryckeri, 1951).

Humphrey, T. M., *Money, Banking and Inflation* (Aldershot: Edward Elgar, 1993).

Jacob, W., *An Historical Enquiry into the Production and Consumption of the Precious Metals*, 2 vols. (London: Murray, 1831).

Jevons, W. S., *A Serious Fall in the Value of Gold Ascertained and its Social Effects Set Forth* (London: Stanford, 1863).

Knolles, R. *Six Books of a Commonweale* (a translation of Bodin's *Republic*), (London: Bishop, 1606).

Kravis, I., 'Availability and Other Influences on the Commodity Composition of Trade', *Journal of Political Economy* 64 (1956), pp. 143–55.

Letwin, W. O., *The Origins of Scientific Economics* (London: Methuen, 1963).

McCulloch, J. R., *A Catalogue of Books, The Property of a Political Economist* (London: privately printed, 1862).

MacIver, R. M., 'Bodin, Jean' in E. R. A. Seligman with Alvin Johnson (eds.), *Encyclopaedia of the Social Sciences* (New York: Macmillan, 1930) vol. 2, pp. 614–16.

Malynes, G. de, *England's View, in the Unmasking of Two Paradoxes* (1603; reprinted New York: Arno Press, 1972).

Monroe, A. E., *Monetary Theory before Adam Smith* (1924; reprinted New York: A. M. Kelley, 1966).

Monroe, A. E., ed., *Early Economic Thought. Selections from Economic Literature prior to Adam Smith* (Cambridge, Mass: Harvard University Press, 1951).

Moore, G. A., introduction to and translation of *The Response of Jean Bodin to the Paradoxes of Malestroit and the Paradoxes* (Chevy Chase, Md: Country Dollar Press, 1948).

O'Brien, D. P., *The Classical Economists* (Oxford: Clarendon Press, 1975).

———, *Thomas Joplin and Classical Macroeconomics* (Aldershot: Edward Elgar, 1993).

O'Brien, G., *An Essay on Mediaeval Economic Teaching* (London: Longman, 1920).

Peronnet, M., 'De L'Or Splendeur Immortelle...' in A. Tournon and G.-A. Pérouse, *Or, Monnaie, Échange dans la Culture de la Renaissance* (St. Etienne: University of St. Etienne, 1994) pp. 45–58.

Phelps-Brown, E. H. and Hopkins, S. V., 'Builders' Wage-rates, Prices and Population: some further evidence' *Economica* 27 (1959), pp. 18–29.

Reynolds, B., introduction to and translation of J. Bodin, *Method for the Easy Comprehension of History* (New York: Columbia University Press, 1945).

Sabine, G. H., *A History of Political Theory*, 3rd ed. (London: Harrap, 1951).

Schumpeter, J. A., *History of Economic Analysis* (London: Allen and Unwin, 1954).

Seligman, E. R. A., 'Bullionists', in E. R. A. Seligman with Alvin Johnson (eds.), *Encyclopaedia of the Social Sciences* (New York: Macmillan, 1930) vol. 3, pp. 60–64.

Servet, J.- M., 'Les Paradoxes des *Paradoxes* de Malestroit' in A. Tournon and G.-A. Pérouse *Or, Monnaie, Échange dans la Culture de la Renaissance* (St. Etienne: University of St. Etienne, 1994) pp. 71–9.

Spiegel, H. W., *The Growth of Economic Thought*, 3rd ed. (Durham, N.C: Duke University Press, 1991).

Spooner, F. C., *The International Economy and Monetary Movements* (Cambridge, Mass: Harvard University Press, 1972).

Tooley, J., introduction and translation of J. Bodin, *Six Books of the Commonwealth* (Oxford: Blackwell, 1955).

Vilar, P., *A History of Gold and Money, 1450–1920*, trans. J. White (London: NLB, 1976).

THE PARADOXES OF THE SEIGNEUR DE MALESTROIT ON THE MATTER OF MONEY

To the King

Sire, having for three years toiled, as much by your Majesty's command as by the ordinance of your *Chambre des comptes*, on the matter of money, I am sent back by the latter to advise you. The strange rise in the prices of all goods which we are today witnessing must induce us to consider this question all the more carefully. Although everyone, great and small, feels this evil in his purse, there are few who can appreciate its source and origin; for the explanation must be drawn up from the depth and abyss of the said money and demonstrated by arguments which are highly paradoxical: that is to say, very remote from the opinion of the vulgar. It has seemed to me, Sire, that in order to treat of the matter in a way appropriate to its nature, and endeavouring to make the fruit of my labours appear more fully to your Majesty, I could not better achieve my purpose than by setting forth the two paradoxes which I have here ventured to present to your Majesty, in order that they may be better received and noticed by all. If they are well understood, everyone will then know the wrong that is done by raising prices and circulating the said money at a rate higher than that prescribed by your ordinances. In this way, your ordinances will be better observed than has been commonly the case; and from this will flow a great and unbelievable profit, firstly to yourself, Sire, and then to your subjects.

Your very humble and obedient subject and servant,

De Malestroit

First Paradox

That we are wrong to complain that the price of everything in France has increased, because no prices have increased during the past 300 years.

Ever since the ancient form of exchange was transformed into buying and selling and the earliest wealth of mankind, which consisted in cattle, was replaced by gold and silver, all things have been valued, sold and appraised by reference to these metals, and they are consequently the true and fair measure of the cheapness or dearness of all things.

We cannot say that something is more expensive now than it was 300 years ago, unless we must pay more gold or silver for it now than they paid then.

But the fact is that we do not now pay more gold or silver for anything than they did then. Therefore, no prices have increased in France since that time.

The premises are clear.

The minor premise is proved in this manner:

At the time of King Philip of Valois, who began to reign in the year 1328, the gold *écu aux fleurs de lis sans nombre*, as good as, and even better in weight and alloy than, the *écu soleil* of today, was worth only twenty *sols tournois*. At that time, an ell of good velvet was worth no more than four *livres*, and it took four *écus* or the equivalent in silver money to pay these four *livres*. Although the said ell of velvet now costs ten *livres*, which is six *livres* more, it still takes only the said four *écus* to pay these ten *livres*, at the rate of fifty *sols* apiece, as fixed by ordinance, or silver money to the same value. Therefore, the said ell of velvet is no dearer now than it was then.

The same reasoning applies to all other non-perishable goods which the merchants call Latin.

If we look at other, more perishable, commodities such as wheat, wine and other similar things, we will find that a similar consideration applies. To make the calculation, however, we cannot reasonably take as our basis the current year, which is perhaps the strangest and most unusual year which there has ever been in France, in that almost all the wheat and wine has been lost: even the wood of the vines and the walnut trees was damaged by frost. We will, therefore, take an ordinary year, as one usually does in estimating things changeable and uncertain, and put a cask of medium quality wine down at twelve *livres tournois*.

Let us turn to King John, the successor of the above-mentioned Philip, who began to reign in the year 1350, and who coined the first *francs à pied* and *à cheval* of fine gold, which were then worth no more than twenty *sols tournois*, and which now exchange for sixty *sols*, which is three times as much. If at that time a cask of medium quality wine was worth four *livres*, it required four of the aforesaid gold francs, or the equivalent in silver coin, to pay those four *livres*. If today we buy the said cask of wine for twelve *livres*, which is the price we have supposed for an ordinary year, to pay the said twelve *livres* requires only the same number of four gold francs at the said rate of sixty *sols tournois* apiece, or the same value in silver coin. It cannot therefore be said that since that time the price of the said wine has undergone any increase at all. And the same is true of wheat and other such merchandise.

We have considered gold; let us now consider silver, and let us take it from an earlier time: that is, from the time of Saint Louis, who began to reign in the year 1227 and who coined the first *sols* worth twelve *deniers tournois* each and therefore called *gros tournois*. These *gros tournois* or *douzains* were all of fine silver, and there were only sixty-four of them to the mark.

As to the *douzains* of today, even the *deniers* coined by Henry II of an alloy of three and a half *deniers fine*, and of seventy-three and a half pieces to the wrought mark: there are 320 of them in a mark of fine silver, which is five times what it was at the time of the said Saint Louis.

One of the said *sols* has become five, and consequently twenty of today's *sols* are worth only four of that time, twenty-five *livres* are worth five *livres*, and a hundred are worth twenty; and so on for the larger or smaller sum.

Hence, if today we pay ten *livres* for an ell of velvet which at the time of the said Saint Louis cost only forty *sols*, we are not paying out more silver than we were then.

The ell of cloth which is now sold for a hundred *sols* is the equivalent of only twenty *sols* in the past.

The cask of wine at twelve *livres* and ten *sols* is no dearer now than it was then at fifty *sols*.

If a capon costs ten *sols* now, they were only two *sols* in the past.

The pint of wine which now costs three *blancs* in the tavern is no dearer than when it cost one *liard*.

A pair of shoes is no dearer now at fifteen *sols* than it was then at three *sols*.

If a day's stay for a man and a horse at an inn in an ordinary year is twenty-five *sols*, it is not more expensive than the five *sols* it might have cost then.

The daily wage of a workman or labourer, which is now five *sols*, is no higher now than it was then at twelve *deniers*.

The gentleman who now has a revenue of 500 *livres* is no richer than he who then had only one hundred.

A plot of land or a house which is now sold for 25,000 francs is not more expensive than it was then at 5,000 *livres*.

All this is so for the reason given above: namely, that 25,000 *livres* now do not contain a greater quantity of fine silver than 5,000 *livres* did at the time of the said Saint Louis.

Thus, the rise in the prices of all things that people suppose to have taken place is nothing but a vain opinion or an arithmetical appearance, with no effect or substance whatever. For we must always return to our first point, which is to know and accept as true that we are not paying out a greater quantity of gold or fine silver for the purchase of anything now than we did in the past. This can be observed and verified throughout, from one period to another and from one reign to the next, from the time of the said Saint Louis down to the present day.

It cannot, then, be said or sustained that the price of anything has increased since the said time.

Second Paradox

That much can be lost on an *écu* or other gold and silver money, even though it is paid out at the same rate as that at which it was received.

One of the things that has most misled and impoverished the French and France, and which has done most to cause the royal ordinances on the value and circulation of money to be disregarded and broken during the past hundred years, has been the taking and fixing of these things at a higher rate than that at which the prince has valued them. This is a matter in which vulgar opinion has always been mistress. For whatever resistance the kings have been able to put up, they have eventually been vanquished and forced to follow, in this regard, the disordered will of the people by raising the *écu* from day to day. Consequently, the *écu*, which was worth twenty *sols* at the time of the said King Philip of Valois, has gradually increased from reign to reign, and step by step, to twenty-five, to thirty, to thirty-five, to forty, to forty-five right up to fifty *sols*, where it is now by ordinance. This has brought incalculable loss and irreparable damage to both kings and their subjects. It has long been a common error, inveterate and implanted in the minds of the greater part of mankind, that they think it not possible to lose anything on an *écu* or other money, either domestic or foreign, provided that they pay it out at the same rate as that at which they received it. These poor people are very far from being right, as I will clearly demonstrate in the same terms as the previous paradox.

At the time of the said Philip of Valois, the *écu* was, as I have said, worth no more than twenty *sols*, and now exchanges for at least fifty *sols*. The gentleman who at that time had fifty *sols* of rents and revenues received two and a half *écus* for his fifty *sols*, or the equivalent in silver money; for which two and a half *écus* he got five eighths of an ell of velvet at four *livres* an ell, which is the price it fetched then and which is equivalent to the four *écus* it is worth at present. Nowadays, for payment of the said fifty *sols* of rent, the gentleman receives no more than one *écu*, or the equivalent in silver money. For this *écu* he will today get only a quarter of an ell of velvet at ten *livres*, which the ell is now worth, whereas in times gone by he had five eighths of an ell. He thus loses three eighths of an ell of velvet on his *écu*, even though he exchanges it for fifty *sols*, which is the same price as that at which he received it. And if he takes or spends the *écu* for fifty-one or fifty-two *sols* his loss will be proportionally greater.

The officer who then had twenty *livres* as wages received twenty *écus*, or the equivalent in silver money, in payment of the said wages. For those twenty *écus* he could get five ells of velvet at the said rate of four *livres* an ell, which was the four *écus* it was worth at that moment. Nowadays, in payment of those twenty *livres* of wages the officer receives only eight *écus* at fifty *sols* each, or the equivalent in silver money, for which eight *écus* he can get only two ells of velvet, at the said rate of ten *livres* an ell, which is its current price, whereas before he would expect to get five. It is obvious, therefore, that on his eight *écus* he loses three ells of velvet, even though he has exchanged the said *écus* for fifty *sols*, the same rate as that at which he received them.

The commoner who at the time of King John had thirty-six *livres* of landed or settled revenue, received in payment of his said revenue thirty-six gold *francs à pied* or *à cheval*, at the rate of twenty *sols* apiece, or the equivalent in silver money, which is what they were worth then. For these thirty-six gold francs he could get nine casks of wine at the then rate of four *livres* a cask, which were four gold francs, worth twelve of our present *livres*, which is the price at which we have estimated the said cask of wine in an ordinary year. If this commoner is now paid gold francs for his revenue of thirty-six *livres*, he will receive only twelve gold francs, which at the current rate of sixty *sols* apiece are worth the said sum of thirty-six *livres*. For these twelve gold francs he will get no more than three casks of wine today, the current rate being twelve *livres* a cask, whereas before he got nine casks. He therefore loses six casks of wine on his twelve gold francs, even though he has spent them at the same rate of sixty *sols* as that at which he received them.

There is a similar loss on all other kinds of gold coin, and in buying all kinds of provisions and merchandise, which, for the sake of avoiding undue length, I shall not here discuss.

Let us now make the calculation with respect to silver money.

The gentleman, or anyone else of whatever rank, who at the time of the said Saint Louis had sixteen *livres* of rent or revenue, received in payment of this revenue five marks of fine silver, or the equivalent in gold money. For as was said in the first paradox, there were only sixty-four pieces, called *sols* or *gros tournois*, to a mark of fine silver. Nowadays, this revenue would be received as only one mark of fine silver, because the sixteen *livres*, which are equivalent to 320 new *sols* or *douzains*, contain at the most only one mark of the said fine silver, which is only one fifth of the silver contained in the original sixteen *livres*. At the time of Saint Louis, sixteen *livres* would buy sixteen ells of cloth at twenty *sols* an ell, as good as, or better than, that which at present costs a hundred *sols tournois*. Nowadays, one gets only three ells for sixteen *livres*, a fifth of the said cloth at a hundred *sols* an ell, instead of the sixteen that one would have got in times gone by. This is a loss of twelve and four fifths ells of cloth on sixteen *livres*, even though one has exchanged each *livre* at the same rate of twenty *sols* as that at which it was received.

If we now take the *sol* or *douzain*, we find that the result is the same; because, for the ten *sols* which the gentleman received in the past in rent or revenue, containing as much fine silver as fifty today, he could get five capons at two *sols* each, whereas for ten *sols* now he gets only one capon. This is a loss of four capons on ten *sols*, even though he exchanged the ten *sols* for twelve *deniers* each, which is the same price as that at which he got them.

If anyone holding an opinion contrary to this paradox were to answer and say that he does not at all care how much an *écu*, a *livre* or a *sol* is worth and that, having a hundred *livres* in revenue or wages, it does not matter in what kinds of gold or silver he is paid, nor at what price he gets them, provided only that he always has the sum of a hundred *livres* and that he exchanges the said money at the same rate as that at which he gets it; then he must, by the same token, boast that he gets as much merchandise today for two *sols* or *douzains nouveaux*, which are almost all copper, as he would have got in the past for two of the said old *sols* or *gros tournois*, which were all of fine silver: and as much at present for one *écu* as he would have got then for two and a half. In saying this he would be introducing and putting in place a third paradox much stranger and more difficult to believe than the first. For he would be saying that all things are cheaper now than they were in former times, inasmuch as one now gives less gold and silver for their purchase than one gave then. This cannot be demonstrated, because it is not true; and it would be better to believe the first paradox, which shows that nothing has become dearer, without fooling ourselves into thinking that things are cheaper now than they were in the past.

The force and intention of these two paradoxes is to show (by the first) that the price of everything, for the king and his subjects, is the same as it was in the past, because we must pay as much gold and fine silver for them now as we did then. But because of the forcing up of the price of gold money, which of necessity produces a weakening and debasement of silver money, the king does not receive as great a quantity of gold and fine silver now as his predecessors did in payment of his domanial and other rights. Similarly, the lords and other subjects of his Majesty who have rents, revenues, wages, estates and salaries, do not receive as great a quantity of gold and fine silver now as they received in the past, but (like the king) are paid in copper instead of gold and silver. For this copper (following the second paradox) one cannot obtain as much merchandise as one could for the same quantity of gold and fine silver. Thus, the loss that people believe themselves to have sustained by the rise in the price of everything does not come from paying more, but from receiving a smaller quantity of gold and silver than they used to.

In this, we clearly see that the more we raise the price of money the more of it we lose; for by this comes the great increase which now affects the prices of all things, which leads to general impoverishment throughout the kingdom.

The movements, causes and progress of this evil will, hereafter, be amply deduced and demonstrated, together with the certain and infallible means of remedying it, to the great good and honour of his Majesty and to the relief and comfort of all his subjects.

END

[THE RESPONSE OF MASTER JEAN BODIN, COURT ADVOCATE, TO THE PARADOX OF MONSIEUR DE MALESTROIT CONCERNING THE INCREASE IN THE COST OF ALL THINGS AND THE MEANS OF REMEDYING IT

For the Book on Money
Jacques du Puys, licensed publisher, to the reader, greeting.

Sirs, it is twelve years since this book was printed and soon thereafter turned into English by command of the Archbishop of Canterbury, Chancellor of England, and judged very useful to the commonwealth. And as the author had foreseen and predicted the inconveniences to which the instability of the currency could give rise, he had counselled that base coin be discredited and abolished and had shown a means of fixing the rate and value of money by reducing it to three simple metals, gold, silver and pure copper, as in fact has begun to be done with regard to copper coinage. And if this had been continued as well for the other metals, the commonwealth would not have fallen into the difficulties to which it now sees itself reduced and which may cause great trouble if they are not very soon remedied. That is why I have resolved, having been requested to do so by many, to reprint this same book, revised, enlarged and fully corrected. Meanwhile, pray accept my good intention in thus serving the public.]

To Monsieur Prevost, Seigneur of Morsan, President for the King in His Court of Parlement

You know, Monsieur, of the complaints commonly made concerning the increasing cost of all things; of the meetings held in every quarter of this city to bring order into the matter; of the pains taken to understand whence such dearness comes; of how Messieurs du Menil and du Faur, advocates to the king, whom nature seems to have consecrated to the public good, have striven to remedy it. Finally, Monsieur de Malestroit, {a man who well deserves to be answered by one greater than I,} employed in this matter by command of the king, published a little pamphlet of paradoxes in which he maintains, contrary to the opinion of the whole world, that there has been no increase in prices during the past 300 years. He has induced a number of people to believe this {and by this means has appeased the complaints of many men}. But having lately read his discourse, I have thought it well to say a word in reply, in order to clarify and illuminate this point which is of great consequence to all in general and to each in particular, provided that you will be the judge of honour, assuring me that M. Malestroit will be in agreement. For to judge a paradox well, or an opinion contrary to what is commonly believed, requires such a judge as yourself, to whom nature has given an intellect so clear and a judgement so complete that it would not be easy to find an equal among a hundred thousand. What I do not at all place among your merits as being a gift of nature, but as having been accomplished by a fine and liberal mind, is the fact that you have such great experience in affairs of state, which so recommends you that everyone knows that you have long ago forgotten your own affairs. How ill this has been expressed by me! For the individual cannot be forgotten by one who governs the public so wisely, as you have shown in the greatest offices of state and, above all, in the government of Provence, which gives a perpetual testimonial that the prudence and incredible adroitness which you employed to manage those people at so perilous a time, with a severity mingled with moderation, merits a government, not of a province, but of a kingdom. This assures me that, in the case which now presents itself, you will not only give sound judgement on the question but will also well know how to find a means of remedying the dearness, insofar as we can see that it is possible for the human intellect to advise prudently, take considered action, and bring matters to a happy conclusion.

{The Response Of Master Jean Bodin, Court Advocate, To The Paradox Of Monsieur De Malestroit Concerning The Increase In The Cost Of All Things And The Means Of Remedying It}

[Discourse Of Jean Bodin On The Increase And Decrease In The Value Of Money, Gold And Silver Alike, And The Means Of Remedying It; And The Response To The Paradoxes Of Monsieur De Malestroit]

Before going any further, I shall briefly set forth M. de Malestroit's arguments. One cannot, he says, complain that a thing is dearer now than it was 300 years ago unless it is necessary to pay more gold or silver for it now than was paid then. The fact is, however, that one does not have to pay more for goods now than they did then, either in gold or silver. Therefore nothing in France has risen in price since that time.

This is his conclusion, which follows necessarily if we grant his minor premise. As proof of it, he says that an ell of velvet at the time of King Philip of Valois cost only four *écus* as good, and indeed better, in weight and value than our *écu soleil*, and that each *écu* was worth no more than twenty *sols* in silver money. Now that the *écu* is worth fifty *sols*, however, one has to pay ten *livres* an ell, which are worth no more than four *écus*. Thus, the said ell of velvet is no dearer now than it was then. He goes on to say that the same is true of all Latin commodities, even our wines and wheat; although he has no proof.

[When he speaks of velvet, the Seigneur de Malestroit deceives himself in saying that an ell cost only four *écus* at the time of Philip the Fair: for it would first be necessary to establish that there was any velvet in France at that time. For the opinion of those who have tried to show it by what Justinian says about purple and dyed goods has not been well received. Moreover, the ordinance of Philip the Fair published in the year 1294 and registered in the *Chambre des comptes*, and not printed, which the Seigneur de Malestroit, *maître des comptes*, might have seen in the book entitled *Ordinances of Saint Louis for the Peaceful State of the Kingdom*, fol. 44, prescribes fully, and in more than fifty articles, the form of dress that each should wear, from the persons of princes down to the lowest servants. But there is no mention, either direct or indirect, of silk, satin, velvet, damask, half silk, samite, or any similar material, although the ordinance permits certain individuals to wear chains and cinctures of gold without any prohibition against wearing silk, be it by men or women, princes or merchants, masters or servants; a matter which the ordinance would not have overlooked, seeing that the first article begins with the following prohibition: 'No female commoner will have a chain; second, no commoner, male or female, will wear gold or precious stones, or a gold cincture, or gold or silver crowns, or silver, or trimmings of vair, squirrel or ermine, which are not forbidden to nobles.'

It is, therefore, misleading to cite the example of velvet, which was not then available in France nor perhaps anywhere else in the world. For many spices were brought from India, whence silk came, and from fortunate Arabia, which is much further away than Brusa, where velvet was invented.] And even if I should grant him the example of velvet, there is no reason consequently to infer the price of all goods from the price of velvet, which must at that time have been the most expensive product of the Levant, since there were almost no towns apart from Damascus in Syria and Brusa in Anatolia (which the ancients called Prusa) where they made velvet and damask.

These things came into use little by little in Greece and Italy; and it is not yet a hundred years since silk mills, which we got from Genoa, were unknown in France. Now that Tours, Lyons, Avignon, Toulouse and other towns in this kingdom are so full of such merchandise that everyone wears them, which was not done then, at least not in so great a quantity, an ell of the best velvet should not cost more than an *écu* at the same rate as before, as I shall presently show. But it is enough for the time being to have shown that velvet must not be taken as an example of other Latin merchandise, and still less of goods in general.

As for wine and wheat, it is quite certain that these cost {three} [twenty] times as much now as they did a hundred years ago. I can say this because I have seen the property register of Toulouse in which a bushel of grain, which was about half the size of ours, was worth no more than five *sols*. Nowadays, the most common price is sixty *sols*, which is {four} [twenty] times dearer than it was then. And, without looking farther afield than this city, we find in the records of the *Châtelet* that a measure of best rental wheat according to the Paris standard cost only 120 *livres* in the year 1524, although two years earlier wheat had been frozen, upon which estimate the judgements of the *Châtelet* were based. In the year 1530, the price rose to 144 *livres*, and by a judgement of the court given in the year 1531 a certain contract made at a lower price was annulled. Now that the ordinary price has gone up by more than a third, contracts made at the price fixed by the judgements of the year 1531 would be declared usurious if the debtor did not have the choice of paying silver for grain at the rate of one twelfth penny. I say nothing of the year 1565 when the ordinary price of a measure of wheat in May was 260 *livres* in straight sale; but I speak only of the ordinary years for the past forty years. We see that rental wheat which cost fifty *écus soleil*, since we are not here speaking in terms of *livres*, now costs twice as much, so that the ordinary price of the best wheat in straight sale is 120 *livres*, which is as much as it cost in rentals forty years ago.

Monsieur de Malestroit should not, therefore, have taken produce as an example. But in order to verify my remarks more fully, let us leave produce aside and turn to the price of land. Land cannot increase or diminish, nor can its natural goodness be altered, provided, as they say, that it is not neglected, but cultivated as it has been since Ceres, the Lady of Sicily, showed us how to make use of it. For it is not likely to be true that land loses its vigour with age, as many think [even if God, in His just vengeance, has for several years made it barren]. Moreover, since God placed France between Spain,

Italy, England and Germany, He provided also that she should be the foster-mother, bearing in her bosom the horn of plenty which never has been, and never will be, empty; which the peoples of Asia and Africa have known well and confessed, as may be seen in all their writings, and also in the oration of King Agrippa when he wished to make the rebellious and mutinous Jews yield obedience to the Romans. 'Consider Gaul,' he said, 'with her 315 peoples surrounded by the Alps, the Rhine, the Ocean and the Pyrenees: that inexhaustible source which furnishes almost the whole earth with all good things. Nonetheless, these warlike peoples have bowed down before the might of this empire, having fought valiantly for eighty years, more astonished by the good fortune and greatness of the Romans than reduced by weariness, seeing that the whole Roman garrison consists of no more than 1,200 soldiers: hardly as many men as they have in their good-sized towns.' From this, we see that France was no more barren at that time than she is now. Let us also show that she is no less fertile today.

Cicero, speaking of the fertility of Sicily, which the Romans called their granary, tells us that the best land there yielded no more than twelve for one, although, he says, it was favoured by the gods. In the judgement of all farmers, we have better land than this today in our own Loire Valley, in Brie, in Saintonge, in La Limagne d'Auvergne, in Languedoc, and even in the Isle de France. Nonetheless, we see that during the past fifty years the price of land has, not doubled, but trebled, so that an acre of the best arable land in level country, which in the old days cost only ten or twelve *écus*, and thirty in the case of vineyards, is now sold at double, indeed treble, the price in *écus* which weigh a tenth less than they weighed 300 years ago. Monsieur de Malestroit will grant me this if he will take the trouble to leaf even cursorily through our records. And, without investigating individual contracts, which one can see everywhere, I call upon you to testify, Monsieur – you who have so often handled all the depositions of the court and all the contracts of the French treasury – that all the baronies, counties and duchies which have been renounced and annexed to the

Crown are not now worth as much in revenue as the price for which they were once sold outright. Everyone knows that the county of Comtat Venaissin is worth twice as much revenue as it was mortgaged for. [Charles the Wise bought the county of Auxerre from the Count, paying 31,000 gold francs, which is approximately the same number of *écus*.] I understand from the councillor, Monsieur Fauchet, whom I take to be a faithful recorder of remarkable antiquities, that in the year 1100 Herpin sold the duchy of Berry to King Philip I in order to accompany Godfrey of Bouillon, and that he sold it for the sum of 60,000 gold *sols*. In our annals also we must take note of the laws of the Lombards, Saxons, Franconians and Ripuarians, in which we find all fines reckoned in *sols*, as when it is said that anyone who kills a free man will pay a hundred *sols*, and that anyone who binds him will pay ten *sols*. I mention this in passing, for I have seen a case under the ancient statutes of the town of Amiens in which the parties, without remarking on it, treated *sols* as the equivalent of our *douzains*; yet, we know that the first silver *sols* were not made until 200 years afterwards, by Saint Louis.

Let us take it that such gold *sols* were of the same weight and value as the gold *sols* of Justinian; for the laws of all his peoples were made at about the same time. They would be at the most only 60,000 *angelots*, or {one hundred} [60,000] gold *reals*, as I shall explain presently. For even the silver *sol* did not weigh much more, and it is probable that the gold *sol* was minted at the same weight; at any rate, I shall take it that it weighs the same as the *sol* of Justinian.

I find also in the antiquities of Italy that the Emperor Henry of Luxemburg sold Lucca to the inhabitants for 12,000 *écus* and Florence for 6,000. Today [as Blondus wrote in the eighth book of the second decade] there are a hundred houses in Florence which are worth three times the amount for which the whole city was then sold. [Furthermore, we find that the ordinances of Philip the Tall concerning the rights of commoners, dated 1318, prescribe that whoever wishes to acquire commoner's rights elsewhere in the kingdom will be required to purchase a house worth sixty Paris *sols*.] And if

Malestroit is not content with such antiquities, let us take the ancient contracts of the *Chambre <des comptes>*, or let us take the customs of France, and even those of my own province of Anjou. Here we find article 499 bearing the following words: 'a load of ore is twenty-five *francs tournois*; a load of rye, twenty-two francs and six *deniers*; a load of barley, twenty-five francs; a kid, three francs and four *deniers*; a capon, twelve *deniers*; a chicken, eight *deniers*; a fat sheep seven francs and six *deniers*; a day's hire of oxen in winter, ten *deniers*.' This custom was settled and made standard in 1508. I find that the custom of Auvergne gives a better account; because a fat sheep with its wool is valued at only five *sous*, a kid at eighteen *deniers*, a chicken at six *deniers*, a rabbit at ten *deniers*, a gosling at six *deniers*, a calf at five francs, a pig at ten *deniers*, a peafowl at two francs, a pheasant at twenty *deniers*, a pigeon at one *denier*, a wagon-load of hay weighing five hundredweight at fifteen *sols*, a day-labourer at six *deniers*, and four in winter, and an ox-cart in winter at twelve *deniers*. Article 555 of the custom of Bourbonnais values a wagon-load of hay weighing twelve hundredweight at only ten *sols*, and at five francs in the meadow. In the custom of La Marche, as settled in 1521, the meat of a whole sheep without the wool is valued at only two francs and six *deniers*, a wagon-load of hay weighing fifteen hundredweight at twelve francs, a wagon-load of wood at twelve *deniers*, a cow at eighteen *deniers*, and a goose at twelve *deniers*. According to the custom of Troyes in Champagne, a bushel of best wheat, Troyes measure, was valued at only twenty *francs tournois*, rye at ten francs, barley at seven francs, oats at five francs, a day's work by a man at twelve *deniers*, and by a woman at six *deniers*.

Here Monsieur de Malestroit cannot deny that the price of everything has increased at least tenfold during the past sixty years, in, I say, whatever money he chooses, as I shall show presently. For if a piece of land could then be sold for only twenty-five or thirty *deniers* complete with lordship and full rights, it follows that the price of land is ten times higher now than it was sixty years ago. And whoever will search out still earlier acknowledgements and records will find that even this was very dear in comparison with the ancient price. I leave aside an infinite number of similar examples, without touching upon what is plain for everyone to see. I think it enough for the time being to have shown the high cost of duchies, towns and counties, and of land which cannot depreciate over time. This will be much more readily understood when the origin and cause of dearness is grasped.

I find that the dearness which we see today has {three} [some four or five] causes. The main and almost the only cause (which no one has mentioned until now) is the abundance of gold and silver, which is greater in this kingdom today than it has been during the past 400 years. I go no further back because the court registers and those of the *Chambre <des comptes>* do not extend back beyond 400 years. The rest has to be gleaned from old histories with little reliability. The second cause of the rise in prices is, in part, monopolies. The third is scarcity, caused partly by the export trade and partly by waste. The {last} [fourth] is the pleasure of kings and great lords who raise the prices of the things of which they are fond. [The fifth is the price of money, debased from its ancient value.] I will touch briefly upon each of these points.

The chief cause of the rise in prices of all things in all places is the abundance of what gives things their value and price. Plutarch and Pliny testify that, after the conquest of the kingdom of Macedonia in the time of King Perseus, the commander-in-chief, Æmilius Paulus, brought so much gold and silver into Rome that the people were exempted from paying taxes and the price of land in the Romagna instantly rose by two thirds. [And Suetonius says that the Emperor Augustus brought so much wealth from Egypt that the rate of usury fell, and the price of land was much higher than it had been before.] It was, therefore, not the scarcity of land, which can neither increase nor decrease, nor monopoly, which cannot apply in such a case, but the abundance of gold and silver that caused the depreciation in value of these metals and the rise in the price of things. It was like the coming of the Queen of Candace, whom holy Scripture calls the Queen of Sheba, into the city of Jerusalem, bringing with her so many precious stones that they were trodden under foot. And when the Spaniard made himself lord of the New World, axes and knives were sold there for more than pearls and precious stones because the only knives they had were of wood or stone, whereas they had plenty of pearls. It is, therefore, abundance which causes devaluation.

On this point the Emperor Tiberius was greatly mistaken in cutting off the head of the man who had made glass soft and malleable for fear, as Pliny says, that if the discovery got abroad, gold would lose its credit. For the abundance of glass, which can be made from almost all stones and many plants, would always have kept its value down. And this is true of everything.

We must show, therefore, that there was not as much gold and silver in this kingdom 300 years ago as there is now; and this can be understood at a glance. For if there is silver in a country, it cannot be so well hidden that princes in their necessity cannot find it. Yet the fact is that King John, in his extreme necessity, could never raise a credit of 60,000 francs (let us take them to be *écus*); and after the battle of Poitiers, when he was held prisoner by the English for eight years, neither his children, nor his friends, nor his people, nor he himself when he came in person, could find his ransom, and he was obliged to return to England while the money was raised. [And the ransom of the King of Scotland, who was captured twelve years later, was only 100,000 gold nobles, which the King of Scotland could not raise. So King Charles V promised to pay his ransom in negotiating the alliance in 1371 with Robert, King of Scotland, as is clear from the treaty.] Saint Louis was in the same difficulty when he was a prisoner in Egypt. It is not likely that the French people, who are naturally inclined to love their king – and especially such a king as this, who has never had, and perhaps never will have, an equal – would willingly have suffered the sight of him as the slave of the Mahommedans, whom they then regarded with extreme horror. Nonetheless, Saladin was forced to release him so that he might find his ransom, retaining as a pledge the consecrated host that the king carried with him; and but for the devoutness of the good king it would have remained forfeit. [I find that there are some who say that it was only a question of 200,000 gold *bezants*, which the Seigneur de Joinville reckons to be 500,000 *livres*; and he says that the queen had the ransom in her coffers. I report this belief it for what it is worth.] We also read in our old histories that, for want of silver, they made leather money with a stud of silver in it, which shows the extreme shortage of silver which then prevailed in France. I report this for what it is worth.

Now, if we turn to our own times, we find that, during a period of six months, the king raised more than 3,400,000 *livres* in Paris, without having to go elsewhere, besides the public funds also found in Paris, and the last of the subsidies, and the income from charges on households, which increase very much. The truth is that necessity forced our prince to give us back the light of peace. [We also find that Philip III assigned to Charles, who then became Count of Valois, 10,000 *livres* as his personal income, and at the peace treaty between King Philip the Fair and King Edward, Isabelle of France was promised, and then married, to the son of the king of England with a dowry of 18,000 *livres tournois petits* and nothing more; and Philip the Tall assigned to his son a personal income of 20,000 *livres tournois* in 1311. And by the ordinance of King Charles V the wealth bestowed on the king's sons is only 12,000 *livres tournois* of income or 120,000 paid as a single sum, and for the king's daughter 60,000 as a single sum. Now, we know that at that time there was more silver than there was at the time of Philip the Fair, for Philip of Valois, grandfather of King Charles V, by the allowance to his son John, willed that, if he had only daughters, the first would have an assigned income of 7,000 *livres*, the second 2,000 as asssigned income and 15,000 as a single sum, and the third 1,000 and 40,000 as a single sum; this bestowal was made in 1331.]

Let us take the age of Charles VII, who was the first to tax the people to pay the soldiers and suffered many mutinies among his subjects, although he had driven the English out and recovered as much in ten years as his forefathers had lost in

200: nonetheless, he could raise only 1,700,000 francs for all charges, as Philippe de Comynes tells us. [And his father, Charles VI raised only 400,000 *livres*, at which the Estates held at Paris in 1444 complained bitterly. Nonetheless, Charles IX raised 14,000,000 in 1572.] Louis XI, having reunited the dukedoms of Burgundy and Anjou and the county of Provence with the crown, took 3,000,000 more than his father, [together with several large confiscations] at which the people felt themselves so oppressed that on the accession of Charles VIII, his son, it was decreed at the request and entreaty of the Estates that half the charges be repaid. [Since then the abundance of gold and silver has, because of the high price of things and the cheapness of silver, caused costs to be greater; and the daughter of King Henry received 400,000 *écus* on her marriage, which is four times as much as Renée of France, daughter of Francis,[a] received when she married, namely, 100,000 *écus*.

And if we ask what had happened to all the gold and silver, the answer is that Italy, for the sake of promoting trade and securing peace among princes, had attracted to herself all the gold in Europe. And in fact we find that, at the time when Charles V ordained that the daughters of the king of France should have only 60,000 *livres* in a single payment as a marriage portion, Galeazzo II, Viscount of Milan, gave 200,000 *écus* for the marriage of his daughter to Lionel, son of the king of England; and his brother Bernabo, who shared with him the viscountcy of Milan, gave 2,000,000 in gold for the marriage of nine legitimate and two illegitimate daughters, although he had five legitimate and two illegitimate sons, as we read in the history of Milan; and his nephew Galeazzo, the first Duke of Milan, married his daughter Valentina to Louis of France, Duke of Orleans, and gave her a dowry of 4,000 gold florins, 667 marks of silver, not counting her jewels, the county of Asti, and a promise that the duchy of Milan would go to Valentina and her heirs in the absence of any male succession. Lodovico Sforza, called the Moor, ruler of Milan, married his niece Bianca Sforza to the Emperor Maximilian,

---

[a] An error: Bodin should have said 'daughter of Louis XII'.

giving her 400,000 *écus* and 60,000 ducats on her marriage in 1494, not counting the 400,000 *écus* he paid after the siege of Milan.] If Monsieur de Malestroit consults the records of the *Chambre <des comptes>*, he will agree with me that more gold and silver has been found in France to meet the needs of the king and the commonwealth between 1515 and 1568 than could be found in the previous 200 years.

And if anyone wishes to say that there is not more gold and silver now than there was, but that the Italians have been lending it to us out of charity for some little time, a case can be made out in rebuttal of this. For it is certain that there have at all times been exiles from that country who, as well as bringing their filth into this kingdom, have always waged war on God and on the poor, striving by all means to grasp at our kings' natural goodness of heart, and making themselves so hated that they were expelled from France and their goods confiscated at the time of Philip the Tall; and since that time our fathers have taxed the bills of exchange known in the chancery as Lombards at double the rate.

We also find that Philip the Fair was the first to impose a tax on salt, which has risen from four *deniers* a pound to forty-five *livres* a hogshead or thereabouts; and this was done at the urging of a Messire Mincion. They would, therefore, have found silver easily enough if there had been as much of it as there is at present, for Philip the Tall did not scruple to demand from the people a fifth part of the {goods} [income] of each.

But, someone will say, where has so much gold and silver come from since that time? I find that the merchants and craftsmen who bring in gold and silver had at that time ceased their activities; for the French, having one of the most fertile countries in the world, had given themselves up to cultivating the soil [and rearing cattle], which is the chief business of France: so much so that trade with the Levant all but ceased, for fear of the barbarians who held the coast of Africa and of the Arabs, whom our fathers called Saracens, who ruled the whole of the Mediterranean Sea, making galley-slaves of the Christians whom they captured. And as for trade with the West, it was completely unknown before Spanish ships appeared in the seas of the Indies. Besides which, the English, who held the ports of Guyenne and Normandy, had closed the routes to Spain and the islands. Moreover, the quarrels between the houses of Anjou and Aragon denied us the ports of Italy.

But in the past hundred and {twenty} [fifty] years, {we} [our fathers] have driven out the English, and the Portuguese, sailing the high seas by the ship's compass, have made themselves masters of the Persian Gulf and in part of the Red Sea, and have thus filled their ships with the wealth of the Indies and fortunate Arabia, frustrating the Venetians and Genoese who take merchandise from Egypt and Syria where it has been brought by caravan by the Arabs and Persians in order to sell it to us retail, and at the weight of gold.

At the same time, the Castilians, having brought under their power new territories full of gold and silver, have filled Spain with it, and have shown the way for our navigators to sail around Africa with a splendid profit. [It is incredible, but nonetheless true, that since 1533 more than a 100,000,000 of gold and twice as much silver has been brought from Peru, which was conquered by the Pyurres <i.e. Piurians>. The ransom of king Atabalira <i.e. Atahualpa> came to 1,326,000 gold *bezants*, while in Peru a pair of cloth breeches cost 300 ducats, a cloak 1,000 ducats, a good horse 4,000 or 5,000, and a jar of wine 200 ducats, as the history of the Indies testifies. Nonetheless, Augustin de Zarate, master of accounts to his Catholic Majesty, has found that the officers of his Catholic Majesty in Peru showed a balance <due to Portugal> in their accounts to the tune of 1,800,000 gold *pezans* and 600,000 *livres* of silver. Besides, there is the trade and incredible profit that the king of Portugal makes in the Moluccas, where cloves, cinnamon and other costly spices grow, having got them by agreement from the Emperor Charles V as a pledge for 350,000 ducats when he passed by rich Bologna on his way to have himself crowned emperor. This the Italians wished to discharge and pay in full, but the emperor did not desire it on account of the alliance between the two houses.]

Now it is a fact that the Spaniard, whose hold on life depends upon France, being forced irresistably to import our corn, linen, cloth, woad, dye stuffs, paper, books, even carpentry and all manufactured goods, searches all the world over to bring us gold, silver and spices. On the other hand, the English, the Scots, and all the people of Norway, Sweden, Denmark and the Baltic coast, who have mines without number, dig metals from the centre of the earth in order to buy our wines, saffron, dried plums, pastel and above all our salt. This is a manna which God gives us as a special grace and with little labour; because for the people of the North, beyond the forty-seventh degree of latitude, there is not enough heat for salt to be made, and below the forty-second degree the excessive heat makes the salt [more] corrosive, especially the salt from the mines of Spain, Naples and Poland, which [very often] does harm to people and to the products cured, so that the salt of Franche-Comté and the rock salt of Spain and Hungary do not have anything like the goodness of our salt. This means that the Englishman, the Fleming, and the Scotsman, who have a large trade in salt fish, often load their vessels with ballast for want of merchandise and come to buy our salt with ready money.

The other reason why such great wealth has come to us during the past 120 to 140 years is the measureless growth which has taken place in the population of this kingdom since the cessation of the civil wars between the houses of Orleans and Burgundy. This has enabled us to taste the sweetness of peace and to enjoy its fruits for a long time, even up to the present religious troubles. For the foreign war that we have had since that time was only a purgation of ill humours necessary for the whole body of the commonwealth. Previously, the countryside and almost all the towns were deserted because of the ravages of the civil wars, during which the English had sacked the towns, burned the villages, murdered, pillaged and slain a good part of the French people, and picked the meat down to the bone; which brought agriculture, commerce and all the mechanical arts to a standstill. But during the past hundred years an immeasurable part of the country has been cleared of forest and scrub, many villages have been built, and towns have been peopled, so much so that the greatest benefit which has accrued to Spain, which is otherwise a wilderness, comes from the French migrants who enter Spain one after another, chiefly from the Auvergne and Limousin. The result is that, in Navarre and Aragon, nearly all the wine-growers, labourers, carpenters, masons, joiners, stone-cutters, turners, wheelwrights, waggoners, carters, rope-makers, quarrymen, saddlers and harness-makers are French, because, except when it comes to war and commerce, the Spanish are amazingly idle, and for this reason love the energetic and useful Frenchman. This was shown by the intervention of the Prior of Capua at Valencia, where there were 10,000 Frenchmen, servants and artisans, who were to be punished for having taken part in the conspiracy against Maximilian who was then Lieutenant-General in Spain; but the magistrates and inhabitants of Valencia went surety for them all. There is also a large number of Frenchmen in Italy.

There is yet another reason for the wealth of France, namely, the trade with the Levant which was opened to us by the friendship between the house of France and the Ottoman house at the time of King Francis I. The effect is that, since that time, French merchants have set up shop in Alexandria, Cairo, Beirut and Tripoli, alongside the Venetians and the Genoese, and have no less credit than the Spaniard in Fez and Morocco; which opportunities were opened up when the Jews, driven out of Spain by Ferdinand, settled in the low country of Languedoc and accustomed the French to trade with Barbary.

{The last} [Another] reason for the abundance of gold and silver has been the Bank of Lyons which, to tell the truth, was established by {King Henry who, when still only Dauphin, borrowed} [King Francis I, who initially borrowed silver at eight per cent, his successor] at ten per cent, then at sixteen, and finally at twenty per cent to supply his needs. Suddenly the Florentines, the Luccans, the Genoese, the Swiss and the Germans, excited by the amount of profit to be made, brought boundless quantities of gold and silver into France; and many of them settled here, attracted as much by the sweetness of the air as by the natural kindness of the people and the fertility of the country. By the same means, the established revenue of the city of Paris, which amounts to {1,400,000 or 1,500,000} [3,350,000] *livres* a year, has attracted foreigners who bring their money to make a profit, and then settle here; which has greatly increased the wealth of this city. The truth is, in my opinion, that the mechanical arts and trade would flourish much more, without being hindered by our trade in silver, and the city would be much wealthier, if we did as they do in Genoa, where the house of Saint George takes money from anyone who wishes to employ it at the {fifth} [twentieth] *denier* and lends it to merchants for the purposes of trade at the twelfth or fifteenth *denier*, which has helped bring about the greatness and wealth of that city, and which seems to me very advantageous for the public as well as for the individual. However, I admire even more the prudence and goodness of two great emperors, Antoninus Pius and Alexander Severus, who lent silver from their reserves to individuals at four per cent, which is only at the twenty-fifth *denier*; and what is more, Augustus lent it without interest to those who guaranteed to pay double if they failed to return the money at the appointed time, as Suetonius says. He thus deprived the financiers of an opportunity to plunder the public; the poor subjects traded and profited much, and the prince was not compelled to borrow, or to alienate his domain, or to exploit his people. But on the other hand the excellent Alexander, managing his affairs in this fashion, lowered the tributes and taxes by thirty parts so that he who paid thirty-one *écus* in tax and subsidy under Heliogabalus (a monster of nature) paid only one under Alexander.

These, Sire, are the means by which we have acquired gold and silver in abundance during the past 200 years. There is much more of it in Spain and in Italy than in France, because in Italy even the nobility engages in trade, and the people of Spain have no other occupation. Furthermore, everything is more expensive in Spain and Italy than in France, and more so in Spain than in Italy. And this holds even for services and manufacturing which attract our people from Auvergne and Limousin to Spain, as I have learned from themselves, because they earn three times as much as they earn in France, for the Spaniard, rich, haughty and idle, sells his labour at a very high price. Clenard testifies in his letters on the subject of expenditure that he paid, on a single item, fifteen ducats a year to have his beard trimmed in Portugal. It is thus the abundance of gold and silver which is, in part, the cause of the dearness of things.

I pass over the other reason for high prices, as being not so important to the case at hand, namely, monopolies of merchants, artisans and labourers when they unite to fix the prices of goods or to enhance their daily wage or the price of their work. And because such associations normally cover themselves with the veil of religion, the Chancellor Poyet wisely advised that we ought to abolish and restrict fraternities, and this was subsequently confirmed at the request of the Estates of Orleans. So there is no lack of good laws.

The third cause of high prices is scarcity, which arises for two reasons. The one is excessive exports from the kingdom, or the prevention of the importation of necessities. The other is waste. So far as export is concerned, it is certain that we had wine and corn on more favourable terms during the war with Spain and Flanders than we did after the war when export was permitted. For the farmer has to make money, the merchant dares not load his ships, the lords cannot store perishables for long, and consequently the people cannot but live cheaply. For our fathers gave us an old proverb, that France is never hungry; that is to say, France is well supplied with the wherewithal to feed her people, even in a bad year, provided that the foreigner does not empty our barns. Now it is a fact that corn is no sooner ripe than the Spaniard imports it, the reason being that Spain, apart from Aragon and Grenada, is very infertile, added to which is the idleness which is, as I have said, natural to the people. Consequently, grain dealers in Portugal have remarkable privileges. Among other things, it is forbidden to arrest anyone who is bringing corn to market. If this happens, the people may overpower the officer, provided that he who is carrying the corn says in a loud voice 'Traho dridigo', that is, I am bringing corn. [Although it is forbidden under severe penalties to take gold and silver out of Spain, this is, as an exception, permitted for the purchase of corn.] In consequence, the Spaniards import a great quantity of corn. Furthermore, Languedoc and Provence supply Tuscany and Barbary with almost all their corn, which causes an abundance of silver and raises the price of corn; for we get almost no other goods from Spain than oil and spices. Also, we get the best medicines from Barbary and the Levant. From Italy we get all our alum and some serges and silk. Yet the low country of Languedoc and Provence has more oil than we need for our provision. And as for serges and silks, there are, in the opinion of the experts, as good made in this kingdom as in Florence or Genoa; and the merchants know well how to profit from them, fixing the price at whatever level they like. As for alum, if we were prepared to exploit the veins of the Pyrenees, it is certain that we would find rich deposits not only of alum but also of gold and silver, seeing that we have favourable reports from many Germans; and Maître Dominique Bertin has shown me on the spot, and given proof to King Henry, that all metals are present there, with an endless amount of copperas, alum, and marcasite. Among other things, it was found that there is more alum than would be needed to supply the whole of France although, as he has shown, more than 1,000,000 of it comes from Italy every year. It is to him that we owe the beautiful black and white marbles, veined woods, jaspers and serpentine marbles that he sends to Paris from the Pyrenees, and he assures me that if he had the influence we would have nothing more to do with Italian alum. If we did this, the Italians would have nothing apart from trinkets, imitation jewels and perfume to draw silver out of this kingdom. One means they have found, having nothing to exchange for our goods, is to sell us perfumes which are so dear that, as you know, a certain Italian *parfumeur* sold some perfume for 400 *écus* worth of gloves to a gentleman of this kingdom, and that was only to meet his personal needs for a year. If I had my wish, I would prefer princes to hold such things in as little esteem as the Emperor Vespasian did. I am sure that the perfumes of Gascony would reduce the price of those of Italy.

As to the fourth cause of high prices: it is the pleasure of princes which determines the price of things; for it is a general rule in matters of state and in commonwealths, as Plato was the first to see, that not only do kings give law to their subjects but they also change customs and ways of life at their will, both in vice, and in virtue, and in things indifferent. I will cite only the example of King Francis I, who had his hair cut short to cure a wound on his head. At once the courtiers and then the whole people had their hair cut short, so that nowadays we mock the long hair which, in earlier times, was the mark of beauty and freedom. (Also, the ancients deemed fair hair to be the pride of the people of the north.) Our first kings therefore forbade their subjects, other than natural born Franks, to have long hair, as a mark of servitude; a custom which lasted until Peter Lombard, Bishop of Paris, removed the prohibition by the authority which bishops then had over kings. This will suffice, in passing, to show that the people always conform themselves to the will of the prince and consequently value and increase the price of everything that great lords favour, although the things themselves are not worth it. [Thus the Emperor Caracalla, as history tells us, gave golden amber an inestimable value because it had the same colour as the hair of his sweetheart.]

We have seen three great princes contemporary with each other and vying with one another to see which of them had the most precious stones, the most learned men, and the best artisans: namely, the great King Francis, Pope Paul III, and King Henry of England. Thus King Francis never wanted the King of England to have Monsieur Budé, no matter how much he asked; and he would rather pay {60,000 francs} [72,000 *écus sol* full weight] for a diamond than let the King of England have it. At once the nobility and the people began to study all the sciences and buy precious stones whatever they cost, with the result that the Italians, having become aware of our appetites, produced more artificial stones in twenty years than all the natural stones ever produced by the Indies. As Cardan writes, they themselves could not conceal their contempt, calling the French blockheads for letting themselves be tricked in this way. Since King Henry scorned jewellery, we have seen the trade in it fall away. It is, therefore, the pleasure of great lords, and not scarcity, which raises the price of precious stones, seeing that such stones cannot diminish or perish, except for emeralds which are a little fragile and pearls which grow black and rotten with age. But when the great lords see their subjects possessing in abundance the things which they love, they begin to despise such things. In addition, abundance of itself devalues a thing, as we see with pearls, in which there is a great trade thanks to the huge number of them which have been imported from the New World. [For we find in the history of the Indies that a fifth of the pearls brought to the emperor in one shipment came to 160 pounds in weight.] Yet in ancient times the pearl was, as Pliny says, the most precious natural jewel. Moreover, a very distinguished man or a thing outstanding in excellence is commonly described as a pearl; and the great Negus whom we call Prester John, lord of fifty provinces, includes in his titles of honour Jochan Belul, that is to say, precious pearl. In ancient times, pearls were thus the most costly things in the world [as Pliny says in one place], as much for their rarity {which was such that they were called *uniones*} as for the estimation put upon them by princes, which was strange and almost incredible. Be that as it may, we know that Queen Cleopatra had two of them each weighing an ounce and valued at 500,000 *écus*. She liquified one of them and swallowed it for a bet; the other was brought back by Augustus as the most splendid spoil of his victory; he had it cut in two and fastened to the ears of Venus. Eight years ago we had a completely white one which weighed little less than half an ounce and was set with five large precious stones. Nonetheless, the whole value was estimated at only 1,300 *écus* which, in the opinion of the lapidaries, was a great deal. This shows that the abundance of pearls has caused them to be devalued, and it is this that makes them cheap.

We can say the same of paintings. The princes of the Levant, and even Alexander the Great, held painting in such high esteem that the picture of Venus rising from the water painted by Apelles, was bought for 60,000 *écus*; Alexander gave him 200 talents of his own money, which were worth 120,000 *écus*. The pictures of other painters were not so highly valued, but the least of them was very expensive. Apelles did not hesitate to buy a picture by Protogenes for 50,000 *écus*. We have pictures by Michaelangelo, Raphael d'Urbino, Durel, and, without going far afield, a picture by Monsieur de Clagny in the gallery of Fontainebleau, an admirable masterpiece; all of which many have compared with the pictures of Apelles. There are many others of remarkable workmanship; but they do not come anywhere near the prices commanded by the ancients, because princes hold them in low esteem, and because all the peoples of the Levant and of Barbary as far as Persia utterly abominate any representation of the things nature produces, for fear of violating the commandment, Thou shalt make no graven image. So that painters, molders, foundrymen, sculptors and illuminators have no place or credit in that part of the world, any more than their works. It is, therefore, the pleasure of great lords which makes the price of things go up.

The last cause of high prices is the waste of what we ought to use sparingly. Silk ought to be cheap in view of how much of it we make in this kingdom, in addition to what we import from Italy. Its high price is due to waste; for we not only dress ragamuffins and flunkeys in it but we also slash it in such a manner that it cannot last or be of any service except to one master; for which the Turks, I have heard, quite rightly reproach us, calling us desperate madmen for wasting, as if in contempt of God, the gifts which He bestows on us. They have, beyond comparison, more silk than we do, but it is more than anybody's life is worth to slash it.

The same goes for clothing, and especially for breeches, where we use three times as much cloth as is necessary, with so much slashing and pinking that the poor cannot use them when Monsieur has tired of them. What is more, we use up three pairs where one would do, and, to complement the breeches, we need an extra ell of material to make a jerkin. Good edicts have been issued, but they have no effect, for, since what is forbidden is worn at court, it is worn everywhere, and the situation is such that officers of the law are intimidated by some and corrupted by others. Together with this, in matters of dress, those who are not attired in the current fashion are deemed to be louts and blockheads. This fashion came to us from Spain, just as the farthingale did, which we borrowed from the Moors, with the result that doors are now too narrow for the ladies to get through. All this is far removed from the ancient modesty of our forefathers who, as Cæsar tells us, wore plain clothes shaped to the body, bringing out the proportion and beauty of the limbs. The Germans, by contrast, wore their clothes loose, which produces incredible waste, and from waste comes scarcity, and from scarcity comes, in part, the high cost of clothing. And then there is the tailoring, which often exceeds the cost of the material by enriching it with embroidery, purfling, lace, fringes, twists, silver thread, purling, germanders, broderie, stitching, back-stitchings and other devices invented from time to time. [For after the prohibition of cloth of gold and silver there were ladies who wore dresses made in Milan and costing 500 *écus* though made with neither gold nor jewels.] And from such finery we turn to the furnishings of the house: to beds of cloth of gold or exquisite embroideries, to sideboards of gold and silver; and, in order to have everything just so, it is necessary to build or rent magnificently, so that the furniture fits the house and one's manner of life is consistent with one's manner of dress. So also it is necessary that the table be furnished with many dishes. Because of the nature of his region, which is colder than Spain and Italy, the Frenchman cannot live on toothpicks as the Italian can. Hence the excessive superfluity of all kinds of meat and delicacies unknown to our forefathers which has prevailed in this kingdom to such an extent that there is no shopboy who does not want to dine at the Moor for one *écu*, his master for two *écus*, a head. [This is one of the most pernicious nuisances to be found in Paris.]

However, these are not the greatest excesses, seeing that in reviewing the cases of the financiers, it was found that one of them sent twelve bundles of shirts to be bleached from Paris to Flanders at one *teston* each; and never gave less than a *teston* as gratuity. [But God was avenged on him, for the executioner, after having strangled him, stripped him of his shirt.] This was one of the reasons that moved the chancellor, du Prat, to make himself the sworn enemy of such pilferers, who corrupt the simplicity of the people and deliberately make things dearer: and the worst of it, so far as I am concerned, is that this is done at the expense of the prince and the people.

I say, therefore, that waste and extravagance of this kind is, in part, the cause of the high price of provisions that we have experienced. I set aside the fact that it is also the source of all the vices and calamities of the commonwealth, because it is necessary to speculate, borrow, sell, wallow in every luxury and, in the end, pay off one's creditors by means of fair compositions or bankruptcies. But if the ancient laws of the Romans, Greeks, Hebrews and Egyptians held in France as they do in [the Indies and] the whole of Ethiopia, so that, in other words, in default of payment, the debtor should be forfeit to the creditor to be sold by him or to serve as his slave, we would not see so many thieves, assignees or bankrupts, nor would the high prices which, as we have seen, are caused by extravagance be anywhere near what they are.

At this point, someone will say that if the prices of things increase partly because of waste and partly also because of the abundance of gold and silver, then {we would finally be all made of gold and} no one would be able to live because of the expense. This is true; but wars and disasters which afflict commonwealths arrest the course of things. As we know, the Romans lived very austerely and, if it must be said, in remarkable poverty for almost 500 years, when they had only heavy brass money, one pound in weight and unstamped, until King Servius. Furthermore, they did not mint silver coin until 485 years after the foundation of Rome, as can be seen in their annals; sixty-two years later, gold coinage came into use. If we look at the prices at this time, we find that a sheep was valued at only ten brass *asses*, which the learned Budé takes to be three and a half *sols* of his time and at most four of ours; an ox cost one hundred *asses*, which he estimates at one *écu couronne*. And that was the price estimated by the *lex Ateria Trapeia*, 280 years after the foundation of Rome. At that time the wage of a foot soldier, according to Polybius, was only two *oboles*, four for a centurion, for a cavalryman one *denier*, which was worth three and a half *sols* [in coin minted at four *deniers* twelve grains. We read in Plutarch that at the time of Solon the price of a sheep was only one drachma, which was a seventh part less than at Rome 200 years later].

As for the price of other provisions, one can judge it by the *lex Fannia* which, in the year 592 after the foundation, curtailed expenses by specifically forbidding the expenditure of more than a hundred *asses*, which is one *écu couronne*, on the banquets which took place during the great games, and ten *asses* at other times on condition that no fowl was served except barnyard chickens; and this edict was published throughout Italy at the request of Didius, tribune of the people. Sixty-four years later, the wealthy Crassus, noticing that provisions were becoming progressively more expensive, allowed the expenditure of one hundred *asses* on festal days, calends, nones and ides, and at weddings 200 *asses* which equals two *écus*: one was permitted to have three pounds of dry meat, one pound of salt meat, as much fruit as one wanted; on other days, thirty *asses*, which equals one *teston*. Twenty-seven years later, when the city was enriched with the spoils of Greece and Asia, the people could not be restrained, in addition to which the prices of everything had increased due to the abundance of gold and silver. Sulla, the dictator, seeing the old ordinances go up in smoke, curbed expenditure as much as he could, and at the same time permitted an increase of two-thirds more than Crassus had allowed, although he reduced the tax on food. Thirty-six years later, Cæsar, the most abstemious lord that ever there was, seeing the whole people given over to excessive banqueting, made an edict by which he forbade the expenditure of more than twenty-five *écus* on weddings, and as for other festal days and holidays, seven and a half *écus*, which was ten times more than Sulla had permitted. Nonetheless, so little notice was taken of his edicts that in order to enforce them he was obliged to go into the market place secretly. Since then, no one has made any ordinance on the subject. Caligula even wanted to give his subjects an example of extreme prodigality, spending in less than a year 22,000,000 of gold, which Tiberius had accumulated.

We see, then, how the abundance of gold and silver and waste raised the prices of everything from the time of Sulla to that of Caligula, which is less than 200 years. We will find that luxury fish, such as mullet, turbot, goldfish, dentex, sturgeon, and conger eel were purchased at their weight in pure silver, as Galen tells us. There was indeed an epicure, who does not deserve to be named, who paid 200 *écus* for a sea mullet weighing only two pounds, which was buying it at its weight in gold. We catch them in our ocean and sometimes in the Loire, into which they stray, at three or four pounds in weight for fifteen or twenty *sols*, because the great lords and the people prefer meat.

From these examples we can judge the cost of all other things. For the peafowl at the time of Varro cost fifty silver *deniers*, which is five *écus*, and a brace of fine pigeons sold for twenty-five *écus*. Since that time the prices of all things have increased tenfold, as we have shown. Pliny goes further, for he says that a certain Hirrius gave 6,000 conger eel, which, length apart, have nothing in common with our lampreys in weight and number, on condition that as many were returned to him, and he did not want to sell any for either gold or silver, which was of little account due to the abundance of it in Rome. For there was no scarcity of things, since everything was brought to Rome from all parts of the world as to a market.

The truth is that extravagance has helped to raise the prices of food; for there are rich people who sometimes do not know what to do with what they have, as in the case of Æsop the tragedian, who, to whet his appetite, had himself served with a dish, valued at 50,000 *écus*, consisting of nightingales, starlings, blackbirds and other song-birds, although such birds are unpalatable and unpleasant. Nonetheless, the cost gave them flavour. [And Athenæus tells of a certain person who, having arrived in Slavonia to eat crayfish, which are well regarded in that country, was told before disembarking that incomparably finer and better specimens were to be had down towards Africa; on hearing which he set sail for Africa to eat them there.] His son, fearing to disgrace his father, imbibed liquified pearls of inestimable value. And we need not be surprised that a tragic actor had so much money, for clowns and comedians were held in so high esteem that Roscius had 36,000 *écus* each year for playing the fool a dozen times before the people, and that is not counting the profit he received from his regular performances [which were worth a hundred times more].

However, in order to demonstrate the abundance of gold and silver more clearly, there is no better example than that of the master cook Apicius, who, having squandered 3,000,000 *écus*, still had 350,000 left, yet nonetheless, fearing that he might die of hunger, poisoned himself, as several historians testify. This leads me to accept as true what is said of Cicero, namely, that he was given a house worth 50,000 *écus* for pleading a case; for, if jesters had such credit with the people, it is not surprising that an advocate such as Cicero should be so well rewarded.

Now, all this gold and silver was got within the space of 120 years; it was the plunder of the whole world, brought to Rome by the Scipios, Æmilius Paulus, Marius, Sulla, Lucullus, Pompey and Cæsar, and especially by the last two. For

Pompey conquered so many countries that he increased the revenue of the empire to 8,500,000 *écus*, which was two and three-fifths more than it was before. Cæsar brought 40,000,000 *écus* to the treasury, above and beyond his extravagant expenditure; for on one occasion he gave 900,000 *écus* to Paulus, the consul, in return for his silence, and, on another, 1,500,000 *écus* to Curio the tribune for joining his party. Mark Antony surpassed him, if what Plutarch and Appian write is true, for he gave his army 200,000 talents for distinguished service, which amounts to 120,000,000 *écus*. This is entirely credible in view of the fact that the Emperor Hadrian, who was a careful administrator, gave 10,000,000 *écus* to his legions, of which there were forty, in order to secure their allegiance.

It is, therefore, no surprise that things were dear, considering the abundance of gold and silver in Rome. However, these extravagancies and luxuries did not last forever, for in less than 300 years the Parthians, the Goths, the Herullians, the Hungarians and other fierce nations plundered the entire empire, including Italy itself, trampled the Romans under foot, burned their city, and pillaged their ill-gotten gains. This is the way of all commonwealths. They are born and grow little by little; then they flourish in wealth and power, and afterwards they grow old and decay until they are completely ruined, as I have shown in the discussion of the state of commonwealths in my *Method for the Easy Comprehension of History*.

We have discussed the reasons for the rise in the prices of things. It remains to show that Monsieur de Malestroit is also mistaken as to the standard of money minted in this kingdom during the last 300 years. For he says that Saint Louis caused to be minted the first *sols* equal to twelve *deniers* and that there were only sixty-four of them to the mark. He also says that at the time of Philip of Valois, the *écu d'or aux fleurs de lis sans nombre*, superior to ours in weight and alloy, was worth only twenty *sols*; that shortly afterwards King John caused to be minted *francs à pied* and *à cheval* of fine gold, which were worth only twenty *sols*; and furthermore that the silver *sol* of that time was worth five of ours. He does not tell us of what standard, of what weight and alloy, the coins were.

On the last point, he contradicts himself. For it is agreed that the old *écu*, which weighs three *deniers* full weight, is worth only sixty of our *sols* as coined by order of King Francis I. Therefore, the old *sol* of fine silver was worth only three of ours. Nonetheless, the *francs à pied* and *à cheval* weigh less than the old *écu* by four grains, and their alloy is no better, seeing that between the one and the other there is a difference of quarter of a carat. Furthermore, by the ordinance of the year 1561, the old *écu* is valued at sixty *sols* and the *franc à pied* and *à cheval* at fifty-five *sols*. Therefore, as to the proportion of the old *sols* to our, he miscalculates by almost half. For if what he says were the case, namely, that the old *sol* of fine silver was worth five times as much as ours, then the old *écu* would be worth a hundred *sols*, and the *franc à pied* or *à cheval* would be worth four *livres* and ten *sols*.

In the second place, Monsieur de Malestroit is mistaken in leaving out the interval of 123 years between Saint Louis and Philip of Valois, during which time Philip the Fair, grandson of Saint Louis, in the year 1300, adulterated the silver coinage to such an extent that a *sol* of the old money was worth three of the new. We find this in our records and likewise in our annals, and in the history of Antonin to which Monsieur de Livres, a man of great learning, has drawn my attention. And although the money was returned to its former value in order to quell popular unrest, the fact is that ten years later it was so badly adulterated that the *sol* was worth only three and a half *deniers* in silver, in that {three parts} [five-eighths] of it were of copper, which is the most debased money we have seen in our time. For in the year 1551 the *sols* minted by order of King Henry II contained three and a half *deniers* of silver. Such a debasement of the coinage has never been known in living memory. We must, therefore, conclude that, since the *sol* was of the same standard, the same weight and the same alloy, and was just as debased 300 years ago as it is at present, Malestroit's proof and his examples can have no force. For although Charles the Fair restored the old standard of the *sol* to twelve *deniers* of the king's silver in the year 1322, nonetheless, he debased it by a good half six months later.

Furthermore, our records tell us that, in the year 1422, the standard of the *sol* was so poor that the silver mark was worth eighty *livres tournois*, which makes 1,600 pieces in a wrought mark. Therefore, one of {our *sols*} [the *sols* of Henry II] is, on this reckoning, worth five of those *sols*, which is quite the opposite of what Monsieur de Malestroit has suggested, to wit, that an old *sol* was worth five of ours, seeing that 150 years ago five *sols* was worth only one of ours. He must, therefore, refer this former remark to certain years only and not to all of them, as he did for the last 300 years.

In short, whoever wishes to leaf through the 'black book' which is in the chambers of the King's Procurator at the Châtelet de Paris, will find that in the year 1420, when the English held Paris, the *écu* was exchanged for sixty *sols*, the *mouton* for forty, and the noble for seven *livres*, which are the rates and values of {today} [the reign of Henry II]. It is true that Charles VII, in November 1422, caused new coinage to be struck at twelve *deniers* so that the silver mark of eighty *livres* was put back to eight *livres* and four *sols tournois*. But in 1453, *sols* at five *deniers* of alloy were minted, which brought the good money down by much more than half.

It is, therefore, a mistake to take as the basis of our calculations a year when money was strongest and to set aside the years when money was weakest, which were incomparably more frequent than the good years. To draw a parallel, it is as if we were to draw conclusions concerning other commodities from the current cheapness of matches in Paris.

I have shown above that the price of things set by the customs of this kingdom, agreed and confirmed for fifty and in some cases sixty years, was ten times less than it is at present. Yet it is certain that the estates and deputies, in agreeing the customs, followed neither the lowest nor the highest price but the most common estimate current at the time, as our laws tell us. Nonetheless, a capon is worth only twelve *deniers tournois* according to the customs of Anjou, Poitou, La Marche, Champagne, Bourbonnais, and other places; a chicken is worth six *deniers*, a partridge fifteen *deniers*, a fatted sheep with wool seven *sols*, a pig ten *deniers*, an ordinary sheep and a cow five *sols* each, a kid three *sols*, a load of wheat thirty, a wagon of hay weighing fifteen hundredweight ten, which is ten bundles for a *sol*, a bundle weighing fifteen pounds. That is the custom of Auvergne. In Bourbonnais, twelve hundredweight are valued at ten *sols*, a tun of wine at thirty, a tun of honey at thirty-five, an acre of woodland fetches two francs and six *deniers* in rent, an acre of vines thirty francs, a pound of butter is worth four *deniers*, nut oil is the same, and so is tallow. As I said above, it was at the time of Louis XII that the *sol* which is now at three *deniers* and twelve grains was at four *deniers* and twelve grains. Thus, the *sol* at the time of Louis XII was worth only one *liard* more than {one of ours} [in the reign of Henry II]; and four *sols* were not worth five of ours; from which it follows that a calf and a sheep with its wool should, at the most, be valued at six *sols* and three *deniers* of our debased money, since sixty years ago they cost only five *sols* throughout France. The same can be said of other things. However, we see that the common value of each is four *livres*, or a hundred *sols*, indeed six *livres* in Paris, which is twenty or thirty times dearer than it was then.

If, then, the fruits of the earth, cattle and poultry cost ten or twelve or twenty times less than they do now, the revenue of lands and lordships was worth less in proportion, and ground rent was cheaper; and for the same reason land was valued at ten times less. For the best common land was valued at only twenty or twenty-five *deniers*, a fief at thirty *deniers*, and a [well furnished] house at {forty} [forty or fifty] *deniers*. Therefore, land which yielded 1,000 *écus* sixty years ago was sold for only twenty-five or at the most 30,000 *écus*. If then the revenue has grown to 5,000 or 6,000 *écus*, land which was then worth only 30,000 *écus* will sell for 150,000 *écus*. As for statute-labour and the craftsman's daily wage, we find that from ancient times they were set, as it were, at a silver *denier* which was worth little more than a Spanish *real*; and in ancient times the wage of a horseman was only a *denier*, as Polybius tells us. Furthermore, a foot soldier received one *denier* a day. This was maintained even at the time of Augustus, as Tacitus writes, although it is true that the gifts made to armies for distinguished service were worth twenty times as much as the wage. This, I believe, is the origin of our expression day-labourer, which applies only to those who hire themselves out by the day; and even in Scripture the master says to those labourers in the vineyard who resented his generosity towards the others, 'Do you not have the *denier* that I promised you for the day?' [In Greece, a drachma was the wage of a soldier and of a day-labourer in a vineyard.] However, as I have said, by our customs established and amended during the past sixty years or so, the daily wage of a man in summer is valued at only six *deniers*, in winter at four *deniers*, and with his ox-cart at twelve *deniers*. Copper money has neither increased nor decreased in weight either before or during the past sixty years. Nonetheless, we find that instead of six *deniers*, the vineyard labourer, the brewer, the labourer, the soldier is not content with five *sols*; even in this country they want eight or ten, complaining that otherwise they cannot live. As for the statute-labour of oxen, the lowest price at which it can be had is twenty francs, which is twenty times as much as it was worth sixty years ago, in whatever money you choose. This is the reason why judges, who have the power to bend customs but not to break them, when assessing taxes, revenues, the value of produce or anything of that kind, refer not to the customs but to the ordinance on the evaluation of produce together with the commonly accepted price, [or else they order the parties to agree on assessors to make a valuation.]

We have spoken of silver money. Let us deal also with gold money, so that anyone may judge at a glance that the rise in prices is not due to any alteration in the coinage.

I find that the finest gold money coined in any country during the past 300 years is no finer than twenty-three and three-quarters carats. Such are the nobles, the old ducats of Venice, Florence, Siena and Portugal, the Turkish *seraph*, the *medins* of the Barbary coast, the ancient medallions of Rome, the old double ducats of Castille, the *moutons à la grand laine*, the old *écus*, the *saluts*, the *francs à pied* and *à cheval*, and the old *angelots*. The *écus couronne* are not anywhere near as fine; the *milrais* and the *écus soleil* are worth more; and then the *Henris* and double *Henris*, the gold *reals*, *pistolets* and double ducats of Portugal are less fine. As for other coins in which there are less than twenty-two carats, that is to say, if they contain more than one twelfth of alloy, be it copper or silver, and less than ten parts of gold, it is not gold, except for the purpose of being worked. Similarly, silver which is lower than ten *deniers*, or rather which contains more than a sixth part of copper alloy and less than five parts of silver, is not silver for money purposes but debased coinage. For this reason, the ancients called gold containing a fifth part of silver electrum.

Let us, therefore, take it that the old *écu* and the *franc à pied* and *à cheval*, which are the coins to which Monsieur de Malestroit refers, are twenty-four carats with a carat to compensate for wear and tear; the *écus au soleil* at twenty-three and an eighth by way of compensation, according to the ordinance of the year 1540; or twenty-three carats and a quarter of a carat to compensate for wear and tear, as are the *écus* minted by the ordinance of King Henry II; they will differ from the old by only one carat. And as for weight, the *écus sol* of the year 1540 weigh two *deniers* sixteen grains full weight, at seventy-two to the mark, as much as the Emperor Justinian put in a *livre*, which caused Monsieur Charles du Moulin, that paragon of jurisconsults, to regard our *écu* as being on the same footing as that of Justinian. But the relation could also be said to be two to three. For just as the *mark* has eight ounces, and the *livre* of Justinian twelve, so the gold *écu* coined by his ordinance, which he calls *solidus*, weighs a third more than ours, just as the *angelot* does. Since then, some have been coined, by the order of King Henry, at two *deniers* fifteen, and then fourteen, grains full weight. Now, the gold franc weighs four grains less than the old *écu* and four grains more than the *écu sol* minted in the year 1540. So if we compare them as to weight, we will find that the old *écu* is worth only an eighth more than the *écu sol*, and the gold franc nearly a ninth more than the same *écu sol*; for there are eight old *écus* in an ounce, nine *écus soleil*, and ten *écus couronne*; of gold francs, there are less than nine of them and more than eight. Also, the old *écu* is, by the ordinance of King Henry II, sixty *sols*, the franc fifty-five, the *écu sol* fifty-two, and the *écu couronne* fifty.

We must, therefore, conclude that if a house, which was sold for 200 old *écus* 120 years ago, is today sold for 800 *écus sol*, which is worth 2,000 *livres tournois* in our debased coinage, deducting the one eighth by which an old *écu* exceeds the *écu sol* in value, we are left with 673 *écus sol* worth 1,750 *livres* at the time of Henry II, or 35,000 *sols* of our money. And if we calculated it in gold francs, it would be necessary to deduct only one ninth of them, leaving 780 *écus sol* at which the house is sold, which is three times more than it cost then. I wanted to calculate this in detail, because Monsieur de Malestroit has not said what proportion there is between the *écus* to accommodate them to our contracts.

So much for the general rise in prices, without touching on particular changes which make the prices of things rise above their ordinary price, such as food at a time of famine, arms at a time of war, wood in winter, or water in the Libyan desert. There is a tomb on the plain of Azoa upon which there is an inscription attesting that a merchant bought a cup of water from a wagon-driver for 10,000 ducats and that nonetheless both buyer and seller died of thirst, as Leo of Africa writes. Or consider items of craftsmanship and hardware in places where such things are not made. They are usually cheaper in towns full of artisans, such as Limoges, Milan, Nuremberg, Genoa, Paris, Damascus and Venice. Another factor is the greater abundance of people and money in one place as against another, as in Istanbul, Rome, Paris, Lyon, Venice, Florence, Antwerp, Seville, and London. Furthermore, food is more expensive where the courts of kings, or great lords or merchants, attract people and money. [This happened regularly at Rome, where there was an abundance of gold and silver and of people who gathered there from all the ends of the earth. Famine was often so bad there that Augustus was forced to expel from the city the crowds of slaves and gladiators and all foreigners, except teachers and physicians; and, in addition, he sent twenty-eight colonies from Rome and despatched them throughout Italy.] Sometimes the change also comes by a new edict, as happened at Rome when the price of houses was suddenly increased by half by the edict of Trajan ordering all those who aspired to honourable status or office to spend a third part of their wealth on purchasing estates in Rome or its environs. All these particular cases are not germane to the general case under consideration.

As we now know that prices have risen and understand the reasons for this, which are the two main points which we had to prove against Malestroit, it remains to seek the least bad of the possible remedies. This is a matter which Malestroit did not touch on, holding as he did that prices have not risen.

First, the abundance of gold and silver, which is the wealth of a country, should in part excuse the rise in prices; for if there were such a lack of it as there was in the past, it is certain that everything would be bought and sold for so much less and that gold and silver would be valued more highly.

As for monopolies and extravagance, I have said what I wish to say above. But it is futile to issue fine ordinances on the subject of monopolies and extravagance in matters of food and clothing, if one does not have the will to enforce them. And they will never be enforced unless the king, of his goodness, compels his courtiers to keep them; for in matters of pomp and extravagance most people conduct themselves according to the example set by the courtiers; and there never was a commonwealth in which health or disease did not flow from the head down to all the members.

As for the export of goods from this kingdom, many persons of distinction strive and have striven, both in speech and writing, to curtail it as far as possible, believing that we can live happily and very cheaply without sending anything out or bringing anything in from abroad. But in my view they are mistaken, for we cannot manage without doing business with foreigners. I admit that we send them corn, wine, salt, saffron, pastel, dried plums, paper, cloth, and rough linen; but in exchange we get from them, first of all, all the metals except iron; we get gold, silver, tin, copper, lead, steel, quicksilver, alum, sulphur, vitriol, copperas, cinnabar, oil, wax, honey, pitch, brazil-wood, ebony, dye-wood, guaiac, ivory, morocco leather, fine cloth, cochineal, scarlet, crimson, all kinds of drugs, spices, sugars, horses, cured salmon, sardines, mackerel, cod, in short, an endless amount of good food and excellent manufactured commodities.

And even if we should be able to do without these commodities, which would not be at all possible even if we had enough of them and to spare, we should still need to trade, sell, buy, exchange, lend and, indeed, give a part of our goods to foreigners, and especially to our neighbours, if only to communicate with them and maintain goodwill between them and ourselves.

I say further that even if we were rich in all the gifts of God, and had received all that man can be granted in arms and law, without fear or hope of anyone, we should still owe them this charity by natural obligation: namely, to share with them the benefits with which God has endowed us, and to teach and shape them in honour and virtue. In this regard, the Romans showed themselves unworthy to rule. When the greatness of their power touched the very heavens and they had extended their empire from the setting to the rising of the sun, certain nations sent emissaries to them to place themselves under their power and render them voluntary obedience. The Romans, seeing that they had nothing to gain from this, declined these offers, as Appian writes. This was a most cowardly act, and the most villainous affront to God ever committed, as if the sovereign right to command and do justice, even over poor and ill-educated peoples, were not the greatest gift of God and the greatest honour that man can receive on this earth. This was certainly very far from sharing their goods and wealth with them, as they ought to have done.

But someone will say that Plato and Lycurgus forbade trade with foreigners, fearing that their subjects would be harmed and corrupted. This is true. But the one had a dream that could never be accomplished, even though he tried; and the other accomplished what no man had ever dared to hope for. And yet, if I am not greatly mistaken, both would have done better to permit trade, as Moses wisely did, thus showing that he was a greater leader than those two. For the light of virtue is so bright that not only does it dispel the shadows of wickedness, but it also increases in brightness the more it is shared. Yet we cannot pride ourselves so much in our virtue as to assume that foreigners will not be able to equal us.

Again, it will be said that, apart from maintaining good relations with them, we should not give our goods to foreigners, and certainly not to enemies. Nonetheless, if, having enough, we did so, we would gain their friendship, which is better than making war on them, since God, against Whom we have blasphemed and made war without respite, sets us an example with His boundless generosity. But because this cannot be got into the heads of those who value nothing but gain, however sordid and dishonest, God has with admirable foresight made provision, for He has distributed His favours in such a way that there is no country in the world so well provided for as not to lack many things. And He seems to have done this in order to maintain all the subjects of His commonwealth in friendship, or at least to prevent them from making war for any length of time, since they always have to do business with one another.

I would certainly suggest, if I were in a position to give advice, that it should be forbidden to trade with the Italians for women's clothing, perfumes, lead, parchment, artificial stones, and fish; and I would exclude all their bankrupts and those banished from their country, unless they were banished for being too virtuous, as was done in Athens and Ephesus. To this end foreigners should display a certificate of approval from the prince or lord [or from some persons of substance and honour]. That would set an example for other peoples to follow and make evildoers tremble by depriving them of any sure refuge in the world. But I see that the {pagans and infidels} [Turks] teach us a lesson on this subject; for Muhammad the Great, Emperor of the Turks, set us a good example in the case of a [Florentine] murderer who, having assassinated Giuliano de Medici during a church service, repaired to Istanbul, seat of the empire. This great lord sent him back to Florence, bound hand and foot, in order that justice might be done. But as long as we open the window to individuals who are expelled, foul air and pestilence will always enter, and there will never be any lack of opportunists who drink the blood, pick the bones, and suck the marrow of the prince and the people. They even go into print to praise and describe as virtues the most execrable vices the world has ever seen; something our forefathers never imagined. Nonetheless such people are welcomed and cherished everywhere.

As for other foreigners, I would not only wish them to be treated with kindness and friendship, but I would also wish the injuries they have suffered to be avenged with every rigour, as the law of God commands; indeed even that we free them from the law of *escheat* to the Crown, {which applies only in this kingdom and in England,} provided that the heir is a resident of the country; the more so because we see that this law brings nothing but dishonour to France and profit to the leeches of the court, besides which it impedes the flow of trade, which ought to be free and unhindered, for the wealth and greatness of a kingdom.

There remains only one argument, to which a brief response is required. They say that when trade flourishes everything in the country becomes dearer. I reject this point, because the imports which replace the goods exported lower the price of what would otherwise be scarce. Besides, to hear such people one would think that merchants give away their goods for nothing, or that the riches of the Indies and fortunate Arabia spring from our native soil. I make an exception of corn, the export of which should be managed more wisely than it is. For we experience high prices and intolerable famines because we do not provide against them. The result, to our great shame, is that France, which ought to be the granary of the West, imports ship-loads of bad rye from, as often as not, the Baltic coast. The way to regulate this is for each town to have a public granary and for the old corn to be replaced every year, as the ancients did in all well-regulated towns [and in this kingdom as well, before the quarrels between the houses of Orleans and Burgundy]. In doing this, we would never experience prices as high as those we have witnessed, because, apart from the fact that we would have provision for lean years, we would curtail the monopolies of merchants who corner the market in corn, often buying it before it is ripe, in order to fix the price at their pleasure.

It was thus that Joseph, supreme lord of Egypt, counteracted seven years of famine in almost the whole world, and Trajan by the same means saved Egypt from a year of famine, despite the fact that Egypt was the bountiful foster-mother of the East.

As for those who wish to dig up all the vineyards and replace them with wheat, or at least to prohibit the planting of any further vineyards, the peasants quite rightly regard such odinances as ridiculous. [And I note that the Emperor Domitian issued an edict on the subject in which he prohibited the planting of any more vineyards and commanded all imperial authorities outside Italy to root up half the vines; but this was never implemented. Moreover, Varro holds that the vine is the most precious inheritance of all]. Furthermore, God, by His good grace, has so arranged things that it is impossible for all land to be devoted either to vines or to wheat. For the best soil for vines is useless for wheat, in that the latter flourishes best in the rich and heavy soil of the plains whereas the former require stony hillsides. Besides, the vine, because of the cold, cannot flourish beyond the forty-ninth degree of latitude. Therefore, all the peoples of the North have almost no other wines than those of France and the Rhine; yet they are so fond of them that they kill themselves drinking them. So, to root up the vines would be to root up one of France's greatest sources of wealth.

But there is a method recommended by experts on taxation which would greatly ease the lot of the people and enrich the kingdom: namely, to impose a proportion of the ordinary charges on foreign trade in corn, wine, salt, pastel, linen and cloth, and principally on salt, wine and corn, which are the three elements on which, after God, foreigners depend for their lives, and which can never fail. The mines of the North and of the Indies will soon be exhausted, and gold, once exhausted, can be restored only after 1,000 years, as the alchemists tell us. But our living resources of corn, wine and salt are inexhaustible. So, if a proportion of the ordinary charges were levied on foreign trade, we would get a much better bargain from it in this kingdom, for the foreigner would take from us more sparingly and, since he cannot do without it, he would buy it with solid silver, which would enrich this kingdom. And no matter what measures have been taken in Flanders against the importation of salt from France, the estates of that country have always complained that their cured products were damaged by salt from Spain and Franche-Comté. And when it happens that the salt ponds and solutions of France are deficient on account of rain or cold, the foreigner still buys our salt at three times the price, simply to have it, regardless of cost. Now, it is the case that salt is cheaper in England, Scotland and Flanders than it is in France, except in Guyenne, which is a serious incongruity in terms of government and management. The same is true of wines and pastels, on which foreign princes impose the most excessive taxes conceivable, which would redound to the profit of the king and the kingdom if one imposed a part of the ordinary charges on foreign trade. [If it is said that foreigners would have just cause to complain of this, because of trade agreements, there is a ready answer: namely, that, in spite of trade agreements, they do not desist from laying imposts on their own merchandise; and, what is more, the ordinances of England and Poland prohibit the export of animal skins, so that the mines of England being exhausted, they have nothing left except wool, cloth and salt fish. Again, they have, with severe penalties, strictly forbidden the export of fleeces, as has also been done in this kingdom, in order that the poorer subjects may have the means of earning a living in the cloth trade, and so that the profit of the work should remain within the kingdom. But these edicts do not hold, because for a sum of money a passport can be obtained, as is done in this kingdom, with which the Italians take out an endless quantity of wool by means of the concessions they obtain, which causes incredible harm to the whole kingdom, for the goods which may not be exported become more expensive abroad, and remain on the hands of the owners and merchants of the kingdom unless they sell them for nothing to those who have the authority to take them away; and the workmen and the poor die of hunger.] This has seemed to me to be a noteworthy method for remedying the increase in the prices of those necessities in this kingdom without which the foreigner cannot live.

At this point I will make a suggestion to counteract the high cost of food: a suggestion which may seem somewhat novel to many; but I am sure that Malestroit, who loves a paradox, will not find it strange. It is that the consumption of fish be restored to the same favour as it enjoyed in ancient times; for it is certain that the poor would thus get beef, pork, mutton and cured meats at a better price, and that the price of poultry would be more reasonable. For us this would be very easy, for France is set between the Ocean and the Mediterranean, which is an advantage possessed by no other people on earth except the Spaniards. But unlike Spain, which has very little water and often suffers from drought, we have a 100,000,000 springs, brooks, rivers, lakes, ponds and fisheries full of fish. Yet we eat fish very reluctantly, and only when the eating of meat is forbidden: so much so that on Easter Day many would rather eat rancid fat than sturgeon. This causes the price of fish to remain constant while that of meat goes up, for fishermen will not invest their time and money, seeing that we do not want fish; and the fish, since nobody else will eat them, eat each other. Indeed, I am sure that they would crowd us out of our cities if they could live on land. This happened to the inhabitants of the islands of Majorca and Minorca, who were so beset by rabbits, which they would not eat, that, as Strabo tells us, they were compelled to send ambassadors to Augustus to request the aid of a legion against enemies who ravaged the whole of the open countryside and ruined the towns from end to end.

Nonetheless, there are some insignificant medical men, whom the good Aristophanes calls dung-eaters, who blame their failings on the poor fish and cry it down abominably; or else, hoping to bring credit to their profession and seeing themselves held in low esteem, they play the tyrant over what people eat. I know nothing of their science and cannot judge whether fish is as unhealthy as they say. Nonetheless, I refer to the excellent Sylvius, who blamed them bitterly and disposed of their objections to eating fish, after having exposed their errors to the light of day. It is true that he counselled against variety in food, and against salt fish, and that he preferred fish to be prepared without water if possible. Furthermore, Galen in two places in his works says that there is no food in the world better or more convenient than rock fish, which are infinite in number; and he holds them in much greater esteem than peafowl and pheasants. This is quite obvious, quite apart from anyone's particular experience, because fish is by its very nature so wholesome that it is not subject to any disease whatsoever. It is never measly like pork or hare, nor scurvy like mutton, nor affected with polyps like the goat; also, it is not subject to dropsy [or scab] like sheep, nor ulcers like cattle, nor epilepsy like quails and turkeys, nor inflammations {and the pip} like chickens and capons, nor lice and sparrows, like pigeons. Also, we note that according to divine law pigs and hares, which are nearly all measly in southern climes, all birds of prey, animals with uncloven feet or indeed animals with cloven feet who do not chew the cud, are prohibited as being infected and unwholesome, but all fish are permitted except certain soft and slimy fish. And it is unbelievable that God should have created 400 kinds of fish, which cost nothing to raise and are nearly all fit for human comsumption, if fish were unwholesome, especially in view of the fact that there are not forty terrestial animals and fowls which are fit to eat. I readily admit that there is nothing worse for the stomach than to eat flesh and fish together for the sake of variety; but they can very well be eaten separately.

Whatever the case, Apicius, the great master-chef, an epicure if there ever was one in the whole world, and Athenæus at the banquet of the wise, tell us that the Greeks and the Romans thought nothing so delicious as the fish which we eat as an act of penance: so much so that great lords took the honourable names of Gilt-head, Muræna, and Pike, and held epicurean banquets consisting of nothing but fish. I cite as an example that of the emperor Caligula which lasted six months and for which the whole Mediterranean was fished. Sometimes peafowl, pheasant, thrush, beccafico, leveret, or roast boar stuffed with all sorts of birds were added for the sake of variety; nonetheless fish took pride of place and were sometimes sold for their weight in silver, as I mentioned above, and were brought to table amid scenes of triumph. And, as Plutarch tells us, Cato complained, already in his time, that a fish fetched more in the market than an ox.

Now, it is the case that the fish of our Ocean are, beyond comparison, larger, fatter and better tasting than those of the Mediterranean, a point which Rondelet has made very well in his book on fish. And those who have tasted fish from both seas at the same table, as happens at Toulouse where the fish comes from both seas, namely, from Agde and from Bayonne, can testify that this is so. And, what is more, there is no seacoast that does not have a variety of fish. The coast of Picardy, where the sea is sandy, has flat fish; the coast of Normandy and Guyenne, which is stony, provides rock fish; the coast of Britanny, which is muddy, has scaleless fish such as lampreys, conger-eels, and haddock. And almost every season has its fish: sometimes fresh herring, sometimes mackerel, sometimes lampreys and the like, and no one ever knows whence come these swarms of billions of herring which arrive at the coasts of France and England, of sardines in Galicia, of tuna in the straits of Istanbul, of anchovies at the coast of Provence, of whales in the Orkneys, of shad on the Barbary coast, of cod in the New World, and of muræna in the sea of Sicily. However, we must confess that the Great Provider of the world has created them only to provide for our needs. I say nothing of freshwater fish which are to be found everywhere.

So if fish were as much esteemed now as in the past, there would be a huge number of fishermen; and we would stock the fish-ponds and hatcheries more carefully than we do. And we would eat fish from September to March without waiting for Lent when the fish begins to spawn and loses its best flavour. This would make meat cheap for the common people, the peasants and the artisans; and, in consequence, poultry would also be cheaper.

I am reminded of the argument of the excellent and astute Doctor Picard who protested to the late King Henry that, if the consumption of eggs were permitted during Lent, there would be no hens or pullets to be found after Easter. For even in England which is full of cattle and fowl, although the caution about meat is removed, they are still compelled to maintain the prohibition against eating meat on certain days of the week, seeing that meat becomes expensive. However, because the queen and the great lords contravene these prohibitions, the people do not respect them as they ought to.

But it seems to me that there is a more convenient policy which dispenses with all prohibitions, for there is nothing more pleasant or more agreeable to man than what is prohibited, when he who makes the law contravenes it. This has the effect that most of the people like meat and dislike fish, because those who prohibit meat live on nothing else. Witness the good Spanish bishop who, as Poggio of Florence says, transformed a capon into fish on a day of fasting by saying a few words, retaining the accidental form and taste of the capon. On the other hand, if the prince once decides to remove the prohibition and nonetheless causes fish to be put on his table, all the great lords and courtiers will follow his example, and then so will the people. That is the only way to bring fish into good repute. To prove what I say I cite no example more ancient than that of the Adrian, of Flemish nationality, who, from being a poor scholar nourished on salt cod, was made pope by the patronage of his pupil, the Emperor Charles V. And because he much enjoyed and heartily recommended salt cod, his courtiers and consistorial Beguines ate it in defiance of their personal preferences to gratify His Holiness and, in a very short time, the people joined in to their heart's desire, as Paulus Jovius writes in his book about fish; the effect was that nothing in Rome was more expensive than salt cod. For shrewd courtiers always imitate princes, even in the most ridiculous matters, as happened with Ferdinand, King of Naples, whom nature had endowed with a twisted neck. To please him, his courtiers twisted their necks like his. Most of the people, even the fools and the ignorant, slavishly followed the fashion and imitated the great. That is the paradox which, it seems to me, is well worth considering on the matter of remedying the high cost of consumables.

My final point, which has no bearing on stabilising the prices of goods, is the stability of money. {Also, it is certain that we shall never see the end of the current abuses until all money is reduced to three kinds, and to the highest standard possible, after all base money is discontinued. This is the only way to eradicate forgers, frustrate the sycophants who cause the value of money to be raised and lowered, freeze as near as may be the value and price of things, in short, to facilitate trade.

I say, therefore, that if all gold coinage was twenty-three carats with no allowance for wear and tear, all silver coinage eleven *deniers* and twelve grains of the king's silver, the rest of the coinage of pure rosette copper, and gold and silver coinage were cast to prevent clipping, one would very easily recognise the soundness of coins by sight, sound, substance, weight and touch, without fire or touchstone; and any falsification would be noticed. And to prevent any alteration in the milieu of money the heaviest gold and silver pieces should be only four *deniers* in weight, like the *angelot* and the *demi-teston*. For it is not difficult to falsify heavy coins, such as the *Portugueses*, the *Joachimthaler* known as *Iocondalle*, or, in ancient times, the gold coins of three and a half marks struck by Heliogabalus, and those struck with the stamp of Constantinople weighing a mark of gold, of which the Emperor Tiberius II presented fifty to our King Childeric.

We know that such coins are easy to falsify from our experience of German thalers of which the majority are nearly eleven *deniers par le bord* and *au milieu* only six or seven *deniers*. We also know the false *teston* at six or seven *deniers* which the common man cannot detect by weight, sound or sight; and if the counterfeiter makes the *teston* at nine silver *deniers*, even the best informed are deceived. Nor should it be said that the game is not worth the candle, for in twelve wrought marks there are three *marks d'empirance*; the expenditure is not so great as to exclude a considerable profit.

As for base money which contains less than three *deniers* and twelve grains of alloy, such as our *douzains* and *carolus*, or four *deniers* such as pieces of three and six *blancs*, there is simply no telling, and the counterfeiter can do what he likes with them. But if silver money were of silver at eleven *deniers* and twelve grains of alloy and each piece weighed no more than four *deniers* and no less than an *obol*, it would be very difficult to falsify it, for the appearance and the sound would immediately disclose the falsification. And to prevent clipping we need only cast the coins; for we see that the old gold and silver coins which come from Spain cannot be falsified without being easily noticed, but most of them are clipped, which cannot be done with coins that have been cast. To be brief, the counterfeiter has no means of making bad money, except through base coinage, which was the cause of so many counterfeiters in ancient Greece, and nowadays in France; for Demosthenes, in his oration against Timocrates, writes that it was the custom of many city-states to mix lead or soft tin with copper and silver. And so he complains bitterly about the counterfeiters of his time.

It will be said that acid can remove whatever silver one wishes without effacing the stamp on the coin. This is true, but the acid costs more than the profit gained on the silver extracted. Moreover, there is always a loss of silver, and the erosion and the weight discloses the falsification.

As for gold coin, it is sufficient that it is twenty-three carats with no allowance for wear and tear whereby one would save on the great expense incurred by refining the gold in fire and by royal cementation, and the coinage would be more robust without perishing over time. We, however, refine the gold to such an extent that, apart from the expense, it is worn out over time and is fragile, and it cannot carry its stamp for long.

Furthermore, setting aside the expenses incurred as well as the fragility and the wear and tear, which apply equally to pure silver of twelve *deniers*, there is a further loss which our goldsmiths and minters do not think of, for they take it for granted that neither gold nor pure silver are diminished by fire. Nonetheless, the truth is that when the alloy is extracted gold and silver go with it and are consumed little by little, just as good blood is also lost when bad humours are extracted. And that this is so is proved by the liquid extracted, as le Cointe proved to us sixty years ago, for, the silver having been liquified, the gold remains twenty-four carats pure; and yet it loses weight if left in the furnace. We must, therefore, conclude that gold is lost and consumed in fire, which our goldsmiths cannot believe, either because they do not have the patience to conduct the experiment for a sufficient length of time, or because they are afraid to make a loss. But if one wishes to take less time about the proof, take an old *écu* and, having reduced it to twenty-four carats with acid refined with salpetre, copperas and sal ammoniac, weigh it and put it in sal ammoniac and arsenic for a while; and then, having removed the salt, put it in a furnace with live sulphur. It will not be long before, the sulphur having been consumed, one will observe that the weight has diminished. If it is then put in arsenic, sal ammoniac and live sulphur, a reduction in weight will be observed each time until it is entirely consumed. However, it is sufficient for the purposes of demonstration that it is reduced, by however little, after being steeped in acid, seeing that the reduction has to be one of refined gold. Furthermore, arsenic alone, which is deleterious to animals, plants and metals, consumes it over time without the aid of fire, which the Emperor Caligula proved to his great loss, as Pliny tells us. Apart from this, it would be contrary to the principles of nature to suppose that a natural substance, and indeed a compound substance, and one as terrestial as gold, could not lose its form because it was inherently incapable of corruption or corrosion. Furthermore, fire reduces everything to ashes, glass, flame or smoke. I shared the opinon of the vulgar until experience taught me otherwise and natural reason compelled me to accept the proof. They say the same about pure silver in pieces of twelve *deniers*. But if pure gold is consumed, the same holds with greater force for refined silver.

So to avoid the loss of gold which occurs when it is refined by royal cementation or in fire, or through use, waste or fragility, it suffices that gold should be at twenty-three carats without allowance for wear and tear. In this way it will have enough body and alloy to last and to preserve its stamp; and it will be better than the gold of the *écu sol* of an eighth of a carat and more. And there is no need to fear that the forger will extract gold from the *écus* with nitric acid refined with sal ammoniac (which they have been doing for some time), for the weight will immediately reveal the deficiency arising from this process. Furthermore, the cost of acid is too great for the small profit derived, and the erosion is evident on close inspection.

And to prevent foreigners from circulating their money at the expense of ours, we must expose it, if it is not of the same alloy as ours; for the coinage of Italy and Spain is very far from its ancient value.

As for coinage of pure brass, the counterfeiter can gain nothing at all from it, for the method and difficulty of forging make it far too expensive. But if the doubles and the *deniers* are of silver alloy, then a great deal can be got from them by extracting the silver and forging a great quantity, as did Pinatel, who pilfered 400,000 francs at one stroke in this fashion. It is for this reason that one should make such coinage of pure brass without silver, tin or powder of rosette copper as I understand in Venice and Spain. For the silver *denier*, or eighteen grains that is in doubles and *deniers*, can only be regarded by the stamp. This has the advantage that the assay of such money as pure rosette copper will become more refined and will not cost so much or involve so much waste. Also it will greatly help the people if it were decided to make four denominations of such coinage without silver, for instance, the *denier*, the double, the *liard* and the *quatrin*, or whatever one might wish to call them. Otherwise, small silver coins at eleven *deniers* twelve grains of the king's silver would be too small and would cost too much to make.

In this matter the Queen of England has made a great mistake in prohibiting all base and brass coinage in her country and in striking coinage of almost pure silver. This is a great disadvantage to the poor, for the smallest coin, which is a very small penny, is worth eight *deniers obole*; so the poor are forced to use small coins of lead and cannot buy goods in small quantities without loss. And it is not easy for a person of small means to give to charity, which is to cut the throats of the poor. On the other hand, in Spain, they coin thirty-six small *cornadis*; and in Venice, and in almost the whole of Italy, thirty-six *bagatins*, which are worth only a dozen of ours. It is even worse in Liège and Lorraine where forty-eight brass *sous* are worth only a dozen of ours, which is a loss to the public in supplying the coinage and brings no profit to anyone in particular, nor to the indigent poor, even in Spain and Italy where food is much more expensive than in France.

As for casting, it is said that it involves too much clipping and waste, for in one hundred marks there are only seventy that can be put in circulation whereas hammering loses only one or two marks. I grant that the expenses are greater, but apart from the fact that cast coinage is more attractive and much easier to make, the clipper cannot filch any of it without its being noticed. As for hammered coin, the counterfeiter can do what he wants with it. Nonetheless, there was a man who, in the presence of the king, demonstrated an alternative to casting, but there was too much business for it to be considered.

So much, then, for the ease and manner of the three coinages of gold, silver and rosette copper which, if minted as I have suggested, would have a value recognised even by children, having a sound, substance, colour, feel and imprint so well established that the forger would never be able to change it. This is a point of great consequence, which is known to all, and which should move us to implement it even if there were no other benefits. Although there is no more harmful pestilence in a commonwealth, we see nothing but counterfeiters and alchemists, who, after having tried to make something from nothing, forge coins to recover their loss: coins which would never have any currency if my recommendations were implemented.

But there is a further point: that the blandishments of the courtiers who cause the value of the coinage to be changed would by these means be confounded. For once base coinage is done away with, although one may wish to restore it later, there is no one who will regret it, as happened in the year 1306 when Philip the Fair first debased the coinage of pure silver, and whom Dante therefore dubbed *falsificatore di moneta*. He had great difficulty in persuading the people of Paris to accept it as currency; for they rose in revolt, pillaged and sacked the houses of Etienne Barbette, and even besieged the king in the Temple, hurling the dinner which he was about to be served into the mud with many insults. And although the king took punitive action, nonetheless, fearing a greater disturbance, he restored the silver coinage on this occasion to its previous value. It is true that ten years later it was once again debased by one half.

I will be told that to weaken the alloy and raise the price of money is a quick way to provide the king with money in times of necessity without oppressing the people. There are two answers. Firstly, it is an imposture and an unabashed courtier's deceit to say that the king and the people gain an advantage, for it is as plain as it can be that both of them lose. Just as taking grapes from a vine without pruning or cultivating it causes it to die in three or four years, so it is when one dilutes the coinage and raises the price. In the second place, the saying, that necessity knows no law, is true only if it really is necessity. However, I have never read that the coin in this kingdom was ever debased out of necessity. On the contrary, Charles VII in his extreme necessity, when in November 1422 he was named King of Bourges ten days after his father's death, caused to be minted the best silver money that ever there was, for it contained twelve *deniers* without any diminution. Then, when he had driven out the English and restored his kingdom to complete and perfect peace, he diluted the silver money by much more than half; for in the year 1453 he caused to be minted *sols* at five *deniers* of alloy. Philip the Fair did the same in that he diluted the coinage by nearly two thirds without any need, apart from the appetite of the flatterers.

I have indeed read that the Romans followed this policy in the First Punic War when the *asse*, a copper coin weighing twelve ounces was suddenly reduced to two ounces, retaining its face value. And in the war against Hannibal it was reduced to one ounce at the same price, and then by the *lex Papiria* reduced to half an ounce at the same value. This was necessary for three reasons. First, because of the great losses inflicted on them by their enemies and the extreme necessity to which they were reduced. Second, because of the weight of the coin; it weighed one pound. Third, because copper money was too pure by seven parts, the whole being eight parts; for by this reckoning a pound of silver was worth 840 pounds of copper whereas, according to the law of Alexander Severus, it was estimated at only a hundred to one, assuming that it was neither leton nor copper. But the first mistake was made by Drusus, tribune of the people, who mixed an eighth part of brass in the pure silver *denier*. Mark Antony did even worse, mixing silver, iron and brass together.

The third advantage to be gained from money coined in the way I recommend is that foreigners will bring in a great deal of merchandise and make it cheap. This is the case in Spain where ducats, double ducats and old *reals* attract the foreigner who sells his merchandise at a low price in order to get such money, although he is forbidden to export it from the country (which ought also to be forbidden in this kingdom), and makes a profit on it in his own country by coining it with the stamp of his own prince. So were we to make the old *reals*, which are twelve *deniers* and two grains of silver, the minters of France would thereby gain at least seven *sous* per mark. And the Flemish would sell us merchandise at a better price in order to bring our *testons* into the Netherlands and coin pieces of forty-three *sous*, much weaker than our *testons*, such that they gain twenty-five *sous* per mark.

On the other hand, if money is too weak for its face value we must deal with foreigners at a financial loss, because they only want money at prices that apply in their own countries. And if one does not have anything to pay in exchange for goods, the country stays poor, like Sparta in ancient times where Lycurgus, having abolished gold, silver and brass, minted a heavy and cumbersome coinage of iron in the shape of rods tempered in vinegar which made it so brittle that it could not even be used to make nails. This was the reason why the country was very poor, for foreigners did not trade there. It is true that, by way of compensation, no prince ever made war on them for the sake of their wealth and that they had no goldsmiths, jewellers, counterfeiters, or cut-purses; but that excellent prince also saw to it that no man dared make the attempt. And even the Spartans, the conquerors of other nations, having forgotten their master's lesson and accepted the use of gold and silver, were never able to get rid of it again, whatever coercion was employed by the kings who were strangled and killed in the attempt. Thus, since we are compelled to use metals to regulate and evaluate all things, we must try as best we can to make it sound, good, and of three metals only, namely, gold, silver and copper, in the manner and for the reasons I have stated.

And we cannot endorse the custom of Mauretania and Guinea, which uses gold dust instead of stamped coin, as I have heard from our merchants who trade in that part of the world, for it is not possible to avoid fraud, seeing that there is no way of recognising gold simply as such and it is necessary to put the dust to the test.

Stamped gold coins are indeed made in Ethiopia and in most of the rest of Africa, but since there is little silver and copper, they use squares of salt as money, as Alvarez writes, which hinders trade because of the weight, cheapness and fragility of salt.

In many other places there are coins of small denomination made of leton or copper which causes great inconvenience because of the cheapness of such materials. But rosette copper, being the most precious metal after gold and silver, should not be added to any other mixture to convert it into leton or copper. And by this means one will be able to make money purely of rosette copper, and make the minting easier, which will not cost a great deal more. Thus, silver coin, which will weigh twelve grains, will be worth twenty-four pieces of the smaller brass coins of two *deniers* in weight, which is the proportion of one mark of silver to one hundred of rosette copper, as established in ancient times by the law of the emperor Arcadius, and which is now in use, more or less, in this kingdom. It is true that in Germany, from where it comes, it is to be had more cheaply, although a long time before, when the *asse* was reduced to half an ounce by the *lex Papiria*, a pound of silver was worth only thirty-five pounds of copper, where shortly before it was worth seventy pounds; and before the first Punic War, a pound of silver was worth 840 pounds of copper, as I said above. But to make the calculation, we need to understand that the Roman *denier* was one seventh and not one eighth of an ounce, as the learned Budé believed. In this, however, he followed the ancient Greeks and Romans who failed to keep him from going astray, because in order to deal in round figures, they made the drachma, which is an eighth of an ounce, equal to a *denier* which is a seventh, which creates a significant error when we are dealing with large numbers. And for this reason, Appian, Pliny and Celsius took care to avoid this error and subtly made the difference clear, showing that a *denier* was worth one and three sevenths of a drachma. This is a fact which George Agricola has drawn to our attention. Budé made a similar mistake in that he took the *mine* for the *livre*, like someone ignorant of our money. Our historians make the same mistake again when they treat the marks of Paris, Boulogne, Venice, Genoa, Provence and Tourraine as being all equal, although there are ounces of difference between them. I wished to mention this in order to clarify the calculations which I have made above, and the proportion of metals, and because many people are too hasty in accepting the opinion of Budé.

But there is an objection to what I have said about the prohibition of base coinage. It is that the poor would be ruined, since base coinage is all that the poor have. It is not my opinion that it should be prohibited all at once, but that none should be coined in the future, and that it should be gradually phased out with less damage.} [For if money, which ought to govern the price of everything, is changeable and uncertain no one can truly know what he has: contracts will be uncertain, charges, taxes, wages, pensions and fees will be uncertain, fines and penalties fixed by laws and customs will also be changeable and uncertain; in short, the whole state of finances and of many public and private matters will be in suspense, which is even more to be feared if the coinage is falsified by the princes who are the custodians of justice and owe justice to their subjects; for the prince cannot, without incurring the infamy of counterfeiter, alter the weight of his coin to the prejudice of his subjects, and much less to the prejudice of foreigners who treat with him and trade with his people, given that he is subject to the law of nations. Thus the poet Dante called Philip the Fair *falsificatore di moneta* for having been the first to corrupt silver money in this kingdom to half the alloy, which was the cause of great troubles among his subjects and set a very pernicious example to foreign princes; whereof he repented too late, enjoining his son, Louis Hutin, in his will to avoid debasing the coinage. And for this same reason, Peter IV, King of Aragon, confiscated the estates of the King of Majorca and Minorca, whom he claimed to be his vassal, for having debased the coinage. And yet the Kings of Aragon themselves made the same mistake. Indeed, Pope Innocent III forbade them, as his vassals, to engage in the practice, in consequence of which prohibition the Kings of Aragon, when they come to the throne, promise not to change either the rate nor the weight of their approved coinage.

But it is not enough to make such declarations if the alloy and weight of coin is not regulated as it should be, so that neither princes nor subjects can falsify it when it is issued, which they will always do if they have the means, no matter what atrocious punishment may be inflicted. The fundamental cause of all the counterfeiters, washers, clippers and corrupters of coin and of the adulteration and debasement of money is simply the mixing of the metals. For one pure and simple metal cannot be confused with another, since the colour, weight, substance, sound and nature of each is different from the others, as I declared when I was deputed by the states, cities and provosts of the Province of Vermandois to the Estates of France. Therefore, in order to avoid the inconveniences I have identified, it is necessary that the coins be of pure metal throughout the commonwealth; and we should publish the edict of the Roman emperor Tacitus prohibiting, on pain of confiscation of body and goods, the mixing of gold with silver, silver with copper, and copper with tin or lead. We may, however, exempt from this law the mixture of copper with tin, which makes bronze and bell-metal, not so much used in old times as now, and also the mixture of malleable tin with copper of which artillery pieces are made. For it is not necessary to mix a twentieth part of lead with pure tin to make it more malleable, for we can cast and work it without any such mixture. The mixture detracts from the goodness of the tin, and the tin can never be separated from the lead. Moreover, this prohibition must hold not only for coins but for all plate and gold-work, in which falsification is even more common than in coin, because it is not so easy to prove it, and the work involved in doing so is often almost as expensive as the material.

Archimedes was mistaken in seeking to discover what the goldsmith had stolen from the great crown of King Hiero without damaging its appearance (the use of the touchstone being unknown at the time). He took two portions, one of gold and one of silver, putting them into a container of water, and by the displacement of the water he estimated the proportion of the gold and silver in comparison with that of the crown and concluded that the goldsmith had stolen a fifth part. But his conclusion was flawed because he assumed that the alloy was nothing but pure silver, whereas goldsmiths, to make the gold firmer and more lustrous, and to keep down the expense, mix it with copper whenever they can. Copper is much lighter than silver, which makes gold look dull and pale; and copper keeps a much brighter colour and in consequence copper has more body and volume than an equal weight of silver by as much as thirteen to eleven; and if the alloy were of copper and silver, it would be impossible to make an accurate judgment without knowing how much there was of either; and even if it were known, a minute error in measuring the drops of water would make a large difference in the volume of metals; and there is no refiner or goldsmith in the world subtle enough to tell by the touchstone how much silver and copper is mixed with gold, if the alloy is of both. And although goldsmiths and jewellers have always complained that they cannot work in gold of under twenty-two carats without loss or in fine gold above twenty-three carats and three quarters, as directed by the ordinance of King Francis in 1540, yet, notwithstanding all the ordinances, they work at twenty and often at nineteen carats so that in twenty-four marks there are five marks of silver or copper, which in time is made into base money by profiteering counterfeiters. It is, therefore, all the more necessary to prohibit any work in gold which is not in accordance with the ordinance, upon the like penalties of confiscation of body and goods, in order that gold used in plate and furnishings be pure. But as it is impossible, as refiners tell us, to refine gold to twenty-four carats without there being a little of some other metal with it, or silver at twelve *deniers* without some alloy, and even the purest refining according to the ordinances is of twenty-three carats and three quarters with an eighth allowed for wear and tear, and of silver eleven *deniers* two grains and three quarters, like the *reals* of Spain, or else eleven *deniers* and eighteen grains, like the coin of Paris in which there is nothing lost; and without any great cost, apart from the difficulty and time it takes; it follows that they may work gold in plate or in coin of twenty-three carats and silver of eleven *deniers* and twelve grains pure, both without any alloy; and in so doing the proportion of gold to silver will be equal, for the alloy will be alike in both, that is to say, that in twenty-four pounds of silver at eleven *deniers* and twelve grains, and in twenty-four pounds of gold at twenty-three carats, there is a pound of other metal in the gold which is not gold and so likewise in the silver which is not silver, be it copper or any other metal, and such silver is called in this kingdom the king's silver, in which the twenty-fourth part is copper. And by the same means the coin of gold and silver will be purer and more durable. In so doing much is gained in the working, in the fire, and by cementation; and waste, fragility and wear and tear are all avoided.

And in order that the just proportion of gold to silver, observed in all Europe and neighbouring regions, of twelve to one or thereabouts, be also kept in the weight of money, it is necessary to coin money of gold and silver at the same weight of sixteen and thirty-two and sixty-four pieces to the mark without any alteration in either direction, to avoid on the one side the difficulty of stamping it and on the other the brittleness of fine gold and silver, if the coin were lighter than one *denier*. On the other hand any coin of either kind is easily counterfeited, because of its thickness, as is the case with gold portugueses and silver dollars which weigh above an ounce, as also the coin of three and a half marks which the Emperor Heliogabalus caused to be made, and that which was coined with the stamp of Constantinople, weighing a mark of gold, of which the Emperor Tiberius presented fifty to our king Childeric. By which means neither changers, nor merchants, nor goldsmiths shall ever be able to deceive the common people or those who do not know the alloy or the weight, for they will always be forced to give twelve pieces of silver for one of gold, and every one of the pieces of silver will weigh as much as the piece of gold of the same stamp, as we see in the simple Spanish *reals* which weigh as much as the *écu sol* which has the weight laid down in the ordinance of 1540, namely, two *deniers* and sixteen grains; and twelve simple *reals* are worth exactly one *écu*. And in order that people be not deceived in changing the said pieces, whether of gold or silver, or take the single for the double, as they often do with the Spanish *reals*, it is necessary that the stamps be different and not similar, as those of Spain are.

However, with regard to silver, in order that the prescribed standard of *sol*, *petit denier*, and *livre* be maintained, as is specified in the edict of King Henry II made in the year 1551, and on account of the payment of rents, amercements, and manorial rights according to the customs and ordinances, the *sol* shall be of three *deniers* weight of the king's silver, as it is called, and of sixty-four to the mark; and four shall be worth a *livre*, as is currently the case, which is the fairest price that can be given. Moreover, every piece can be divided into three so that each weighs a *denier* and is equivalent to four *petits deniers*. It will be called a common *denier*, so that the *sol* is always worth twelve *deniers*. In consequence, we may see an end to the complaints of the lords concerning the payment of their seigneurial rights, which payment was traditionally made in good silver money, since they will be paid in *sols* of the kind we had at the time of Saint Louis, that is, sixty-four to a mark of the king's silver.

And as for other landed revenues and mortgages, which were purchased for silver, let them be paid according to the value of the *sol* which prevailed at the time of purchase, which was only four *deniers* a hundred years ago and is now only a third of the ancient *sol*, which it will be necessary to put back into use. Such was the silver drachma current throughout Greece, namely, the eighth part of an ounce, which we call a *gros*, and of the same weight as the *sols* which Saint Louis caused to be minted, which were called *gros tournois* and *sols tournois*, by which all ancient contracts and agreements are ordered, and many treaties not only within the kingdom but also among foreigners. For instance, the treaty between the Berne and the three small cantons states that a soldier's pay shall be a *sol tournois*. It was the same in this kingdom, and for that reason it is called *solde*; and it was like the pay of the Romans, as Tacitus tells us, and of the Greeks, as we read in Pollux, for the drachma is the same weight as the *sol tournois*. The Venetians have followed the ancients in setting the ounce at eight *gros* or drachmas, and the drachma at twenty-four *deniers*, and the *denier* at two *obols* or twenty-four grains, as we do in France and as is done in Spain and Africa. From this rule we must not depart, as it is very ancient in Greece and in the regions of the Orient.

It is true that the ancient Romans, having their ounce equal to that of the Greeks, that is, of 576 grains, divided it into seven *deniers* of their money, their *denier* being worth an Attic drachma plus three-sevenths. Here Budé was mistaken. He said that there were eight *deniers* to the ounce and that the Roman *denier* was equal to the Attic drachma and the Roman pound equal to the Attic *mine*, although he is certain that the Roman pound had only twelve ounces and the Greek *mina* sixteen ounces, like the merchant's pound in this kingdom. George Agricola has shown this very well by the calculations of Pliny, Appian, Suetonius and Celsius. So if we coin pieces of gold and silver of the same weight, denomination, and alloy, that is, so that there is no more alloy in gold than in silver, their prices can never either go up or down, as they do more often than there are months, at the pleasure of those who have influence with princes and who borrow all the money they can and then raise the price of money. One such, having borrowed 100,000 *écus*, raised the price suddenly by five *sols* in the *écu* and thus made 25,000 francs. Another reduced the rate of money in March and raised it again in April, after having collected the quarter's rent. We will also, by these means, prevent all falsification of the coinage; and even the most stupid and ignorant will know the worth of any coin by the sight, the sound, and the weight, without fire, graving-tool or touchstone. For seeing that all nations for these 2,000 years or more have always kept and still keep an equal proportion of gold to silver, it will be impossible for either the individual or the prince to raise, lower or alter the prices of gold or silver coins, if base coinage is eliminated from the commonwealth, and gold is set at twenty-three carats.

However, to help the common people, it is necessary to coin a third kind of money of pure copper without calamine or any other admixture of metal, which has been begun, and as is done in Spain and Italy; or else to divide the mark of silver into 1536 pieces, each piece being of nine grains. For the Queen of England has banished all base money and reduced all coins to two kinds only, the smallest silver coin being a penny, which is worth about eight *deniers*; but this takes away the means of buying anything for a smaller price; and, what is worse, people cannot give less than a penny in charity to the poor, which prevents many from giving anything at all. However, it would be far more expedient to have no coin but of gold and silver, if it were possible to coin money smaller than a penny, or to divide the mark of silver, as they do in Lorraine, into 8,000 pieces which they call *angenines*, of which 200 are worth only one *real*, and forty are worth one *sol* of our base money. And they are of very fine silver. But if they were made half as small, they would be more solid and of the alloy I have suggested, and they could be cut and stamped in one operation.

Since the price of copper varies from one country to another and from time to time, it is not suitable for making money, which ought to be as constant and unchangeable in price as it can be. Also, there is no metal more subject to corrosion which consumes both the stamp and the substance. And as for the value, we read that during the Punic Wars a pound of silver was worth 840 pounds of pure copper at twelve ounces to a pound; and then the *denier* of pure silver, which was a seventh of an ounce, was raised from ten pounds of copper to sixteen, as Pliny tells us, which was at the rate of 896 pounds of copper to one pound of silver, a pound being twelve ounces. Afterwards, the smallest coin, which was a pound of copper, was reduced by a half, by the *lex Papirius*, while retaining the same value; and when silver became very abundant it was reduced to a fourth, retaining its value, which was 224 pounds of copper for a pound of silver, which is about the value of copper in this kingdom where a hundred pounds at sixteen ounces to the pound are worth only eighteen francs. And in Germany where, in many places, the furniture and even the churches are covered with it, it is even cheaper. But it is more expensive in Italy and also in Spain and Africa, where there is much less of it. This is very far from the estimation which the Emperor Arcadius made of copper. He valued a pound of gold at a hundred pounds of copper, which cannot be done except by means of supply, that is, by reducing the quantity of this metal in comparison with silver.

It will be said that the abundance of silver can also cause a reduction in its value. In fact, we read in Livy that, in the treaty between the Ætolians and the Romans, it was stipulated that the Ætolians should pay a pound of gold for ten pounds of silver; and yet by an ordinance of Arcadius, a pound of gold is valued at fourteen and two fifths of a pound of silver, for he would have them pay five *sols* of gold for a pound of silver, making seventy-two *sols* in a pound, so that five *sols* is just a fourteenth part of a pound and two fifths more. And at present the price is twelve for one, and a little bit less. It is true that hitherto a mark of gold has been valued at 185 *livres* and a mark of silver at fifteen *livres* and fifteen *sols tournois*, so that one mark of pure unwrought gold is equal to eleven marks, five ounces, twenty-three *deniers* and five grains of unwrought king's silver. In northern countries, where there are many silver mines and very little gold, gold is dearer; and according to the evaluation made at the pope's court, a mark of gold is worth twelve and five-fifths marks of silver, which is more or less the rate of gold to silver that obtained 2,500 years ago; for we read in Herodotus that a pound of gold was valued at thirteen pounds of silver. The Hebrews in their laws put a *denier* of gold at twenty-five of silver, the gold coins being double the silver ones, which were twelve and a half for one. We also read that at the time of the Persians and when the Greek commonwealths flourished, an ounce of gold was worth a pound of silver, for, as Julius Pollux tells us, the Daric *stater* which weighed an ounce was worth a pound of silver. From this we may conclude that the price of these two metals is at their ancient value.

However, the value of gold was increased under the later emperors because gold was wasted by gilding everything. Thus, Nero gilded his great palace throughout, which had galleries 1,000 paces long; and after him Vespasian gilded the Capitol at a cost of 7,200,000 *écus couronne*; and even Agrippa gilded the whole roof of the Pantheon to prevent the copper from corroding, as one also does with iron to prevent rust. And even silver is often gilded, although it never suffers from rust. And if princes do not prohibit gilding, it is inevitable that the price of gold goes up, given that silver, having no hold, is not, or is very rarely, used for silvering.

Besides which, the mines of the North produce much silver, but no gold, and those of the New World produce more silver than gold. Nonetheless, the change in price which occurs over time is very slight, and it cannot militate against the alloy of coins minted of these two metals being the same in all countries, thus eliminating all base coinage. Moreover, trade, which now extends more than ever before to the whole world, cannot permit of any significant variation in the value of gold and silver, except by the common consent of all nations. For even at the time of Augustus, the rate of gold to silver was the same in the East Indies and in the West; and the King of the Indies, being informed of the fact, praised the justice of the Romans, as Pliny says.

But it is impossible to stabilise prices if we retain base money, which is everywhere different and unequal, for just as the price of everything falls as the value of money decreases, as the law says, so it rises when the price of money goes up. And it must rise and fall, because there is no prince who keeps the alloy of base money the same as in other commonwealths, or even in his own, in that the alloy of the *sol* is different from that of the *teston*, *petits deniers*, double *liards*, pieces of six and three *blancs*, which never remain in the same condition.

The attempt that was made in this kingdom to debase the silver coinage by mixing a twenty-fourth part of copper with it was intended to encourage merchants to bring silver into this kingdom, which does not have any. This gave the twenty-fourth part of silver to the foreigner, for eleven and a half *deniers* in France was as much as twelve *deniers* in another country. But there was no need for it, considering the wealth of France which people will always come to get, bringing gold and silver from all quarters. This mischief took deeper root at the time of Philip the Fair who debased the silver coin by a half in the year 1300, adding as much copper to it as there was silver; later, it was reduced to a third, so that the new *sols* were worth only a third of the old ones, and in the year 1422 the alloy of the *sol* was so debased that a mark of silver was worth 80 *livres tournois*, and had 1,600 pieces in a wrought mark. It is true that in the same year Charles VII recovered his crown which had been taken from him and, in order to maintain his credit, caused a new strong and good coin to be made in the month of November so that a mark of silver was fixed at eight *livres*; but finally, in the year 1453, he caused *sols* to be coined at five *deniers* of alloy, since which time they have been steadily debased to such an extent that, in the year 1540, King Francis I had them made at three *deniers* and sixteen grains of alloy, and King Henry at three *deniers* twelve grains, so that the old *sol* of king's silver was worth almost four of the new ones.

Other princes have done no better, for the German *creutzer* which was formerly of silver at eleven *deniers* and four grains is now at four *deniers* and sixteen grains. The *sol* of Wurzburg and the *Reichs grosschen* is six *deniers*, that is, it is half silver and half copper. The *schessind*, the *rapin*, and the Strasbourg *denier* is four *deniers* and twelve grains; the *rapesemin* is four *deniers* and three grains, and the silver florin is eleven *deniers* and four grains, as are the pieces of five and of ten creutzers. The Flemish *sol* or *patard*, twenty of which are worth twenty-four of ours, is only three *deniers* and eighteen pence of alloy, and more than two thirds of it is copper. The four *patard* piece is seven *deniers* and ten grains of alloy, the *Geldern brelingue* is eight *deniers* of alloy, and a third part is copper. In former times the *sol* or *gros* of England was ten *deniers* and twenty-grains, and all this base coin never continued at one rate or at the same weight for more than twenty or thirty years. And hence comes the difference between the *livres tournois*, great, small and medium, as well as the *livres* of Normandy, of Brittany, and of Paris, which are all different, as is shown in the taxes of the papal court. And in Spain, the *livre* of Barcelona, Toledo and Majorca, and in England the pound sterling, is worth eight of ours. And in Scotland there are two different kinds of *livre*, one sterling and the other ordinary. And there is no prince in Italy whose monetary *livre* is not different from the others. Similarly, although the mark is generally eight ounces, the ounce of the Low Countries is eight grains less than ours, that of Cologne is nine grains less, and that of Nuremberg six grains. And on the other hand, that of Paris is one ounce more. The mark of Naples has nine *gros*, that of Salerno has ten; and there is almost no town in Italy whose mark is not different from the others. This makes the value of their coins very diverse, being so different in their weight and alloy, which means that the poor are severely troubled and lose a great deal in exchange, as do all those who do not understand the parity, as the bankers call it: that is to say, the value at which money is exchanged from one place to another. That is why they say of a man of business that he understands the parity, as being a very difficult matter.

For they have, by their debasements, wrapped the subject of money up in such obscurity that most people understand nothing about it. And just as craftsmen, merchants, and everyone in his art, often disguise their work, like many physicians who speak Latin before women and use Greek characters, Arabic terms, and Latin abbreviations in notes, and sometimes blot their paper so that it cannot be read, fearing that if their prescriptions were revealed they would be held in low esteem, so the mint-masters, instead of speaking plainly and saying that two parts out of twelve in a quantity of gold consists of copper or some other metal, say that it is gold of twenty carats; and instead of saying that a piece of three *blancs* is half copper, they say that it is silver of six *deniers fine*, two *deniers* in weight, and fifteen *deniers* of currency, thus giving to *deniers* and carats an essence, quality and quantity which are contrary to nature. And instead of saying that a mark has sixty pieces, they speak of five *sols de taille*. Then they make one coin stable, another unstable, and a third imaginary, although none are stable. And all the variability and fantasy comes from having reduced the weight and impaired the purity of gold and silver. For the ducat which is current in Venice, Rome, Naples, Palermo and Messina, and which is imaginary money, was once a real gold coin weighing an *angelot*, or a *medin* of Barbary plus four *deniers*, which is precisely the imperial of Flanders of the same weight and alloy as the ancient ducat worth ten silver *carlins*, and the *carlin* ten *sols du pays*, at 46 pieces to a mark of gold, and six to the ounce. This they divide into thirty *taris*, and the *tari* into twenty grains, which is one *gros* on the ounce more than the common ounce, which has only eight *gros*. The law calls this gold coin a *solidus*, which like the *angelot* has forty-eight pieces to the mark, and seventy-two for the Roman pound of twelve ounces, which has been current for a long time, as is evident from the laws of the

Greeks, the Germans, the English, the French and the Burgundians. And it is nothing other than the French *écu soleil*, that is, *solidus*. For the mint-masters, not properly understanding the word *solidus*, have for the past fifty years stamped a sun upon it; but the common people, knowing the language, retain the old sense and still call it *écu sol*, which in the old days weighed four *deniers*, like the *angelot*. But since then princes, bit by bit and grain by grain, have brought it down to three *deniers*, which is the old *écu*; and at the time of King John, the old *écu* being diminished bit by bit, as the old *écu sol*, by three grains, *écus* weighing two *deniers* and twenty grains were coined of the same alloy as the ancient ones which were called *francs à pied* and *à cheval* (for at that time the French were called Franks, just as throughout the East the peoples of the West are still called Franks). At that time the Burgundian *écu*, called the *ride*, was also coined of the same weight and alloy. It continued in circulation until the time of Charles VIII when the French *écu* was reduced by six grains in weight and three quarters of a carat in fineness; for the old *écu* was of twenty-three carats and three quarters and the *écu couronne* was of twenty-three carats. Afterwards, King Francis I, correcting the *écu couronne* a little, coined *écus sol* of two *deniers* and sixteen grains and of the same alloy as the *écu couronne*, except for an allowance of one eighth for wear and tear. These continued in circulation until King Henry, who added four grains of weight to it; and Charles IX then diminished it by five grains in the year 1561.

But the old *écus* or ducats of Venice, Genoa, Florence, Sienna, Castille, Portugal and Hungary kept the alloy of twenty-three carats and three quarters, and their weight of two *deniers* and eighteen grains, until 1540 when the Emperor Charles V debased the Spanish *écu* by one and three quarters carats and by three grains in weight, causing the *écus* of Castille, Valencia and Arragon (known as *pistolets*) to be coined at twenty-two carats, and two *deniers* and fifteen grains in weight, thus setting a very bad example for other princes to follow. Which the princes of Italy did by making coins of twenty-two carats or less and weighing two *deniers* and sixteen grains, such as the *écus* of Rome, Lucca, Bologna, Saluzzo, Genoa, Sienna, Sicily, Milan, Ancona, Mantua, Ferrara,

Florence, and the new *écus* of Venice. It is true that Pope Paul III began to make *écus* coined in his name of twenty-one and a half carats, and two *deniers* and fourteen grains in weight; and those struck at Avignon at the same time under the name of Alexander Farnese, legate and the pope's grandson, are even more debased and five *deniers* lighter in weight.

This inflicts untold harm on the subjects and brings profit to the counterfeiters, coiners and merchants who take good money out of the country and make base money with the stamp of another place. This is particularly common with silver coinage of high value and more than eleven *deniers* pure, like the *reals* of Castille which contain eleven *deniers* and three grains of pure silver; from which other princes have, until now, made considerable gains, for if they are converted into French *testons*, on 100,000 *livres* they make a profit of 6,500 *livres* without debasing the French *teston* which is ten *deniers* and seventeen grains fine. And by the same means the Swiss, who converted French *testons* into the *testons* of Solothurn, Lucerne and Unterval, gained upon each mark forty-one *sols* and eleven *deniers tournois*. For the *testons* of Lucerne, Solothurn and Unterval are only nine *deniers* and eighteen grains, which makes them twenty-three grains in the mark less than those of France, which were worth twenty-five *sols tournois*. And as for weight, those of France are at least twenty-five *testons*, which makes the weight of a *teston* of Solothurn less by five eighths of a *teston* in a mark, which is worth four *sols* and three *deniers tournois*. And because the said *testons* can be evaluated only as silver of base alloy, known as billon, being less than ten *deniers fine*, counting fourteen *livres*, seventeen *sols* and four *deniers tournois* in a mark of fine silver, the French *teston*, because it is more than ten *deniers fine*, is evaluated as silver of high alloy, which at the same rate is worth fifteen *livres* and thirteen *sols tournois* in a mark of fine silver; and because of the difference in silver of high and base alloy, the said *testons* are less than those of France by twelve *sols* and eight *deniers tournois* in a mark of *testons*. Similarly, the *testons* of Solothurn are worth forty-one *sols* and eleven *deniers tournois* in the mark less than those of France, yielding for each piece of the said *testons* one *sol*, eleven *deniers* and nine twenty-sixths *tournois*. Because the *teston* of Berne is nine *deniers* and twenty grains *fine* per mark, it is worth a *denier tournois* more than that of Solothurn. But gaining only ten *sols* in the mark is nonetheless a very good profit. The Flemings do the same, converting French *testons* into the *reals* of Flanders.

Every prince has made good provision in his ordinances, prohibiting, under severe penalties, the export of gold and silver; but it is impossible to enforce these ordinances, and a great deal is exported, by both land and sea. And even if one kept so strict a watch that no gold or silver at all was exported, the subjects would always find ways to debase, deform, alter and smelt gold and silver coin, so long as there is diversity of alloy, be it by permission granted to certain goldsmiths or by contravention of the law. For they pocket the deficit of alloy yielded in their work, as much by the abatement which is permitted to them as by the enamel and solder which they use, using in their work the good sort, and mocking the laws and ordinances made to establish the value of a mark of gold and of silver, and setting what price they please upon their work, so that it is always sold at a higher price by the goldsmith than the ordinances allow, silver by forty or fifty *sols* and gold by twelve or thirteen *livres* on the mark. Consequently, gold and silver is bought dearer from the goldsmith and the merchant than it is from the mint-master, who cannot go beyond the king's ordinance either in buying his material or in coining. And as soon as the material is coined into money better in weight and alloy than that of neighbouring princes, it is smelted and gathered together by refiners and goldsmiths to be made into plate or to be coined by foreigners according to their own standard. In this the money-changers play a ministering role and, under colour of providing people with money, they trade with goldsmiths and foreign merchants; for it is certain and has been found true that in the last twenty-five years, since the *petit sol* was abolished, there have been coined in this kingdom more than 25,000,000 *livres*, apart from pieces of three and six *blancs*, which cannot now be found, because the refiners and goldsmiths found a profit in them.

For this reason those who have a great deal of gold and silver plate can make no use of it, for having bought it very dear from the goldsmith, they are unwilling to sell it at so great a loss. Even Charles IX lost a great deal, having turned his plate into coin; whereas, before, the alloy of silver coin was always the same as the goldsmith's alloy, so that one could lose nothing in the plate except the workmanship. This still remains a common proverb among us: In silver plate there is nothing lost except the workmanship. Therefore, to prevent these inconveniences it is necessary that the alloy of coin and that of gold and silver workmanship be the same, that is, twenty-three carats, without allowance for wear and tear, in gold and eleven *deniers* and twelve grains in silver.

A means to mitigate these abuses was found by farming out the revenues of the mint and the confiscations and amercements which issue from forfeiture, which were farmed out in 1564 for the sum of 50,000 *livres* a year. However, it was abolished at Moulins in 1566, and the mints were farmed out to those who offered to coin the greatest quantity of gold and silver marks. By this means, some boughs and branches were cut off; but so long as the root of the abuse remains, these frauds will never cease. The root of the abuses is the confusion of the three metals: gold, silver, and copper. When that ceases, no subject or foreigner will be able to commit any fraud without it being soon discovered. For just as there was in this kingdom no money of copper or of pure rosette copper, since none was coined, so if there is no base coinage and the minting of it is forbidden, the base coin of the foreigner will also be expelled altogether. But as long as the prince and the commonwealth coin base money, there is no hope that foreigners and subjects will cease to counterfeit in private or to receive all foreign coins.

There is another benefit, both public and private, which flows from my suggestion that the mixing of metals should be prohibited. It is that we avoid the loss of silver, which counts for nothing in gold of fourteen carats and above, which is incurred through the expense of refining caused by the process of royal cementation or through water separation. For we need at least sixteen *sols* to divide a mark, and yet the loss is very great in a large sum, as all the florins of Germany are only sixteen carats, or sixteen and a half at most, so that in 100,000 marks there is a loss of 33,000 marks, and of fourteen carats, 40,000 marks and more.

In addition, the abuses of the officers of the mint will cease with regard to the savings and debasements from which the wages of the officers were paid. To put a stop to this, King Henry II of France ordered that they be paid by the district receivers. Although the ordinance was sanctioned, it was annulled by Charles IX upon the remonstrance of the *Chambre des comptes* of Paris which gave the king to understand that, instead of making a profit on his mints, he made a loss of 10,000 *livres* a year, in that the officers were paid yet did almost no work.

However, the true way to remedy this is to suppress all officers of mints, except those in a single town where they should coin all the money and be paid by the district receiver, seigneurial rights remaining, of which the ancients knew nothing. Nothing was deducted from the money, not even the right of brassage, which is really very necessary. Or a tax might be laid on the subjects for the coining of money, in order that the seigneurial rights and the rights of brassage be abolished, as was done in Normandy in the old days and is still done in Poland, in order to mitigate the harm and incredible loss suffered by the subjects. Furthermore, by these means the variations in the prices of gold and silver marks, which causes a million abuses, will cease. And foreign coins will be received only to be smelted, without taking account of seigneurial rights or brassage, and notwithstanding letters obtained by neighbouring princes requesting that their money be exchanged at the same price as in their own territories. And in order to remove all occasion for falsifying, altering or changing the accepted standard of gold and silver coin, it is necessary to coin all the money in only one city, where the judges of the mint shall reside, and to suppress all others (unless the monarchy or republic is so large that it is necessary to have more). Here all the refiners will work under pain of death if they work anywhere else; for they are the source of the greatest abuses. And information should be given by indictment to the ordinary judges to punish all the abuses committed there; for it is well known what abuses have been committed in the coining of money in this kingdom and at places of work for lack of magistrates to whom information is given confidentially, especially after the suppression of the *generaux subsidiaires*. It is therefore necessary to imitate the ancient Romans who, for all the subjects of Italy, had only the temple of Juno where three kinds of money, pure and simple, were coined, namely, of gold, of silver and of copper; and they had three mint-masters who caused the coining and the refining to be done in public and in the presence of each other. And in order that no one should be deceived as to the value of the coins, there was also, at the request of Marius Gratidianus, a place where coins could be assayed. We also read that, in this kingdom, an ordinance made by Charlemagne forbade the coining of money except in his palace. But since the Kings Philip the Fair, his son Charles, and King John established several mints in this kingdom and many masters, guards, provosts and other officers in each mint, the abuses have also multiplied.

But at this point I may be told that the Persians, Greeks and Romans coined pure money of gold, silver and copper at the highest value they could, and yet there was no end to the falsifying, as we read in Demosthenes' speech against Timocrates. I reply that it is very difficult to purge the whole commonwealth of such people, but that for every thousand now in existence, there will be only ten, once the difficulty which prevents everyone from knowing the value of gold and silver is removed by the means I have indicated. And if any prince should be so ill advised as to alter the goodness of his coinage for gain, as did Mark Antony, who coined silver money that was very base, it will soon be rejected, quite apart from the blame heaped on him by everyone and the danger of his subjects rebelling, which was great at the time when Philip the Fair debased the coinage. Whatever the case, it is certain that there were never fewer counterfeiters than at the time of the Romans who had no gold or silver money that was not of high value. For even the tribune Livius Drusus was blamed for presenting a request to the effect that an eighth part of copper be mixed with the silver coin, or as we say, that coin be made of ten *deniers* and twelve grains fine; which shows that even in those days they would not permit any confusion of gold and silver, and that silver was of the highest alloy, as was also the gold, as we may see in their medallions of gold which are of twenty-three and three quarters carats; and there are even some with the stamp of the Emperor Vespasian which are only one thirty-second part of a carat short of twenty-four carats, which is the finest gold possible. But, for the reasons I have given, it is sufficient that gold be of twenty-three carats and that silver be eleven *deniers* and twelve grains pure. This removes the excuse that, not being a fire-master, one requires a quarter or at least an eighth as allowance for wear and tear, which is the cause of much abuse, though we must allow two *ferlins* per mark on money coined with a stamp.

Again, some may say that it is more expedient to coin doubles and *deniers* of base alloy to avoid the heaviness of copper money. I say that if the coining of base money is permitted, however small the denomination, it will drag in its wake the *liard* and the *sol*, and so forth in endless repetition. And even if only doubles and *deniers* were coined, this would always provide an opportunity for counterfeiters to deceive the ordinary people for whom this money was struck. They know nothing about it, and because of its low value they do not trouble to enquire as to its substance or value before accepting it. I have a letter from Jacques Pinatel to King Henry II in which he says: 'Sire, I wish to advise you that in one of your mints, in the last six months, douzains have been coined which are debased for each mark on the weight of twenty *sols* and on the alloy of four *sols*. When it pleases your Majesty, I will show you the work, and I will acquaint you with the loss inflicted upon you and your subjects, and which will grow greater if your Majesty does not prevent it with all rigour.' It was then that, at the command of the king, he coined pieces of six *blancs* of four *deniers* of alloy and two grains allowance for wear and tear and four *deniers* and fourteen grains in weight. This was the best base money then in France, in consequence of which they were soon melted down, and few of them are now to be found.

Everyone knows that the loss the king and the people incurred, of twenty-fours *sols* upon the mark, amounted to more than twenty-five per cent. And yet the same Pinatel, having obtained underhand a commission from the governors of the mint in 1552, caused to be minted at Villeneuve d'Auvignon, and at Villefranche de Rouergue, doubles and *deniers* which were evaluated at only twelve *sols* to the mark; and it was proved that, by this means, he had stolen little less than 40,000 *livres* and had purchased his immunity for 15,000 *livres*, which he gave to a lady who, though she did not secure a pardon for him, had his punishment deferred.

I therefore say that we must not permit base money of any kind whatsoever, if we will purge the commonwealth of counterfeit money. Furthermore, by this means we will prevent the harm inflicted on the poor by the discontinuation of coinage or the depreciation of its value, after it has been debased. And there would be no credit with princes for those who urge the profit they can make from their mints, as did a certain officer of the mint who suggested to the *Conseil des Finances*, and also wrote to King Charles IX, that he could make a great profit from his mints and bring relief to his people. And in fact, by his calculations, it was found that every mark of pure gold wrought should give the king eight *livres tournois*, whereas he only received twenty-five *sols* and four and sixteen twenty-thirds *deniers*; and for a mark of the king's silver wrought he should get forty *sols tournois*, instead of which he got only sixteen *deniers* in the form of *testons*. His advice was to coin money of the king's silver of twelve *sols tournois* current, and of thirty pieces to the mark weighing six *deniers* and nine grains full weight, the halves and the quarters at the equivalent; and gold coin at twenty-four carats, a carat as allowance for wear and tear in thirty pieces to the mark, and of the same weight as the silver at six *livres tournois*. And yet he would also have coined base coinage in small denominations to the value of three *deniers* and 320 pieces to the mark, and of three *deniers* current, and all other kinds of base money under ten *deniers fine*, fixing the mark at fourteen *livres tournois*. This was his advice, but it was rejected as it deserved; for it is absurd to think that the king can get so great a profit from his mints and yet help his people, if what Plato says is true, that no one gains but another loses. And the loss by necessity has to fall upon the subjects, since foreigners do not incur it.

It is imperative that some great prince should, through his ambassadors to other princes, bring it about that all princes by common consent forbid the coining of base money, setting the value of gold and silver coin as specified above, and using a mark of eight *gros* or drachmas, and of 570 grains to the ounce, which is the most common. This should not be difficult, since the Catholic king and the Queen of England have already prohibited all base money; and moreover all the gold money of Spain, apart from pistolets and Portugese money, is of the highest possible alloy; and all the silver money is eleven *deniers* and three grains, which is as good as it can be.

And it would be a good idea to have all coin cast in the form of a medallion, as did the ancient Greeks, Romans, Hebrews, Persians and Egyptians. For the cost would be much less, the ease would be greater, the roundness would be perfect (to hinder clipping), and it would not be subject to bending or breaking. Furthermore, the stamp would last forever. We would not be troubled with hammering, there would be no need of a cutter, there would be no loss in shearing, nor margin of error in the weight, as, for instance we have to allow at least two *ferlins* per mark made with a stamp. Moreover, more could be made in one day than can, at present, be made in one year. It would also remove the opportunity for counterfeiters to mix the metals as easily as they do with the press and the stamp where the metal is stretched out to cover the thickness. The mould makes all medallions of the same metal equal in size, weight, breadth and form. So if a counterfeiter wanted to mix copper with gold more than the alloy of twenty-three carats, the volume of copper being, in equal weight, two and an eighth times bigger than gold, or two and an eighth times lighter than gold of an equal mass, the medallion would be much larger and would thus make the falsification apparent. For it is most certain that if a mass of gold equal to a mass of copper weighs 1,551 *ferlins*, the mass of copper will weigh only 729 *ferlins*, which is a proportion of seventeen to eight in gross weight, as I have learned from François de Foix, the great Archimedes of our time, who first established the true proportions of the metals in weight and volume. We make the same point about silver which, given equal weight, is greater in volume than gold, or that a quantity of gold is one and four fifths heavier than the same quantity of silver, which is 1551 to 998, or nine to five; and the ratio of copper to silver is eleven to thirteen or, precisely, 1,229 to 866. This is, in weight and volume, more or less the same as other metals, except for lead which is heavier than silver in that it differs by fifteen to fourteen, or more precisely by 929 to 866. However, it cannot be used for counterfeiting because it separates itself from all metals except for tin. Even less can tin be used, since it is like poison to all other metals; and it cannot be cast for silver, since it is lighter by as much as nine to fourteen or, to be precise, as 600 to 929. Nor can it be disguised as gold, which is heavier than tin, the mass being the same, or less in body, the weight being the same, in the ratio of eighteen to seven, or exactly 1551 to 600, which makes it two and four sevenths heavier.

As for iron, the counterfeiters cannot use it by smelting, because it cannot be mixed with either gold or silver, and laminated iron is not difficult to detect. Pliny calls it ferrumination, and it was used by the counterfeiters of his time. And, in fact, the Sieur de Villemor, commissaire of war, showed me an ancient medallion of iron covered with silver in this fashion. But, on closer inspection, the weight and the volume revealed the deception, for silver is heavier than an equal mass of iron, or smaller in volume than an equal weight of iron, in a ratio of four to three or, to be precise, of 866 to 634. And as for gold, ferrumination can serve no purpose for counterfeiters, for gold is smaller in volume than iron of equal weight, or heavier in equal mass, by sixteen to nine, 1556 to 634. Nor is it to be feared that quicksilver can be used to falsify these two metals, although it is as close to the weight of gold as seven to eight, or 1,158 to 1,551, because the counterfeiters do not know how to fix it without causing it to evaporate.

So much for the form of coins and the benefit to be got from casting them, as was done in ancient times. It was only when their mines of gold and silver were exhausted and these two metals were worn out, lost, hidden, or dispersed, that the ancients were compelled to make coins so thin that they could only stamp them with a hammer, which subsequently gave rise to many abuses. But just as the first men, having little gold and silver, stamped it with a hammer and then, when they got a greater quantity, began to cast it, so we too should return to casting. We did indeed begin casting, but it was found that the imprint of the mark was not good, that there was always thirty marks of clippings for every hundred of material instead of one or two with the hammer, and even the sound was different from that of hammered coin; and what is more, it was found that the coins were not all of the same weight, because the sheets were made thinner in one place than in another.

As for what I have said, that the mark of gold and silver should be divided into pieces equal in weight, without any fractions of pieces in the mark, *deniers* in the piece, or grains in the *denier*, the advantage, not only for the exchange of marks and pieces but also for evaluation, weight and the fixing of the rate, is very clear. It follows the example of the ancients, for the gold or silver piece weighing four *gros* or drachmas, which is half an ounce, will be equal to the Hebrew shekel; and the piece of two *gros*, or thirty-two to the mark, will be equal to the Attic *stater*, the ancient Philip, the *rose noble*, and to the gold medallions of the ancient Romans which the law calls *aureus*. And the one *gros* piece, or *sol tournois*, or drachma of sixty-three to the mark, will be equal to the Attic drachma and to the Hebrew *zuza*, which in Greece and throughout the East was the daily wage of a brassier. It is true that the silver *denier* of the Romans, a soldier's daily wage at the time of Augustus, was heavier by three sevenths, which is a little more than the simple *real* of Spain.

And if the alterations and changes are harmful and pernicious if carried out all at once, we could proceed with it by degrees, coining money, as I say, so that everyone has time to get rid of his base coinage at the least possible loss. In connection with these difficulties, when I was at the Estates of Blois as deputy for the province of Vermandois, I was called, together with the first president, three governors of the mint and Marcel, superintendent of finances, to remedy the abuses of money, and in the end it was decided that everything that I have said above, which I stated in summary form, was very necessary. And yet the difficulties and diseases of the commonwealth were such that they would not allow of it. This was as much as to say that it was better to let the patient perish slowly than to make him drink a disagreeable medicine that would cure him.

I agree that the silver in base money will come to only half when it is purified to eleven *deniers* and twelve grains; but it will be for ever, once the law is established and kept, as I have said. And if it is not done, then the commonwealth will inevitably be ruined.]

And even if base money were abolished all at once, provided that the king bore half the loss and the people the other, it would still be much more advantageous to the people than to coin debased money and, having put it into circulation, depreciating it. I know of no man of sound judgment who does not think that it is better to extract the bad humours by bleeding than to languish forever in a fever which never ceases to redouble its onslaught. For we see that, since the year 1538, without going further back, 10,000 people were ruined when the *vaches de* {*Bretagne*} [*Foix*] were depreciated and that, ten years later, all the clipped base coin was abolished. At the time of King Henry II, *sols* were minted at three *deniers* and twelve grains of alloy [and at the time of Charles IX at three *deniers* of silver] which were not worth the old clipped base coin nor the depreciated vache. And yet the price of the base coin was soon raised, without improving the alloy, to please the people, like a sick person given something cool to drink, for depreciation comes at a very high price. {Furthermore, counterfeiters have a thousand ways of altering base money of different alloys, as the alloy of the *denier* to that of the double, and of the double to that of the *liard*, of the *liard* to the *sol*, and of the *sol* to pieces of three and of six *blancs*, which contain four *deniers* of the king's silver; but one does not any longer notice that the mint-masters have found profit in converting them into other base coin.

Now, the worst is that in such deceptions the commonwealth and the poor are ruined and only paymasters, mint-masters, counterfeiters and usurers gain. For some lend base money at high interest and then find a way to get it depreciated in order to be paid back in good money; others buy the prohibited base money at a very low price, for people are forced to sell at the pleasure of money changers and mint-masters, if it is not sold by the mark. Others borrow from everywhere, having got wind of the intention to raise the value of money, or they themselves urge princes to this purpose, as I have learned a great lord of this kingdom, whom you know, Monsieur, who had a 100,000 *écus* in his coffers. He managed the affair so well that he caused the price of an *écu soleil* to be suddenly raised from forty to forty-five *sols* and thus made 25,000 francs at a single stroke. And although the king benefits from it for a while, nonetheless it happens that the poverty of his people later redounds upon him. As the Emperor Hadrian said of the Treasury, it resembles the spleen in that it can grow only at the expense of all the other members of the body. Similarly, the prince cannot benefit in this way without the people suffering a great deal, and he himself even more. This would not happen if there were no base money. For if the price of gold were raised, it would be necessary to lower the price of silver, which is not in the power of princes unless it were by the common consent of all monarchs and sovereign lords. And if a prince does it in his own country, he loses trade, or he impoverishes himself and his subjects who are, as I have said, thus forced to trade at a loss with foreigners. Thus we find no prince who changes the proportion of gold to silver established throughout Europe, which is about one to twelve, so that a gold mark of twenty-four carats is worth twelve marks of silver of twelve *deniers* without allowance for wear and tear, which is more or less the price in Spain and Italy, where a pound of gold is worth eleven and two thirds pounds of silver; in Germany it fetches somewhat more than twelve, for where there is more silver it is worth less. The ancient value and proportion of gold to silver, which was established in Greece and Asia more than 2,000 years ago (as Herodotus tells us) was thirteen pounds of silver to one of gold. In the treaty of Ætolia, 600 years later, it was decreed that the Ætolians should pay ten pounds of silver for each pound of gold, unless there is a numerical error in Livy, seeing that 300 years later, or thereabouts, we find that a pound of gold is worth fifteen pounds of silver which would be far too great a change for so short a time, unless gold was much more pure than silver, which, of course, it is not. For I have seen gold medallions of Vespasian (to whom Pliny dedicated his work) which are of twenty-four carats, and there is not a variance of as much as one thirty-second of a carat according to the masters and governors of the mints who have tested them. I do not find that gold has ever been at a higher price, and since then it has always been lower, because by the decree of Alexander Severus a pound of gold was equal to fourteen and a half pounds of silver, and since that time the price has gone down to twelve pounds, which is just about the fair proportion of the true price. For if we take the lesser price, namely ten to one as it was at the time of the treaty of Ætolia, and the highest it has ever been, namely one to fifteen at the time of Pliny, we will find that the mean between the two is one pound of gold for twelve and a half of silver. We accept the exact price of one to twelve which is almost common to the whole of Europe, Asia and Africa, except that in northern countries, where silver mines abound and there is very little gold, the price of gold is a little higher; and, on the other hand, towards the southern countries and the Indies, where there is more gold, the price of silver is higher than in cold countries. But the proportion does not normally vary by more than 1/24 more or less, which is a necessary and convenient justice almost like an ordinance and common law decreed at the request of commonwealths in general in order to maintain the intercourse, trade and friendship between them. Which is the reason why the king of India, having been told by a Roman ambassador that the proportion of gold to silver which prevailed in his own country was maintained also by the Romans, praised their justice. For money is properly speaking a law; thus the Greeks gave money and law the same name, just as we speak of law <*loy*> and alloy <*aloy*>. And just as the law is sacred and must not be violated, so money is sacred and must not be altered, once it has been given its true standard and its just value.}

It would therefore be a barbarous injustice and an inevitable loss to the country if the prince were, at his pleasure, to change the price of gold and silver, raising or lowering the value of money minted at the same degree of soundness from these two metals{. For}[; and there would be no neighbouring prince or people who would be willing to trade with him, except in kind. And to show that the three metals, coined in the manner I have suggested, would maintain their natural and convenient proportion,] it is evident in that there is as much to be said for gold of twenty-three carats, at the price of fine gold, as there is for silver of eleven *deniers* and twelve grains, at the price of pure silver of twelve *deniers*. {And if a prince so ill advised should be found, he will ruin his people, his country, and himself.}

But maintain the rate and standard of money that I have recommended, and a million {losses} [lawsuits] incurred through the payment of obligations will cease, be they in good or bad money, in gold or in silver, in old *écus* or in new. And by the same means, revenues and rents will be secured, the evaluation of goods will be better regulated, the uncertainties of changing money will be removed, the path of trade will be smoothed, [the prince and the magistrates will be obeyed, the financiers and deceivers will be thwarted,] {France will be enriched, the courtiers frustrated,} the counterfeiters will be expelled, and the poor will find [infinite] relief.

There, Monsieur, are the policies which, in my opinion, are necessary, or at least obvious, concerning the increasing price of goods and how to bring it under control. To determine whether they are practicable, we need only submit them to the touchstone of your superior judgement which will test them better than the Lydian stone, or than fire can test gold. This has increased my confidence in submitting the whole to the scrutiny of the public. For is there anyone who would disapprove of that to which you have decided to give your approval? It is not that I hope to be believed on these matters; that would be too ridiculous for words. Even less do I wish to contradict anyone. I wish only to ask those who are more experienced in affairs of state to take a bit better care than hitherto in what they do; and also to encourage Monsieur de Malestroit [and those who have some concern for the public good] to continue to pursue this excellent subject. In consequence of which, sovereign princes, who have the power to make law, together with those who counsel them, will, I believe, be more resolute in what must be done for the honour and growth of the commonwealth. First, they should listen to the just complaints and grievances of the poor which come from all quarters. The poor suffer the pain but, for the most part, they cannot tell whence it comes. They should also listen to those who do have a better judgement on the matter but who cannot get a hearing, nor have any means except by writing to disclose the disease to those who have the means the remedy it.

THE END

NOTES

Introduction

General references in addition to those given in the bibliography include F. P. Braudel and F. Spooner, 'Prices in Europe from 1450 to 1750', *Cambridge Economic History of Europe* 4 (Cambridge University Press, 1967), pp. 378–486; H. Hauser, ed., *La Vie chère au XVIe siècle: la réponse de Jean Bodin à M. de Malestroict, 1568* (Paris, 1937); E. James, *The Origins of France: from Clovis to the Capetians, 500-1000* (London: Macmillan, 1982); Seigneur de Joinville, *History of Saint Louis* (Harmondsworth: Penguin, 1963); R. J. Knecht, *The Rise and Fall of Renaissance France 1483–1610* (London: Fontana, 1966) and his other publications on Francis I; D. and M. Frémy, *Quid 1997* (Paris: Robert Laffont, 1997); S. Mennell, *All Manners of Food: Eating and Taste in England and France from the Middle Ages to the Present* (1985); H. A. Miskimin, *Money, Prices, and Foreign Exchange in fourteenth-century France* (New Haven: Yale University Press, 1963); *New Cambridge Modern History*, vol. 2 (Cambridge University Press: 1965), hereafter NCMH; the invaluable *Oxford Classical Dictionary* (Oxford: Clarendon Press, 1966), hereafter OCD; *Oxford Companion to French Literature*, (Oxford: Clarendon Press, 1959), hereafter OCFL; N. J. G. Pounds, *An Economic History of Medieval Europe*, 2nd ed. (Harlow: Longman, 1994), which contains a useful bibliography; and S. Runciman, *A History of the Crusades*, vol. 3 (Harmondsworth: Penguin, 1954; reissued 1971); P. Spufford, *Money and its Use in Medieval Europe* (Cambridge University Press, 1988) is an invaluable guide to many different currencies with an excellent bibliography.

Bodin's response is not just a discussion of money and economic theory, for he was a polymath, presenting a wide range of *vignettes* of history and social life of the period. Indeed, he has been acclaimed by Trevor-Roper as 'the undisputed intellectual master of the later sixteenth century'.

Notes to Text

Page 39

Malestroit: Jehan Cherruyt de Malestroi(c)t, comptroller of the royal mint in Paris. In 1563 the *Chambre des comptes* began an enquiry into the depreciation of the *livre tournois* and the rising cost of commodities. probably in association with this, *parlement* ordered an enquiry in 1565, into depreciation as a result of poor harvests and resulting high local grain prices. From these enquries Malestroit, a *maître des comptes* (a magistrate (*maître*) in the *chambre des comptes*) published his own explanation in *Les paradoxes du Seigneur de Malestroict, Conseiller du Roy, & Maistre ordinaire de ses comptes, sur le faict des Monnoyes* of March 1566. He argued that the rising cost of commodities in

France was an illusion caused by the depreciation of the *livre* and that prices in terms of silver and gold had not really changed for 300 years (first paradox); that price inflation was a result of the increase in the number of copper *sous* in a gold *écu* and that people were only losing money because rent and wages had not increased comparatively (second paradox). Jean Bodin challenged this in 1568.

J. C. de Malestroict, *Paradoxes inédits du Seigneur de Malestroit touchant les monnoyes, avec la response du president de la Tourette*, ed., A. de La Tourrette and L. Einaudi (Turin, 1937), includes, 'Mémoire sur le faict des Monnaye proposez et leur par le maistre des comptes de Malestroict au Privé Conseil du Roy tenu à Sainet-Maur-des-Fossez, le 16 jour de May 1567'. Appropriately, he wrote that currency 'was a mystery few people can understand' (1567)!

money: the money of account, ie. the terms in which values and monetary transactions and royal accounts were recorded, was completely distinct in France from the time of Charlemagne (q.v.) to the eighteenth century, from the money in actual circulation. Even when the Carolingian emperors and their successors still minted nothing but *deniers* and *oboles* (ie. half *deniers*), accounts were kept in *livres*, *sous* and *deniers*. Twelve *deniers* were counted as one *sou* and twenty *sous* were counted as one *livre* (cf. the English penny, shilling and pound). A greater variety of coins was issued by the later Capetiens, but their value was never neatly tailored to the traditional £.s.d. accounting system (P. Spufford, *op. cit*, pp. 27, 33-4, 229-30). For a description of the medieval monetary system including money of account see N. J. G. Pounds, *op. cit.*, pp. 115-22, 428-32.

To make matters more complicated, from the beginning of the Capetian dynasty, the coinage was not uniform throughout France, so that any accounting system had to specify which particular coin was adopted as its basic unit. In addition to the royal and provincial coins, foreign coins also circulated in France.

Actual coin was either gold, silver or billon (q.v.), eg. *écu* (q.v.), *teston* (q.v.) and *douzain* (q.v.).

Majesty: Charles IX, King of France 1560-74, b. 1550, son of Henry II, succeeded his brother Francis II. Malestroit published his pamphlet in his reign.

Chambre des comptes: an administrative court similar to a Public Accounts Committee, with ten presidents and sixty-two *maîtres des comptes*, which revised the public accounts of the kingdom, exercising jurisdiction over accountants and even some control over the king.

Page 41

gold: Croesus (560-46 BC) of Lydia initiated the use of gold and silver for coins. Local supplies meant that bronze was the earliest coinage of Rome, though gold (from c. 217-209 BC) and silver (from 269 BC) were increasingly used. Gold coins were issued sporadically from the time of Sulla but became regular coinage under Julius Caesar. After a period of about 550 years (c. 700-1250) when no gold was minted in western Europe, gold currencies were introduced partly for commercial convenience and partly for prestige. In the later Middle Ages the highest value actual coins in France were gold, with more and larger gold denominations appearing in the fifteenth century. From 1500-46 gold coins were about two-thirds of the total annual coinage of royal mints. From 1546 to 1600 the average fell to seventeen per cent.

silver: by the sixth century BC, silver Greek coinage was minted from silver from the Paeonian mines in the Balkans, from Laurium and the Greek islands, southern Italy and Sicily, until Philip II of Macedon popularised the use of gold. Silver was popular for Roman coins from 269 BC and was the main metal for coins between eighth and the thirteenth centuries in Europe. In France, silver coins were used to the fifteenth century, often debased.

Philip of Valois: Philippe VI *aka* Philippe de Valois (1293-1350). First French king of the Valois dynasty, ruled from 1328, after the death of Charles IV. Elder son of Charles of Valois and grandson of Philip III, first cousin of Louis X, Philip V and Charles IV. Grandfather of Charles V. His claim to the French throne was disputed by Edward III of England from 1327 to 1377. He took considerable profits from debasing coinage from 1336.

ell: a measure of length (114.3 centimetres).

écu: Saint Louis limited the circulation and validity of feudal money, imposed royal coinage and created the nominally fine *écu d'or* in 1266, a hammered coin of good alloy (3.55 grams). The *écu* issued by Philip de Valois was worth twenty *sols* or a *livre*. The king is shown with a royal *fleurs de lis* on a shield. The *écu d'or* repeatedly appreciated in value. In 1351 it weighed 4.47 grams. From 1516 the gold *écu* was frequently devalued (1516) at forty *sous*, in 1550 at forty-six *sous*, fifty *sous* in 1561 and sixty *sous* in 1575 (R. J. Knecht, *op. cit.,* p. xiii).

The silver *écu* dating from the sixteenth century was worth three *livres*. The gold *écu d'or au soleil*, also known as the écu au soleil was the principal and largest gold coin in circulation in sixteenth-century France. It was issued from 1475 weighted 3.5 grams, in 1515 weighed 3.40 grams, and in 1586, 3.31 grams. The *écu à la croisette* was essentially the same as the *écu au soleil*, whilst the *demi-écu* was half the weight and value of the *écu*.

Latin: Cotgrave defined 'Latin marchandise' as 'excellent good stuffe; or the best, or most utterable commodities, tearmed so by Marchants' (*A Dictionarie of the French and English Tongues*, London, 1611, reprinted University of South Carolina Press, 1968).

wheat: France was essentially self-sufficient in grain, with a surplus available for export. Figures for grain prices 1510-9 and 1540-9 for Paris, Lyon and Toulouse reflect fluctuations and inflation (R. J. Knecht, *op. cit.,* pp. 7, 304). After 1520, wages did not keep up with the grain prices whilst the population continued to increase; this led to the *Grande Rebeyne* in 1529; there was a grain famine in 1545 with associated disturbances; grain was more abundant in 1557. In the 1560s, bad harvests meant that prices rose steeply. R. J. Knecht, *op. cit.,* p. 305 and H. A. Miskimin, *op. cit.* give useful information on wheat prices.

wine: wine consumption increased in the sixteenth century with more hostelries, and a rapid expansion of vineyards and production for export. Indirect taxes (*aides*) were imposed on consumers by the crown (R. J. Knecht, *op. cit.,* p. 22).

Page 42

livres tournois: the principal money of account and the currency in general circulation in (South of) France from the tenth century. *Livres*, *gros* and *deniers* were minted in Tours from the tenth century to 1204. The lighter *livre parisis* (ratio 4:5) prevailed in the North until Languedoc was absorbed by the crown. *Denier parisis* were issued by kings from Louis VII to Charles V. Both continued side by side, with the *livre parisis* being valued at twenty-five per cent higher than the *tournois*. *Parisis* gradually went out of use but the *tournois* ceased to be minted in Tours only in 1772. H. A. Miskimin, *op. cit.* gives full details of the fourteenth-century French mints.

King John: Jean II *le Bon* (1319-64), King of France, of the House of Valois (r. 1350-64), son of Philip VI of Valois, captured by the Black Prince, eldest son and heir of Edward III of England, at Poitiers in 1356. For his release, John II had to consent to disadvantageous but inconclusive treaties of Brétigny and Calais (1360) and ransom demands, but he continued to be held prisoner in England and died in captivity in London.

sol: also called *sou*, one *livre* equalled twenty *sols* and one *sol* equalled twelve *deniers*. In 1266 the *sol* (*sou*) became the silver *gros tournois* (c. 4 grams).

franc: name given to various coins from early times. Under John II, a gold coin (*franc d'or*) bearing *Francorum Rex*, equivalent to the *livre tournois*, was minted in 1360 to commemorate his ransom from the English, but the *franc d'or* ceased to be struck by the early fifteenth century. Henry II reintroduced it as a silver coin worth twenty *sols* or a *livre*. From that time, the term *franc* was used as the equivalent of *livre* of the money of account (OCFL, p. 489). The nominally fine gold *franc à cheval* (3.89 grams) was issued from 1360 by John I, as part of his chivalric aspirations, to pay his ransom after Poitiers.

Saint Louis: Louis IX (1215-70), King of France, son of Louis VIII (r. 1226-70). His mother, Blanche de Castille, acted as regent until he attained his majority. He defeated Henry III of England at Saintes when Normandy was returned by England to France. He reformed the French coinage about 1262. He eventually died in Tunis on the Fourth Crusade and was canonised in 1297.

denier: French coin of silver or base metal of very small value, corresponding to the *denier* of the money of account. The name was also applied to a variety of other coins at different times, eg. silver *deniers* of Rome from 1188 and in Germany in the twelfth century; roughly equivalent to a penny (Seigneur de Joinville, *op. cit.*, p. 361). The *maille* is a small coin worth half a *denier*.

gros tournois: silver coins produced from the time of Saint Louis to Charles VI (4.22 grams in 1266-1322; 1329-64 weighed 2.55 grams).

douzain: an actual very common French coin worth twelve *deniers*, made of billon, which represented the *sou*; the principal unit of account in the retail trade.

fine silver: pure silver or *argent-le-roi*, which was standard nearly pure silver, defined as having a fineness of twelve *deniers* (ie. twelve parts of twelve).

Page 43

blancs: white money (*album*), wholly or partly made of silver.

liard: a small coin first issued under Charles VI, worth three *deniers*.

Page 46
mark: *marc* 'not a coin but a denomination in weight of gold or silver, usually regarded as equal to 8 oz' (or 4,608 grains) (Seigneur de Joinville, *op. cit.*, p. 362); the measure adopted in the eleventh century in place of the *livre* of twelve ounces, for stating weights of bullion (OCFL, p. 489). Weights were expressed in terms of the number of coins struck from a standard weight, a pound or *marc*.

Page 47
copper: billon coins (of copper and silver) accounted for seven per cent of the French coinage minted in 1568. Pure copper coins began to be minted in 1578, the year of Bodin's second edition: F. C. Spooner, *L'Economie mondiale et les frappes monétaires en France 1493-1680* (Paris: Armand Colin, 1956), p. 525.

Page 49
Master Jean Bodin: (1530-96), political philosopher; see 'Introduction' (above) for full details. After 1576 he produced various books on the dangers of sorcery (1580), God in nature (1597) and on religion. For the scourge of debasement in the late Middle Ages, see P. Spufford, *op. cit.*, pp. 289-319.
Archbishop of Canterbury: Matthew Parker (1504-75), chaplain to Anne Boleyn in 1535; supported Lady Jane Gray's claims and deprived of office by Queen Mary. Queen Elizabeth I appointed him Archbishop of Canterbury from 1559. A noted moderate who used his patronage to check the spread of Puritanism. He was succeeded in 1576 by Edmund Grindal (c. 1519-83) but suspended from 1576-83 for refusing to support Elizabeth I's orders to suppress prophesyings, ie. at the time of Bodin's second edition of 1578.

No English translation has yet been traced but Gerrard de Malynes' response, *England's View, in the Unmasking of Two Paradoxes; with a replication unto the answer of Maister Jean Bodine* appeared in 1603 (reprinted New York: Arno Press, 1972), seven years after Bodin's death, and gives a précis of Malestroit (pp. 11-21), an abstract of Bodin's reply (pp. 50-63) and a critique of Bodin's response (pp. 63-120), saying his explanations are beside the point. Possibly not completely understanding Malestroit but agreeing that the latter was mistaken, Malynes (fl. 1586-1648) contends that the paradoxes contradict each other by definition. He criticises Bodin for not answering the problem directly; his own answer was based on the importance of international foreign exchange transactions. He gives an account of the economic and geographical conditions to show England's relative position (pp. 120-48) and urged restriction on trade to attract foreign exchange.
Chancellor of England: Nicholas Bacon (1509-79). In 1558 Queen Elizabeth I appointed him as Lord Chancellor, then known as Keeper of the Great Seal. He strongly opposed the claim of Mary, Queen of Scots (1542-67, d. 1587) to the English throne.

Page 51

King: Bodin wrote the first edition during Charles IX's reign. At that stage, he felt assured of the stability of the French monarchy. The second edition appeared during the reign of Henry III.

Henri III (1551-89) Duke of Anjou, King of Poland (1573-4); third son of Henry II, succeeded his brother Charles IX as King of France in 1574 and like Charles IX was dominated by his mother, Catherine de Médicis, who had ordered the St-Barthélemy massacre of Protestant Huguenots in August 1572. Italianate, dubious, given to favourites, he was a considerable patron of literature. During his reign the quality of coinage was improved. Henry III, the last king of the House of Valois, was assassinated at St-Cloud in 1589 by a Dominican friar, Jacques Clément. He died without issue.

Faur, M^r du: Guy du Faur de Pibrac (1529-84), born in Toulouse, magistrate, advocate and moralist, versed in classical culture and with a distinguished career. He was nearly put to death at the time of Henry II for his bold advocacy of religious toleration. He was one of the three envoys of Charles IX who defended the Gallican church at the Council of Trent (1545-62). He also wrote quatrains full of wisdom and gentlemanly conduct. Between 1576-9 he was part of the palace academy gathered together by Henry III.

Page 52

Provence: am ancient French province in South France. Its annexation in 1481 was significant for the development of Levantine trade, in competition with the Italian ports. In southern France the imitative florin (q.v.) (*Dauphiné*) was used as a basis for accounting in the 1340-60s, and actual coins included the *courronal*, worth seventy-five per cent of a *denier tournois*, and the *patae*.

Page 53

velvet: Florence probably produced velvet from AD c. 1100, well before 1285. It is practically impossible to distiguish between Italian and Ottoman velvet (*katīfe* and *çātma*) and silks of the sixteenth century.

Philip the Fair: Philippe IV *le Bel* (1268-1314), King of France (1285-1314), and of Navarre as Philippe I (1284-1305) ruling with his wife Jeanne [Joan] I of Navarre. Succeeded his father, Philip III, belonged to the Capetian dynasty. Grandson of Saint Louis. He reformed the coinage (1306), which had long been advocated by the church. In later years, he began to seek advice from his subjects on monetary policy. There was a great expansion and building between 1150 and 1300, especally during his reign, when most of the major cathedrals and many churches of France were rebuilt or constructed. Not to be confused with Philip, Archduke, the Fair (1478-1506), King of Castile (r. 1504-06).

Justinian: Flavius Petrus Sabbatius Iustinianus, great Roman Emperor of the East (AD 527-65) who built Santa Sophia and other great buildings in Constantinople. He ordered the codification of Roman law (*Digesta, Institutiones*, and *Novellae*). Falsifying money was firmly repressed by edict. The manufacture of silk in Asia Minor began during his reign: previously it had been imported from China to the West.

purple and dyed goods: ie. richly or brightly coloured. Under the Roman empire dyeing became one of the great luxury trades, and vast sums were spent on red, purple and violet dyes. Even during the last decades of the Outremer and later, purple dye from Tyre (es Sur) was fashionable.
ordinance (1294): in 1294 a ten-year war began with England which severely strained Philip the Fair's resources.

Page 54
Ordinances of Saint Louis: two ordinances (1254 and 1256) outlined the duties of royal officials; further ordinances forbade duels, prostitution and counterfeiting, stabilised the currency, and compelled the circulation of royal coinage. Following the treaty of Paris of 1258, Saint Louis reorganised the administration of the kingdom and promoted its commercial interests.
material: cloth was the second most important export, after sugar, from the Levant and Egypt after the First Crusade. The silk-worm had been cultivated round Beirut and Tripoli (Syria) from the end of the sixth century and flax grown in Palestine. Samite (from *shāmī*, 'Syrian') was made in Acre, Beirut and Lattakieh; Tyre was famous for cendal or zendado fabric; Nablus for renowned for its linen (N. J. G. Pounds, *op. cit.*, pp. 301-20).
vair: a kind of fur, like the grey miniver, used in the Middle Ages for lining and trimming ceremonial costumes; probably the skin of a squirrel with a grey back and a white belly. Valuable furs were traded long distances from Ireland and Russia. In Florence, ordinary women were forbidden to use some types of fur.
spices: the *Assises de Jérusalem*, the code of law arranged for Godefroi de Bouillon (c. 1099) mention various spices including cinnamon, cardamum, cloves, mace, musk, galangale, nutmeg, also indigo, madder, aloe-wood and ivory which were traded with the West (W. Van Heyd and F. M. Raynaud, *Histoire du commerce du Levant au Moyen Age*, 2 volumes (Leipzig, 1937, new edition 1967), pp. 563 ff). Portugal (q.v.) tried to enforce a monopoly on the spice trade. Estimates of exports of spices to Europe via the Ottoman empire 1500-60 indicate spice consumption rose by a hundred per cent.
Brusa: Bursa [Prusa] in Anatolia, still famous for the manufacture of cloth and sericulture, which exported luxury silks to Europe in the Middle Ages. Silk was 'not just another commodity, but a symbol of authority' (C. Lopez, 'Silk industry in the Byzantine empire', *Speculum: Journal of Medieval Studies* 20 (Canbridge, Mass.: Medieval Academy of America, 1945), pp. 1-42)). In c. 1130, skilled weavers came to Palermo from Greece and Turkey and produced elaborate brocaded fabrics of silk interlaced with gold (damask). Following the conquest of Sicily in 1266, many of these weavers fled to Lucca, which became well-known for it silk fabrics with elaborate floral designs. In 1315, the Florentines captured Lucca. By 1450 over 46,000 workers were employed in the Italian weaving and silk (damask and satin) industry centred on Florence. By the mid sixteenth century, a successful industry in velvets and brocades was established in Genoa and Venice.

136 Notes

Genoa: enjoyed fantastic prosperity as a seafaring city state, rivalling Pisa and Venice, with entrepôts on the Mediterranean, Atlantic and Black Sea in the thirteenth century, until deprived of these by Turkey in the sixteenth century.
Tours: (population c. 30,000 c. 1300), important luxury silk textile industry was established in the late fifteenth century in Tours but its prosperity was ruined 1562–95 by the Religious Wars.
Lyons, angl. of **Lyon**: (population 10,000–20,000 c. 1300), medieval mint. From 1420 it was famous for its fairs and banking. Luxury silk production was established in 1536 to provide employment after the rioting of 1529 and became the provenance of Calvinists in Lyon before 1567.
Avignon: the capital of the marquisate of Provence. About the same size as Lyon in the early fourteenth century. Avignon remained a papal possession until 1791.
Toulouse: medieval mint; the oldest provincial university (associated with Dolet, Bodin and Scaliger) was established in Toulouse in 1229 by the Count of Toulouse, partly as a bulwark of orthodoxy against the Albigensian heresy.

Page 55
property register of Toulouse: between 1510–9 and 1540–9 the price index for grain rose from one hundred to 173 (R. J. Knecht, *op. cit.*, p. 304).
Châtelet: originally a defence on the North bank of the Seine of the Pont au Charge, later the two courts (*Grand* and *Petit*) and prison where the *prévôté*, assisted by a *lieutenant criminel* and a *lieutenant civil*, ruled Paris for the crown.
Paris standard: each region of France had its own system of weights and measures in the sixteenth century. For example, Knecht indicates the Paris *setier* of grain equalled 156 *litres*. Twelve *setiers* equals one *muid*. The *parlement* of Paris controlled the supply and quality of supplies to Paris and most of North France, except Normandy (R. J. Knecht, *op. cit.*, p. 19). Weights based on wheat grains (0.053 grams) were known as Paris grains.
Ceres, the Lady of Sicily: Sicilian agrarian cult of Demeter, the Greek corn-goddess, identified with the ancient Italian goddess Ceres (origin of 'cereal'). Sicily exported wheat, wine, oil, cattle and horses from Greek times.

Page 56
King Agrippa: Agrippa II (AD c. 27–before 93); a speech supporting Titus in AD 68 reported by Josephus, *Of the Wars of the Jews*, bk. 2, ch. 16.
Cicero: Marcus Tullius (106–43 BC), lawyer, orator and writer.
Loire: longest of the four great rivers of France, via Orléans, through a plain famous for the *châteaux de la Loire* to Tours, Saumur, Nantes to the Atlantic.
Brie: site of a famous Renaissance fair. At such fairs, money-changers were important figures; foreign money was allowed to circulate freely, and commercial suits could be heard by special judges; at the end of each fair, a period was allowed for the settling of accounts (R. J. Knecht, *op. cit.*, p. 7).
Saintonge: former province of western France, based at Saintes, incorporated into France in 1375.
Languedoc: until 1542 the royal lands were divided into four fiscal districts *générales* (Languedoïl, Languedoc, Normandy and Outre-Seine-et-Yonne) with

an additional four *recettes-générales*. Under the edict of Cognac (1542) the four were subdivided into sixteen *recettes-générales*.

Page 57
Comtat Venaissin: area around Avignon, from *Comitatus Avennicinus*. Made itself a republic at the end of the twelfth century to escape the domination of the Counts of Toulouse. Captured by Louis VIII in 1226 and ceded to the Count of Provence. In 1309, Clement V was expelled from Rome and established himself at Avignon where seven popes resided until 1377/8. Then followed two antipopes who were driven out in 1403(8). After the Count of Toulouse was defeated at Avignon by Louis VIII in 1226, he pledged the Comtat Venaissin with the Holy See as a security against his treaty obligations. It was Avignon's proximity to the Comtat, which drew Clement V (1305-16) there in 1309, when he was driven from Rome by sedition.
Charles the Wise: Charles V, *le Sage*, b. 1337, (r. 1364-80), King of France of the House of Valois, after the death of his father John II. He managed to restore some order to France during the Hundred Years' War (1337-1453) and strengthened the crown at the expense of the nobility.
Auxerre: capital of Yonne *départment* and famous for Chablis wine; a county between 1364-80; united to France by Louis XI in the 1400s.
Mr Fauchet: probably Claude Fauchet (1529-1601), magistrate, historian and critic; he would no doubt have been compiling his *Antiquités gauloises et Françoises*, published 1579-99, when Bodin was preparing the second edition of the present document.
duchy of Berry: former province in the Paris basin, capital Bourges, now in the *départments* of Indre and Cher. The district was bought by Philip I in 1100, probably from the Viscount of Bourges, was made a duchy in 1360, and gave title to various French princes. The Duke of Berry, Jean d'Este, (1340-1416) had a large coin collection.
Philip I: Philippe I (1052/3-1108), King of France (1059/60-1108), elder son of Henry I (r. 1031-60) of France, belonged to the Capetian dynasty.
Godfrey de Bouillon: Godefroi de Bouillon (1058/60-1100), one of the leaders of the First Crusade (1096-9), and first King of Jerusalem (1099). He was commemorated in the 'Cycle of the Crusade' poems.
Lombards: of Lombardy, a region in northern Italy. Part of the Charlemagne's Frankish empire from AD 774, later ruled by Spain (1535-1713).
Saxons: Germanic people, who fought against Charlemagne in the eighth century AD and infiltrated central Europe until the twelfth century.
Franconians: of Franconia, one of the early medieval German dutchies; by the twelfth century, referred only to East Franconia (Würzburg). Basis for the *kreis* (administrative district) set up in the early sixteenth century.
Ripuarians: a division of the Franks.
Amiens: c. 1000, capital of Picardy; medieval mint until c. 1447; capital of the Somme, famous in the Middle Ages for its textile industry.
real: réal, large silver coins of Castille (3.48 grams), first issued by Pedro I (1350-69).

Emperor Henry: (c. 1269/74–1313), Henry IV, Count of Luxembourg. Henry VII, Holy Roman Emperor (1312–3), took the Lombard crown in Milan (1311) and the cities of Piedmont and Lombardy. He was unable to subdue the Florentines fully.

Blondus: Flavius Blondus *aka* Flavio Biondo (1392–1463), humanist historian. Author of *Histories* (thirty-two books), a reliable chronological history AD 410 to 1442.

Philip the Tall: Philippe V *le Long* [the Tall] (c. 1293–1322). King of France from 1316 to 1322, and King of Navarre as Philip II from 1314. Second son of Philip IV, *le Bel* (1285–1314), belonged to the Capetian dynasty.

Page 58

Anjou: historical province of France in the Loire valley; occupied by England many times, returned to the crown in 1480. First a county, often gift of kings to their relations; then duchy (from 1360) when John II gave the countship to his son Louis in 1351 *also* titled French nobility, royal princes of the blood, the first being Francis (r. 1566–76). Bodin was born in Angers, its chief market town.

Auvergne: region based on animal husbandry in central France, with several important counties by the thirteenth century. Two of these were united by Charles, Duke of Bourbon in 1503, and were annexed to the crown in 1532.

Bourbonnais: region in central France, attached to the crown in 1531.

La Marche: Marche Limousine, Latin *Marchia*, province of ancient France between Berry and Bourbonnais to the North of Poitou; produced *deniers* in its mint by 1211; given to the Bourbons-Montpensier, confiscated by Francis I in 1525; united with the crown in 1531.

Troyes: the capital of the Counts of Champagne until its formal union with France in the reign of Philip VI (1328–50) with its own mint. It sided with the Burgundians after Agincourt. From about 1480 to 1635 it was a flourishing artistic centre, especially sculpture, although severely damaged by a fire in 1524. Because of the importance of its fairs during the twelfth century (a period of rapid development in mercantile commerce) the measures, as well as the currency of Troyes, were adopted as international standard.

Page 59

abundance of gold and silver: the increasing volume of silver and gold in circulation during the sixteenth century was increasingly the result of imports from America. Unfortunately there is no very accurate way of measuring the increase in the amount of precious metals in circulation resulting from this influx. R. Trevor Davies, *The Golden Century of Spain 1501–1621* (London: MacMillan, 1964), pp. 299–300, gives information on the total bullion imports from America, calculated in English pounds at par of sterling eg. 1503–5 £213,400 all gold; 1546–50 £3,167,600 fifteen per cent gold and eighty-five per cent silver; 1566–70 £8,131,100 three per cent gold and ninety-seven per cent silver, with an additional ten to fifty per cent bullion smuggled into Spain.

Plutarch: academic philosopher and biographer (AD c. 46–after 120), wrote a life of Aemillius Paullus, AD c. 105–15.

Response to the Paradoxes of Malestroit 139

Pliny: the Elder, Gaius Plīnus Secundus (AD 23/4–79). Encyclopaedist, sole extant work of his 102 volumes is his *Naturalis Historia* (AD c. 77).
Macedonia: the connecting link between the Balkans and the Greek peninsula. Alexander the Great raised Macedonia to the status of a world power. It collapsed before the expanding power of Rome (167 BC). It was annexed as a province by Rome in 146 BC, though its culture continued to survive.
Perseus: King of Macedon (r. 179–68 BC), who fought against Rome and the Aetolians, in his expansion of Macedon in the Third Macedonian War. He was defeated by Aemilius Paullus and captured at Samothrace.
Æmilius Paulus: Lucius Aemilius Paullus Macedonicus ended the Third Macedonian War (AD 171–68) at Pydra. He symbolises the union of Roman tradition with Hellenism.
Suetonius: Gaius Suetonius Tranquillus (AD 69–c. 140) historian who wrote *De viris illustribus* (AD 106–13) and *De vita Caesarum* (AD c. 121).
Augustus: Emperor (63 BC–AD 14). C. Octavius, adopted son and heir to Julius Caesar. 27 BC transferred the State to the free disposal of the Senate and People but kept Spain, Gaul, Syria and Egypt. Overthrew Antony and became master of Egypt in 23 BC.
Candace: for the Queen of Sheba see I Kings 10:1–3; 2 Chronicles 9:1–2; Acts 8:27.

Page 60
New World: after 1493 began the rise of Spain as a colonial power in the New World and the influx of Spanish-American gold into Europe (E. J. Hamilton, 'Imports of American gold and silver into Spain (1530–1660)', *Quarterly Journal of Economics* vol.43 (May 1929), pp. 436 ff). Ferdinand and Isabella issued the Medino del Campo ordinances to regulate Spanish coinage in the New World in 1497. In the 1560s prices rose steeply, partly due to the influx of American silver. Bodin argued that increased gold and silver from the New World was a major cause of the Price Revolution, although inflation began before its discovery (R. J. Knecht, *op. cit.,* p. 305). Despite all the silver and gold from Peru, Spain was not a rich country. American treasure helped to pay for emperors' wars and enriched Genoese bankers, when it might usefully have been invested into Spain's economic infrastructure.
pearls: an item of conspicious display from the Persian Gulf, demanded by the wealthy of medieval Europe in exchange for silver; later supplemented by supplies from the New World.
Tiberius: Emperor Tiberius Julius Caesar Augustus, born 42 BC. Suetonius, Tacitus and others wrote of his reign. He exercised rigid economy and therefore accumulated great wealth.
Poitiers: Edward, the Black Prince, defeated the French in 1356 and captured John II at the end of the first phase of the Hundred Years' War.
King of Scotland: David II (1324–71), succeeded his father Robert I, the Bruce, in 1329 and married Joanna, sister of Edward III, King of England (1327–77). Most of his reign was marked by costly intermittent warfare with England and he spent eighteen years in exile in France from 1334, where he was maintained

generously by King Philip VI, whose campaigns against Edward III he joined in 1339 and 1340. Captured at Neville's Cross, Durham in 1346, he was not released until 1357, in return for a ransom (100,000 marks) which proved more than the Scottish government could pay. Attempts to cancel the ransom by offering the Scottish throne to England made him enemies in the Scottish parliament and with Robert II. In order to raise his ransom, constitutional changes were made whereby representatives of the royal burghs were asked to join the barons and clergy on the Grand Council.

noble: English nominally pure gold coin 1344–1464 (in the reigns of Edward III to James I). Scottish standards were similar to but separate from sterling from 1280.

alliance (1371): fortified by this agreement, which marked the beginning of a long alliance between the two countries, Robert II successfully defeated the English at Otterburn (1388).

Robert, King of Scotland: Robert II, the Steward (1316–90, r. from 1371), first of the Stewarts and regent (1334–5 (joint), 1338–41, 1346–57).

Saint Louis...prisoner in Egypt: Louis IX surrendered to the Egyptians at al-Manṣūra on 5 April 1250. The terms of his ransom were the cession of Damietta (on 30 April 1250), and for his large captured army he had to pay 500,000 *livres tournois* (about one million *besants*). This was later reduced to 400,000 *livres tournois*, half to be paid at Damietta and half when the king arrived at Acre. If he failed to raise the ransom, he was expected to renounce Christ, which he refused to do. He had only 170,000 *livres* in his coffers, so the Egyptians held the king's brother, Alfonso of Poitou until the ransom was raised. Only after the Templars (a military and religious order founded about 1118 for the protection of pilgrims and the Holy Sepulchre in Jerusalem) were threatened with violence, did they agree to provide the rest of the ransom, and the king was released on 6 May 1250 (S. Runciman, *op. cit.,* pp. 270–4).

Saladin: Bodin was wrong in associating Saladin (Ṣalāḥ ad-Dīn Yūsuf ibn Aiyūb) (r. 1169–93) with Saint Louis' ransom, although Saladin founded the Egyptian dynasty of the Aiyubids (1171–1250). Sultan Eṣ-Ṣāliḥ Aiyūb (1240–50) died whilst the ransom for Saint Louis was being raised. His son, al-Muʿaẓẓam Tūrānshāh, was responsible for the capture of Saint Louis and his army at al-Manṣūra. During the negotiations for Louis' release in 1250, Tūrānsgāh was murdered by his Mamlūk bodyguards.

Page 61

bezant: a fine gold coin (*solidus*), later *bezant* (from 'Byzantium'), derived from the Greek 'talent'. First minted in Byzantium (Constantinople) by Constantine the Great AD c. 309, a continuation of late Roman coinage and continued in a period of great monetary activity until the eleventh century. A *solidus* weighed twenty-four carats thus pure gold was described as twenty-four carats fine. Gold *bezants* varied in value between a sovereign and a half-sovereign; silver *bezants* worth from a florin to a shilling (1963 values) (Seigneur de Joinville, *op. cit.*, p. 361). Smaller denominations in Byzantium were in silver and bronze; after the eleventh century, the gold tended to be replaced by electrum.

Response to the Paradoxes of Malestroit 141

Seigneur de Joinville: Lord/Sieur of Jenn, b. 1224/5, joined Saint Louis' crusade. His *Life of Saint Louis* was written when he was over eighty years old. In his account, Queen Margaret gave birth to Jean Tristan in Damietta when Saint Louis was marching on Manṣūra. She had to buy all the food in Damietta at a cost of over 360,000 *livres* to prevent the Italians leaving and thus preserving the city as a useful bargaining counter (S. Runciman, *op. cit.*, pp. 271-2). An account by Jean Sarrizin and its anonymous continuation gives a clear account of events.

leather money: in crises, currency has been produced from a variety of materials, including leather, paper, cloth and so on (A. Del Mar, *History of Monetary Systems* (Orono: University of Maine, 1983), p. 182).

Philip III: Philippe III, *aka* Philip the Bold, *le Hardi* (1245-85). Capetian King of France 1270 to 1285; succeeded his father Louis IX.

Charles, Count of Valois: father of Philip de Valois. The House of Valois was the Valois-Orléans line of the Capetian dynasty.

King Edward: Edward I (1239-1307), son of Henry III of England, King of England from 1272-1307, bankrupted by wars with France, had to yield Gascony to Philip IV in 1293. He eventually made peace with Philip IV (1299) and married Philip's sister, Margaret, in 1298 at the same time as arranging the marriage of Isabelle of France and his fourth son, Edward II.

Isabelle of France: Isabella of France (1292-1358), in 1308 married Edward II (1284-1327), weak King of England (1307-27), which led to peace between the two kingdoms. Daughter of Philip IV of France. Her eldest son was Edward III of England. Despite the development of international banking, gold coins were essential for great political payments in the fourteenth and fifteenth centuries, such as for her dowry and John II's ransom.

Philip the Tall ...son: There is some confusion here. the king in 1311 was Philip the Fair (Philip IV, 1285-1314) who left three sons. Philip the Tall, who ruled as Philip V (1316-22 had no son.

Charles VII: *le Victorieux*, b. 1403, son of Charles VI, ruled during his father's mental incapacitation (r. 1422-61); his reign marked by struggle to recover French domains in North and South West from the English and Burgundians with his champion, Joan of Arc; his reign saw the end of the Hundred Years' War.

Page 62

Philippe de Comynes: Commynes/Comines (*c.*1447-1511), historian, moralist and diplomat for Charles the Bold, Louis XI and Charles VIII. His *Mémoires* (publ. 1524) are full of vibrant personal memories of his diplomatic missions.

Louis XI: (1423-83), succeeded his father Charles VII as King of France (r. 1461-83). An astute ruler, he encouraged early printing, established a postal service, extended the royal dominions almost to France's present limits (except Brittany and Lorraine). In conflict with Charles the Bold, Duke of Burgundy, the last of the powerful feudal vassals of the kings of France, who was in alliance with England. Obtained Cerdaña and Roussillon from Juan II of Aragón as security for a loan of 300,000 crowns. During Louis XI's reign the change from a medieval social system to the modern state was accelerated.

Burgundy: John II made his fourth son, Jean *sans Peur*, Duke of Burgundy. Powerful not only in France, the Burgundians controlled the Netherlands between c. 1000 and 1482. Around 1410-8 France suffered from dissentions between the Armagnacs and the Burgundians. In the reign of Charles VI the Armagnacs supported the House of Orléans against the House of Burgundy. When Henry V of England invaded France in 1415 the Burgundians supported him.

Provence: in 1246 Provence was inherited by Charles of France, Count of Anjou, later King of Sicily and Naples, who was on Saint Louis' crusade. Queen Joanna I of Naples and Countess of Provence sold Avignon to Pope Clement VI in 1348, and later it passed to *le bon roi* Count René, Duke of Anjou (1408/9-80), who was titular King of Naples, the two Sicilies and Jerusalem and last independent Count of Provence. (He also wrote a treatise on *Tournois*.) René's successor bequeathed his count-ship to Louis XI and in 1487 Provence was formally united to France.

Charles VIII: *l'Affable*, King of France, b. 1470 of the House of Valois (r. 1483-98), succeeded his father Louis XI. He invaded Italy to assert the rights of the French crown to the Kingdom of Naples.

King Henry: Henry II gave 400,000 *livres* for the marriage of his eldest legitimate daughter Elisabeth (1545-1568) to be paid in three instalments, six months apart when she married Philip II of Spain on 18 June 1559 as his third wife (F. J. Baumgartner, *Henry II, King of France 1547-1559* (London: Duke University Press, 1988, pp. 247-9).

Renée: Renée de France (1510-75), Duchess of Ferrara, second daughter of Louis XII and Anne of Brittany. Under the treaty of Paris (24 March 1515), Charles of Hapsburg, Duke of Burgundy and son of Archduke Philip the Fair, grandson of Emperor Maximilian I, was promised Renée's hand (R. J. Knecht, *op. cit.*, pp. 96-7). She was also promised to Henry VIII of England. In June 1528 she married Ercole d'Este, son of Alfonso d'Este, Duke of Ferrara.

Galeazzo II: Galeazzo Visconti, Lord of Pavia, Vicount of Milan (1354-78) ruled with his brother Bernabò (q.v.). In 1367 he arranged the marriage of his only daughter Violante to Lionel (q.v.) with the dowry settled at 200,000 gold florins, the city of Alba and various castles in Piedmont.

Lionel: Lionel (1338-68) of Antwerp, Earl of Ulster (1346-62), Duke of Clarence (1362), second son of King Edward III of England. Married Violante (Yolande) in Milan in 1368. After several months of festivities, Lionel was taken ill and died.

Bernabo: Bernabò Visconti, brother of Galeazzo II, Viscount of Milan (1354-85). Savage, wild but strictly just, the strangest of all the Viscontis, he acknowledged thirty-six children, sixteen of them legitimate. He made political marriage arrangements for his children including that of Louis II, eldest son of Louis of Anjou, to his daughter Lucia, with a large dowry and troops; another daughter was betrothed, with a substantial dowry, to the Count of Valois.

Galaezzo: Jean Galéas (Gian Galeazzo) Visconti (1351-1402), first Duke of Milan (1378-1402). When he married Isabella de Valois, the French gave the county of Virtù as dowry, whilst Galeazzo paid 100,000 florins, mostly raised by taxes on the Milanese.

Response to the Paradoxes of Malestroit 143

Milan: governed by the Visconti family (1277-1447) and then under the Sforzas (1450-1535). Louis XII invaded Italy to claim the duchy of Milan (between 1498 and 1515) because of his claim through Valentina (q.v.). Charles V had partial control in the 1530s and its retention was seen by Hispano-Italians as the key to Spanish power in Italy and formed a military outpost for Spain. Prince Philip was given the duchy in 1546 but after forty years of wars, Milan was in ruins and had to be heavily subsidised by Spain. France renounced its claims on the duchy in 1559 (G. Ianziti, *Humanistic Historiography under the Sforzas: politics and propaganda in fifteenth-century Milan* (1988)).
Valentina: Louis of France married Valentine Visconti (1366-1408), the charming and beautiful daughter of Giangalaezzo Visconti, first Duke of Milan, and of Isabella de Valois (d. 1372), daughter of John II le Bon. Negotiations began in 1386, the contract signed in 1387 with a dowry of 450,000 florins and the city of Asti. By a series of fatalities, her heirs were to be the sole legitimate heirs of Giangaleazzo and also of the French crown. Through descent from her, Louis XII based his claims to Milan.
Louis of France: (1371-1407), Duke of Touraine (1386), of Orléans (1392), bestowed by Charles VI of France on his brother Louis as an appanage of the crown, third son of Charles V. Assassinated in 1407, he was grandfather of Louis XII by one son and great-grandfather of Francis I by another.
florin: Florence issued its famous large, nominally pure gold coin, *fiorino d'oro* (c. 3.5 grams) between 1252 and 1533. In England, the half mark sterling equalled eighty old pence or a third of a pound sterling was known as the noble or double florin. Florins, like ducats (q.v.), became the staple of foreign exchange throughout medieval Europe and Mediterranean.
Lodovico Sforza: Ludovico Maria *Il Moro* (the Moor) (1451/2-1508), Duke of Bari. A ruthless prince of the powerful Sforza dynasty, he paid an enormous sum to Emperor Maximilian for the duchy of Milan (1494-8). Charles VIII gained his support for France's campaign to seize Naples (1494-5). In 1498 Louis XII, a descendant of the first Duke of Milan, with the help of the Milanese, conquered Milan. Ludovico was captured in 1500 and died in prison in France (C. M. Ady, *A History of Milan under the Sforza* (London; Methuen, 1907).
Bianca: Bianca Maria Sforza of Milan, sister of Gian Galeazzo, married Emperor Maximilian in 1494 with a dowry of 300,000 ducats, then added an extra 100,000 ducats to give 'more solemnity and lustre to the deed', ie. the price of the imperial investure and diploma which confirmed Lodovico with all the privileges of Gian Galeazzo Sforza II (1469-94), erstwhile Duke of Milan.
Maximilian: Maximilian I, Archduke of Austria, German King, King of the Romans, then Holy Roman Emperor (r. 1493-1519); of the House of Hapsburg. He secured the Netherlands by his marriage to Mary, daughter of Charles the Bold, Duke of Burgundy (d. 1482). He gained Hungary and Bohemia by treaty. He arranged the marriage of his son Philip to the Spanish infanta Juana (the Mad) in 1496, and his daughter Margaret to the Spanish crown prince in 1497, which secured him control of Spain and its colonies. He fought against France in the Netherlands and Italy. He also possessed a large coin collection (G. Benecke, *Maximilian I, 1459-1519* (London, Routledge and Kegan Paul, 1982)).

Page 63

Lombards: bills of exchange were introduced in medieval Europe (See N. J. G. Pounds, *op. cit.*, pp. 418–22). Medium short-term credit for moderate sums but with high rates of interest (twenty to forty per cent), were available from a range of money-lenders, including 'Lombards' from Asti. Philip V of France, 'the Tall' (1316–22) tried to suppress usury in 1315 at the beginning of a major famine.

salt: most salt in Europe in medieval times was obtained from salt-pans on the Atlantic and Mediterranean coasts, then transported by boat. The salt-marshes of the Atlantic coast supplied northern France, England, the Netherlands and Baltic states. Supplies from salt-springs were obtained from the Danube Valley of upper Austria and Bohemia (politically tied with Hungary until 1526).

The French crown controlled the sale and distribution of salt, particularly in the North and central provinces and imposed a tax (*gabelle*).

cultivating the soil: due to demographic pressures, there was a strong inducement to increase agricultural production especially between 1470 and 1540 with land clearance schemes and extension of arable land.

Levant: the Italian maritime cities had developed commercial links with the Levant since the time of the First Crusade. French trade links developed after its success. There was an increasing demand in medieval Europe for spices, silk, wood and dyes. By the twelfth century, and aided by the stable environment developed by Saladin, Italian trade with Egypt was flourishing, especially in Alexandria. Slaves, metal and wood from Europe were traded for Oriental goods. In 1536 Süleyman signed a secret treaty with France giving the French similar commercial rights as the Venetians. This formed the basis of long-term French dominance in the Levantine commercial world. After the economic crisis of 1557, the spice trade developed direct with the Levant through Mediterranean ports rather than through ports like Antwerp.

Saracens: group of tribes in North Arabia who pillaged the Roman frontier of Syria: later applied to militant Arabs and Muslims. The period of Islamic expansion in the Middle East between AD 632–1038 is known as the Saracen.

Page 64

Guyenne and Normandy: Henry VI of England (1421–71) married Margaret of Anjou in 1445 but Maine and Normandy were lost to the French; Guyenne lost by 1453. Calais was retaken in 1558.

quarrels with house of Anjou and Aragon denied us the ports in Italy: Sicily and Sardinia were part of the medieval Aragonese empire, but from 1494 the French tried to intervene in Italy. Ferdinand II of Spain acquired Naples in 1503. Rival claims to Naples led to four wars between Emperor Charles V and the French kings. Philip II of Spain (1556–98) reinforced Spanish claims in Italy with the Council of Italy (1558), with Spanish viceroys in Sicily and Naples. Philip II's rights restored in 1559, with Spanish influence replacing French.

Aragon: kingdom in North East Spain, united with Castile in 1479, but retained some parliamentary and administrative autonomy until the eighteenth century.

Persian Gulf: Portuguese control of Persian Gulf and the Red Sea, seized in 1500-10s, was later supplanted by Ottoman and Muslim commercial interests. From 1538, there was sporadic warfare between the Portuguese and Ottomans along the Red Sea and Persian Gulf. Hadim Süleyman Paşa captured Bandar Diu, the Portuguese base in Gujerat, then controlled Aden, Yemen and the Red Sea. Masawwa was seized in 1557.

... sail around Africa: the Cape of Good Hope was rounded in 1487 by Barthélemy Diaz, a Portuguese navigator. In fact the development of the spice trade by this route continued to be in the hands of the Portuguese rather than the Castilians and they continued to negotiate treaties with the Ottoman empire to secure the spice route via the Sed Sea and Egypt.

Peru: Spanish colony from 1530 after the Inca empire was conquered, where most gold reserves were found apart from those of New Granada (Colombia) and Upper Peru (Bolivia). In addition, the famous Potosi silver mines were discovered in 1545, and the mercury mines of Huancavelica in 1563.

Piurians [Pyurres]: Piura is a coastal province in Peru.

Atahualpa [Atabalira]: *aka* Atahuallpa (c. 1502-33), last Inca Emperor (c. 1527-33), victorious in a civil war with his half-brother Huáscar; captured in 1532, and held to ransom. He offered a room full of gold and precious objects in return for his freedom. This was melted down on the instructions of the Spaniards who accumulated twenty-four tons of gold and silver, the largest ransom ever received. Once the ransom was acquired, he was executed by Francisco Pizarro.

ducat: Venice produced gold ducats (3.5 grams) from 1284. The gold florins of Florence and ducats of Venice were international currency in late medieval times.

Augustin de Zarate: Spanish historian (d. 1548), secretary to the council of Castile, treasurer-general for Peru (1543). Published *History of the Discovery and Conquest of Peru* (Anvers, 1555; tr. into French 1706).

Portugal: from 1502, Portuguese international trade under rigid royal control expanded into South East Asia between 1512 and 1520, from their base in Malacca, and into India, West and East Africa, Brazil, Middle East and China in the 1500s-30s. They bought silk, pepper, cloves, nutmegs and mace to the West; they even tried to find the mythical island of gold in 1519 near Sumatra. The rapid expansion, and involvement in local wars led to overstocked markets and a fall in the price of goods they wished to sell. This led to a monetary crisis in 1557 and subsequent weakening of the state. The flood of silver through Spain from the New World after 1545 was also available to Portugal.

Moluccas: in the Portuguese sphere of influence from 1512, the clove and spice trade with the Molaccas (Spice Islands) was developed from 1521 by Spanish explorers. This led to war between Portugal and Spain in the area. Charles V, at war with France and almost insolvent, ingeniously sold his claim to the Moluccas, which led to the treaty of Zaragoza in 1529. For the sum stated by Bodin, he pledged all the rights to Portugal and an arbitary line fixed 15° E of the islands. It was not until the 1560s that Spain explored the Pacific in earnest.

Emperor Charles V: (1500–58), King of Aragon, Castile and Naples (as Charles I of Spain, 1516–56), House of Hapsburg (1516, Hapsburg ruler of the Netherlands, elected Holy Roman Emperor (1519–56/58)), son of Philip the Handsome and Juana the Mad. Gained control over the Low Countries, Naples, north Italy, central Europe, Aragon, Castile, and the Spanish colonies in America. Though preoccupied with campaigns against the Reformists, he saw himself as Charlemagne's heir with a dream of a united Christian Europe and a crusade against the Turks. Abdicated his claims to Spain 1555–56 and the Netherlands and succeeded by his son Philip II (1556–98).

Page 65
Naples: Italian city, attacked by French 1525–8; inherited by Charles V and Philip II; Francis I abandoned its claims in the treaty of Madrid (1526). France again abandoned its claims in 1559.
Franche-Comté: in Philip VI's ordinance of 1340, salt was produced in Franche-Comté (the ancient Bourgogne), designated for payment of the salt tax (*gabelle*) as *Dans les pays de saline*.
population of this kingdom: there was a rise in France's population and growth of towns in the early sixteenth century. Bodin recognised the inflationary aspect of this growth for the rise of commodity prices, but also blamed the increase in the amount of gold and silver in circulation.
Orleans: a name borne by younger princes of royal blood from the fourteenth century, when Charles VI gave the duchy to his brother Louis. Burgundy (q.v.).

Page 66
French migrants...Spain: many peasants from the Auvergne worked seasonally in Spain, though most villages were self-contained (R. J. Knecht, *op. cit.*, p. 9).
Navarre: the Spanish part of the Kingdom of Navarre was annexed to Ferdinand's kingdom only in 1512.
idle: 'In Spain alone is manual labour held dishonourable for which reason idlers and bad women abound' (Alejo Venegas, 1537).
Valencia: an independent kingdom of Spain from 1010 to 1238 but thereafter held by the kings of Aragon. United with Castile in 1479 under Ferdinand and Isabella, which resulted in a long period of peace when many fine buildings were erected. Other academics may be able to shed further light on the episode mentioned here but I was not able to trace the incident cited in any mainstream texts during the relevant period 1547/7–50, unless it refers to the suppression of the *Germania* in Valencia in 1525?
Maximilian...Lieutenant-General in Spain: made Lieutenant-General in Spain in 1547 by Emperor Charles V, who was determined that his son Philip should succeed him as emperor instead of his brother Ferdinand. He summoned Philip to Germany, sending Ferdinand's son Maximilian II (d.1576) to govern Spain in his stead (1547/8–55), which led to an acrimonious dispute between Charles and Ferdinand (R. T. Davies, *op. cit.*, p. 107).
Friendship...Ottoman house: Europe, polarised by dynastic conflict between the Hapsburgs in Austria, Germany and Spain, and Francis I of France meant that

Response to the Paradoxes of Malestroit 147

Turkey was a welcome ally to the French. Sultan Süleyman (1494–1566, r. 1520–66) hoped to expand into Europe as part of his counter-crusade against the expansionist Christian ambitions of Charles V. Both rulers gloried in the arts (J. M. Rogers and R. M. Ward, *Süleyman the Magnificent* (London: BMP, 1988)). Francis I, from prison in Pavia (1525) proposed a double attack with his forces on the Italian coast and by Süleyman on Hungary (1526) (q.v.). France urged Süleyman to attack Vienna (1529) and Germany (1532) so that Francis I could regain Milan; meanwhile Charles V captured Tunis in 1535. In the 1530s there was a real danger that Rome might be taken by the Turks. In 1543 the fleet of the Turkish captain Barbarossa (Hayreddin, 1457–1546), was placed at France's disposal. With the French ambassador aboard, it seized Nice, wintered in Toulon, attacked Barcelona, Tuscany, Spanish Naples and Sicily (1544).

King Francis I: François Ier (1494–1547), King of France (r. 1515–47), son of Charles, Count of Angoulême, and Louisa de Savoie. In 1514, he married Claude de France, daughter of Louis XII. In 1515 he reconquered lost French possessions in Italy but had to surrender them for his liberty when he was taken prisoner by Emperor Charles V in 1525. In 1526 he was engaged to marry Eleanor, sister of Charles V. He promoted the cultural concepts of the Italian Renaissance in France, and encouraged authors such as Marot, and Rabelais; he founded chairs in Greek, Hebrew and classical Latin and developed the royal library. His reign also saw the influx of Italian luxury goods into France.

Beirut: in northern Syria but not a major port in medieval times. Local iron mines near Beirut and the production of silk led to the wealth of traders there.

Tripoli: a port on the Syrian coast. Almost as soon as the crusading states were developed, the count of Tripoli, amongst others, began to mint *dīnars* (*Saracenate besants*) in gold with about two-thirds the amount of gold found in the Fatamid *dīnars*, and became known locally as *souri*. These circulated widely through the Middle East. It is difficult to know where this gold came from, possibly purchased with silver which was plentiful in Europe, from Moslems who obtained it from the gold mines of Sudan.

Jews: in March 1492 all Jews unwilling to receive baptism were banished from Aragón and Castile. By July the exodus to Portugal, North Africa and France began, with great suffering. Under this Spanish Inquisition, the Moors subsequently suffered a similar fate and forced conversions led to insurrection in the south.

Ferdinand: II 'The Catholic', King of Aragon (1479–1516). The two Kingdoms of Castile and Aragon were united by the marriage of Ferdinand to Isabella of Castile in 1469. Grenada, the last Moorish stronghold, was defeated in 1492.

Barbary: coastal region of North Africa, associated with corsairs, *condotteri* and free-booters (S. Lane-Poole, *Barbary Corsairs* (London, 1890). Tunis was temporarily under Hapsburg control from 1535. After 1538, Barbarossa united Algers and Tunis under the Ottoman sultanate.

Bank of Lyons: banks existed in France from the thirteenth century and developed as agencies for credit and exchange in the fifteenth century. Francis I raised huge loans at Lyon's fairs from 1542, with sixteen per cent interest charged (R. J. Knecht, *op. cit.*, pp. 8, 218). By 1575 there were about forty banking houses there, of which the Bonvisi of Lucca were the most important.

Page 67
Genoa, house of Saint George: the *Casa di San Giorgio*, established in 1407, was a public bank that held as its capital the funded debt of the republic of Genoa. It was the most sophisiticated credit institution in late medieval Europe.
Antoninius Pius: Emperor Titus Aurelius Fulvius Boionius Antoninus (AD 86-181), Antonin le Pieux, senator, Proconsul in Asia AD 133-6; adopted by Hadrian in AD 138 as his successor, beneficent ruler (r. AD 159-61).
Alexander Severus: Marcus Aurelius, Emperor AD 222-35; the title under which Alexianus, nephew of Elagabalus (q.v.) was known. Virtuous and honest, he rehabilitated the finances of Rome, and reformed senatorial powers. However, he was also weak and ineffective and was eventually murdered along with his domineering mother.
Heliogabalus: Elagabalus, the Roman Emperor (r. AD 219-22), real name Bassianus, a treacherous, religious pervert. During his three-year rule, Rome witnessed incredible debauchery and extravagance (with two great temples built to the Sun-god); eventually murdered by the Praetorians.
Clenard: Nicolas Clénard *aka* Clenart *aka* Kleinharts (1495-1542), Orientalist and linguist and Orientalist who studied Arabic in North Africa and Spain, Greek and Hebrew; writings include *Peregrinationum* (Louvain, 1551).

Page 68
Poyet: Guillaume Poyet (1473-1548), Chancellor of France under Francis I; responsible for the ordinance of Villers-Cotterêts (1539). His attempt to abolish confraternities was not particularly effective.
fraternities: 'associations of masters, apprentices and journeymen formed principally for religious or charitable purposes' (R. J. Knecht, *op. cit.*, p. 208). In 1561 the crown reminded confraternities that their funds could only be used for religious and charitable purposes (not for political unrest).
war with Spain and Flanders: Cateau-Cambrésis treaty (1559) between Henry II of France and Philip II of Spain, settled boundaries and ended a long rivalry.

Page 69
alum: indispensable mordant for fixing dyes and used in making copper; until the fifteenth century it was imported from Constantinople and Aleppo; then found (1431-53) in papal mines at Tolfa, traded in Antwerp by Italian contractors; in the mid-sixteenth century found in Germany, Spain and France.
copperas: 'green iron-sulphate crystals.' (OED).
marcasite: '(white iron) pyrites' (OED) found in Saxony, Bohemia and France.
Vespasian: Titus Flavius Vespasianus, Emperor AD 69-79. He strictly exacted tributes from the provinces in order to make the state solvent and devised new taxes to raise revenues. In Rome, magnificent buildings such as the Temple of Peace and Colosseum were erected, elsewhere roads and buildings were built and art and education encouraged. He punished maladministration and strengthened

frontiers. Blunt, straightforward and honest, he was a typical countryman. His reign restored the prosperity (and sanity) of the Roman empire after Nero's rule.
Plato: (c. 429-347 BC), Greek political philosopher and metaphysicist. Author of *The Laws* and the *Republic*, on role of princes and commonwealth. In *The Republic*, Plato argued that communism among the guardian class is a necessary condition of perfect unity. In each city trading and teaching should be practised only by resident foreigners.

Page 70
Peter Lombard: Bishop of Paris (c. 1100-c. 1160), wrote his theological study *Sententiae*, in Paris University (1150-2).
Emperor Caracalla: Aurelius Antoninus, Marcus (AD 188-217), commonly called Caracalla, became Emperor in AD 211.
Pope Paul III: Alessandro Farnese (1468-1549), Pope (r. 1534-49). At first his patron was Cardinal Rodrigo; he then travelled as a diplomat; patron of the arts, built the Palazzo Farnese and enjoyed ceremony before being made Bishop of Parma in 1509; after his ordination in 1519 his private life was above reproach. He patronised the arts, restored the university of Rome, improved the Vatican library and Sistine chapel. He was conscious of the decadence of the church and called the Council of Trent in 1545. He led the church from the corrupt splendour of the Renaissance towards a more austere post-Reformation epoch.
King Henry of England: Henry VIII (1491-1547), King of England 1509-47. Met Francis I on the Field of the Cloth of Gold in 1520, to show his support for the French against Emperor Charles V. On bad terms with Rome under Pope Clement VII, who objected to Henry's attempts between 1527 and 1534, to divorce Catherine of Aragon, aunt of Emperor Charles V and led to subsequent break of the English Church from Rome. The dissolution of the monasteries and appropriation of their riches between 1535 and 1540 temporarily made the English government very wealthy.
Mr Budé: Guillaume Budé *aka* Guglielmus Budaeus (1467-1540), French classical scholar influenced by the spirit of the Renaissance and friend of Erasmus. Guillaume Budé persuaded Francis I to set up the Collège de France, initially as part of the Sorbonne. Writings include *Commentarii linguae Graecae* (1529) and *De Asse* (Venice, 1522), six volumes, on ancient money and measures.
Cardan: probably Gerolamo Cardano *aka* Jerome Cardan (1501-76), Italian physician and mathematician.

Page 71
Negus: in 1150 a letter (no doubt a forgery) purporting to be written by Prester John to Emperor Manuel circulated through Europe, giving an account of Negus' wealth and piety. Philip, doctor to the pope, went to Abyssinia at the pope's behest in search of information, but without concrete result.
Cleopatra: second daughter of Ptolemy, a Macedonian princess with no Egyptian blood, mistress of Julius Caesar and of Mark Antony.

150 Notes

Alexander: III of Macedonia 'the Great' (356-23 BC). His conquests led to the application of a unified currency system, with the consequent extinction of local coinage (except in bronze).
Apelles: early Hellenistic painter (fourth century BC) of Colophon and later of Ephesus. Pliny dates him as 332 BC. Taught first by Ephorus of Ephasus and then joined the Sicyonian school. Court painter of Philip II of Macedon and of Alexander the Great. Paintings in Cos described by Herodotus. Regarded as the greatest painter of antiquity and inspired many Renaissance painters though none of his work including his famous picture of Venus (Aphrodite) survives.
talent: in 440s BC Athens the talent was equal to 6,000 *drachmae*. A normal week's wage was three and a half *drachmae*.
Protogenes: Greek painter from the late fourth century BC, contemporary and rival of Apelles, for whom none of his carefully executed paintings survive.
Michaelangelo: Michaelangelo di Locovico Buivarroti Simoni (1475-1564), Italian Rennaissance sculptor, painter, poet and architect with an unrivalled influence on the development of western art. Sculptures in Rome and Florence; Chief architect of St Peter's in Rome, painted the Sistine chapel ceiling (1508-12) and frescos (1534-41) and author of over 300 sonnets and madrigals.
Raphael: Raffaello Sanzio (1483-1520) born in Urbino, master painter and architect of the Italian High Renaissance in Florence and Rome. Urbino had become a major centre of culture around 1482. Francesco Primaticcio's work at Fontainbleu reflects Raphael's influence.
Durel: probably Albrecht Dürer (1471-1528), one of the greatest German Rennaissance painters, with a vast quantity of work, including altar-pieces, portraits and religious works; printmaker of copper engravings and woodcuts. Following his visit to Italy in 1494-5, his work exhibited the Renaissance spirit but promoted the Reformist ideals. He worked for Emperor Maximilian I (1512-9). By 1515 he was exchanging work with Raphael.
Fontainebleau: a castle established before the twelfth century, a favourite place for kings of France. Charles V established a library there in 1363, which later became the basis for the *Bibliothèque nationale* in Paris. The *château* was developed by Francis I and then by Henry IV. After 1527, Francis I used a group of Italian artists to rebuild and decorate it, including Serglio, G. B. Rosso, Francesco Primaticio, Vignola and Nicolo dell'Abate, with Gilles Le Breton as architect. Lists of artists of the *École de Fontainebleau* (1530-89) do not include a painting by Mr de Clagny in its gallery. The gallery disappeared in 1739.

Page 72
Cæsar: Gaius Julius (102/100-44 BC), Roman dictator and orator, whose armies overran most of Europe, including Italy, Spain, Gaul and England, North Africa and Asia Minor. Author of *De Bello Civilo* and *De Bello Gallico* (58-52 BC). He produced sumptuary laws and introduced the Julian calendar.

Page 73
cloth of gold: cloth embroidered with gold (also silver and silk) threads was produced in Paris, Cologne, Florence, Venice, Milan and Lucca in the Middle

Ages (N. J. G. Pounds, *op. cit.*, p. 320) as well as Ottoman Bursa. In medieval France, brocades of gold and silver were reserved for those of royal blood.

teston: *teston d'argent*, a silver coin issued from 1514 (weight 9.555 grams), under Louis XII, bearing for the first time, the head of the king on the obverse. Worth ten *sols tournois* in 1515. *Testons* remained the principal silver coin until Henry III introduced the franc (q.v.) in 1576.. Between 1516 and 1575 the value rose from ten *sols* to fourteen *sols*, whilst the gold *écu* was devalued. Based on the *testoni* with their excellent portraits of Italian rulers such as the Duke of Milan, Galaezzo-Maria Sforza in 1474, were minted in the fifteenth century between the Alps and Apennines and were used like gold coins.

du Prat: Antoine Duprat (1464-1535), Chancellor of France from 1515 for Francis I; later Chancellor for Milan; lawyer, Archbishop of Sens, later a Cardinal. Hardworking and shrewd, he ruled during Francis' captivity.

Ethiopia: the first diplomatic relations with Europe were established by Emperor Zara Yacob (1434-68). Francisco Alvarez (q.v.) also explored the country.

Page 74

brass money: In c. 289 BC mints were set up to cast both currency bars and coins in bronze. The coins weighed one pound and had the face value of one *as*. In 269 BC Rome struck her first silver coins.

Servius: Servus Tullius, sixth King of Rome, traditionally 578-35 BC, who was supposed to have reformed the army into centuries, and property owners into classes. The property rates were based first on agricultural produce or land, later reckoned in money terms. The ancient writers give various monetary scales; probably they changed over time. His constitution is probably a fictitious precedent for the laws of the fourth century. Until c. 450 BC Rome reckoned values in terms of oxes and sheep, then in uncoined bronze (*aes rude*) until after 300 BC.

asses: Latin, *as*, meaning a weight, hence a bronze coin, see above.

lex Ateria-Trapeia: Roman law (454 BC) which fixed the maximum fines which magistrates could impose.

Polybius: (c. 203?-c. 120 BC) Greek historian of Rome who wrote a *Universal History* in forty books on the period 220/219-145/144 BC, which was a source for Livy, Plutarch and others.

Solon: (c. 640/35-c. 561/560 BC) Athenian statesman and poet, though most of his writings have been lost. He reformed the coinage and weights and measures to bring them in line with those of Euboea and the western Greeks (Plutarch, *Solon*). His legal code formed the basis of the Athenian constitution.

drachma: Athenian silver coins, unit weight c. 4.25 grams. About 650 BC, Pheidon of Argos reformed his currency by making the Aeginetan unit the value of two *drachmae*, replacing iron (q.v.) tokens with silver ones (ninety grains silver equalled a drachma). Other mints, such as Attica, had different standards. In Athens Solon made the Euboaean drachma into a commercial weight. As Roman influences increased, so Greek coinage disappeared. Silver coinage continued in Athens until the time of Augustus, with some cities issuing bronze coins. Coins in various Greek cities were issued for festivals and imperial visits.

The drachma continued to be a basic unit for the eastern Mediterranean from Augustus' imperial mint of Antioch.
lex Fannia: the Roman law *sumptuaria* (161 BC) which limited the amount to be spent on entertainments.
écu (à la) couronne: nominally fine gold crown issued between 1388 and 1475, declined in weight from 3.99 grams.
Didius: Titus, consul by 98 BC, *tribunus plebis* (103 BC), later proconsul in Spain, later consul. Died in the Social War (89 BC).
Crassus: Lucius Licinius Crassus, consul in 95 BC, constitutionalist and senator who supported the reforms of Drusus.

Page 75
Sulla: Lucius Cornelius Sulla (138-78 BC), dictator, won considerable reputation in the Social War, defeated Mithridates who paid Sulla indemnity and surrendered his fleet. Sulla rewarded his troops generously. The *as* reduced to half an ounce and then ceased to be struck, whilst the *denarius* suffered serious debasement in the Social War but later recovered under Sulla. During his dictatorship, secured in 81 BC after civil war in Italy, he made financial demands on his erstwhile enemies. Plated coins were still produced by forgers, whilst provincial mints became more numerous and important.
Caligula: Emperor Gaius Julius Caesar Gemanicus (AD 12-41), nickname Caligula. After a serious illness in AD 37 his character became unstable; he governed autocratically with much cruelty and was in fear of assassination.
fish: there were 150 species of fish known to Greeks and Romans and a fish diet was popular. In the Roman empire immense sums were paid for luxuries such as sturgeon and turbot.
Galen: (AD 129-c. 199) of Pegamum, gladiator-physician in Asia Minor, then court-physician in Rome; wrote philosophical treaties and medical books on neurology, pathology, anatomy and dissection, eg. *Uses of the Bodily Parts of Man*. Presented pharmacological and dietetic doctrines, some of which were translated into Arabic in medieval times. In the Renaissance, many editions of his works appeared, including the Aldine edition (1525) and Johann Günther's of 1541-52.
Varro: Marcus Terentius Varro (116-27 BC), librarian, writer and philologist. He wrote *Rerum rusticarum libri* in three volumes (37 BC), book one on general agriculture, book two on cattle and sheep and book three on smaller livestock breeding, including fish and birds. His works were a mine of information for medieval compilers.

Page 76
Æsop: tragedian, said to have been a slave in Samos in sixth century BC. By end of the fifth century BC most Greek fable was in general ascribed to Aesop.
Athenæus: (fl. AD c. 200) of Naucratis in Egypt. His only extant work, 'The Learned Banquet' was completed around AD 192.

Roscius: Quintus Roscius Gallus (d. 62 BC), famous comic actor from Solonium who also played tragic parts. According to Pliny (*Naturalis Historia,* bk. 7, section 128) his earnings were enormous.

Apicius: a gourmet under Augustus and Tiberius; the *De Re Coquinaria* under his name was compiled some time after his death.

Cicero: Cicero (q.v.) spoke for Roscius (c. 77 BC) and other *causas nobiles*. In 68 BC he acquired a villa in Tusculum which he retained until his death.

Scipios: the Scipios, outstanding men of action, included Scipio Aemilianus Africanus Numantinus, Publius Cornelius (185/4–29 BC), second son to Aemilius Paullus, who was adopted by the orator, Publius Cornelius Scipio, elder son of Scipio Africanus Major (236–184 BC) before 160 BC. They served variously in Spain, Carthage and Africa, the Levant, Egypt and the East

Marius: Gaius Marius (157–86 BC), as consul developed commercial and military interests in Africa, northern Italy, introduced army reforms, fought against Mithridates. Quarrelled with Sulla over the last command, which jealously led to the first great Civil War in Rome.

Lucullus: Lucius Licinius (c. 117–56 BC), Sulla's *quaestor*. He campaigned successfully in the Aegean, Africa and the Levant; continued the war against Mithridates in the East and settled financial crises in Asia. After 63 BC he spent his life in Rome dedicated to elegance.

Pompey: Gnaeus Pompeius (106–48 BC), son of Strabo. Military genius who served in the army of Sulla and subsequent emperors, in successful campaigns in Sicily, North Africa, Spain and in Asia. He destroyed pirates, defeated Mithridates, founded colonies in the Levant and set up the basis for the future Roman organisation of Asia.

Page 77

Paulus: probably Lucius Aemilius Paullus, consul in 50 BC when he was bought by Julius Caesar with 1,500 talents, which he needed for the Basilica.

Curio: Gaius Scribonius Curio, on his election as tribute in 50 BC he was bribed by Julius Caesar's agent, Balbus. In the Civil War he won Sicily for Caesar and died in Africa fighting loyally for him.

Mark Antony: Marcus Antonius (c. 82–30 BC), Roman Emperor. A natural soldier whose great generosity made him a great leader of soldiers, a skilful politician but at times ruled by his 'irascible temper' (Plutarch, *Antony*).

Appian: of Alexandria, (AD c. 110) held office in Alexandria, wrote an account of the Roman conquests, with an ethnographic content.

Hadrian: Publius Aelius Hadrianus (AD 76–138), Roman Emperor (AD 117–38). Spanish-born but adopted by Trajan, he reorganised the army and the judiciary; developed a graded and salaried civil service with salaried knights. After serving in Syria in Trajan's Parthian War, he returned to Rome in AD 118 and gained public support by bestowing favours, including financial assistance to senators and a ceremonial cancellation of debts to the state.

Rome: the mid third century AD witnessed the economic and political collapse of Rome, with depreciation of the coinage, decline of industry, compulsory requisitions and labour, whilst coins were partly replaced by payments in kind.

154 *Notes*

Picts, Scots and Saxons invaded Britain; Gaul was overtaken by Franks and Burgundians, Spain by Vandals and Suebi. The rule of Rome in the West ended when the German Odocer deposed Romulus Augustulus (AD 476), though East Rome continued in Byzantium (q.v.) until 1453.

Parthians: land-owning military aristocracy of Parthia, based on Seleuceia, which ruled from the Euphrates to the Indus; used Greek culture and methods of administration until there was an Iranian reaction about AD 10. Acted as middlemen in trade between China and Roman Syria.

Goths: a German tribe which began to raid the Roman empire AD c. 238. Under Alaric the Visigoths invaded Italy and sacked Rome (AD 410); then into Gaul and Spain and set up the Kingdom of Toulouse. The Ostrogoths entered Italy in AD 493 and set up a kingdom there; Goths also raided Transylvania.

Herullians: the Herules, a Germanic people, who under the leadership of Odoacer, destroyed the Roman empire in the West in AD 476, when he deposed Romulus Augustulus.

Hungarians: Roman rule in the first century AD extended through Transdanubia and the area formed a buffer zone (Pannonia) between the empire and barbarians to the East. In the fourth century AD, the Romans began to withdraw from Pannonia, leaving it to the Vandals and Jazgians. In AD 430 Hungary was invaded by Huns, whose empire reached its zenith and then fragmented with the death of Attila (AD 453).

Method for the Easy Comprehension of History: in 1566 Bodin wrote *Methodus ad facilem historiarum cognitionem*, which advanced novel ideas on the study of history and looked at the most enduring forms of law.

Page 78

carat: weights were expressed in ancient, Byzantine and medieval times in carats (*siliqua*, seed of the carob).

ordinance (1561): in the 1560s, the government attempted to reinstate the worth of particular coins in terms of standard money of account, the *livre tournois*. Thus the *écu soleil*, valued at two *livres* ten *sols* in 1561, which was equated at two *livres* twelve *sols* in 1568.

Antonin: *Antonine Itinerary* (about early third century AD with later additions), an important work on ancient geography, included a listing of places in the Roman empire, and their distances.

Mr de Livres: this may possibly refer to Guillaume Budé (q.v.) who was the first to hold the title *maître de la librairie*, Keeper of the Royal Library.

Henry II: Henri II (1519–59), of the House of Valois, succeeded his father Francis I as King of France in 1547; husband of Mary, Queen of Scots. France was bankrupt in 1559 with a debt of forty-two million *francs* and Spain was suffering a similar financial crisis. He died in a tournament held to celebrate the treaty of Cateau-Cambrésis.

Page 79

1420: Henry V of England invaded France in 1415, supported by the Burgundians. By the treaty of Troyes (1420), Henry was betrothed to Catherine,

Charles VI's daughter, along with the right of succession to the throne of France. He entered Paris in 1420 and the English controlled the city until 1436 .
mouton: or *agnel*. Magnificently designed gold piece (*mouton d'or*, 'Paschal Lamb') first struck under Louis IX, with the *Agnus Dei* on the obverse, worth ten *sols*; in 1314 the *agnel* weighed 4.68 grams; in 1355 the *mouton* weighed 4.65 grams. P. Spufford (*op. cit.*, p. 408) indicates they were first issued from 1311 under Philip IV.

Page 80
Louis XII: (1462-1515), House of Valois, son of Charles d'Orléans, grandson of Louis d'Orléans the brother of Charles VI, succeeded Charles VIII, (r. 1498-1515), *le Père du Peuple*, second husband of Anne de Bretagne; invaded Italy to claim the duchy of Milan; recognised Spanish claims to Naples (1504).
Tacitus: Cornelius Tacitus (AD c. 55-c. 115), historian, discusses *pax Augusta* in his *Annals* and shows the lower ranks as loyal heroes, in contrast to the cringing nobles.
Scripture: Matthew ch. 20, vv. 1-16, especially v.13.

Page 81
seraph: corruption of Ottoman Turkish *sharīf* (Arabic *sharīf*, noble), Turkish gold coin. Later described by Florio in 1656 as 'a Turkish coyn, worth about a French crowne'.
medins: *medin*, *medine* (various spellings), originally a silver half-dirham first issued in the fifteenth century by Sultan al-Mu'ayyad (from whose name the term ultimately derives). Later, a copper coin worth one fortieth of a piastre.
Castile: Castile used gold, silver and billon royal coins in the fifteenth century; the union of Castile and Aragon (1479) and influx of New World precious metals led to an abundance of gold and the popular silver *réal* or 'pieces of eight'.
Henris: *écu d'or* struck under Henry II in 1550, at which time it replaced the *écu* for ten years.
pistolet: a Spanish gold coin, worth about twenty *livres*.

Page 82
ordinance (1540): Francis I's ordinance of 1540 which Bodin supported in the *États* in 1576 as a rational programme of protection; a fiscal tariff, including control of striking of coins by a *graveur-général des monnaies*.
ordinance of King Henry II: possibly relates to the appointment by Henry II in 1547 of a 'general engraver of coins' to design medals and coins (R. J. Knecht, *op. cit.*, p. 261) as part of his cult of ancient Rome.
M͏ʳ Charles du Moulin: legist, author of *Commentaries on the Customs of Paris*, from 1539 (J. L. Thireau, *Charles Du Moulin, 1500-1566* (Geneva: Droz, 1980)).

Page 83
Leo of Africa: Leo Africanus *aka* Giovanni Leone *aka* al-Ḥasan ibn Muḥammad al-Wazzān az-Zayyātī *aka* al-Fāsī (c. 1485-1554), Islamic scholar and traveller

in North and West Africa. Born in Granada, captured by Pope Leo X he was baptised a Christian in 1520, though he died a Muslim in Tunis. His greatest work *Descrittione dell' Africa* was completed in 1526 (published 1550).

Istanbul: Constantinople (q.v.).

Antwerp: Brabant mint with a population of about 100,000 by 1550s. From 1501 to 1549 the commercial development of Antwerp was tied in with the Portuguese international spice trade and a favourable balance of trade. Initially this was exchanged for Baltic grain, later metals (copper and silver) and wines from South Germany; cloth, lead and tin from England; French wines and salt. It overtook Bruges as the commercial hub of the Low Countries in the fifteenth century, its fortune associated with that of the Holy Roman Empire. By 1540s–50s, Antwerp handled seventy to eighty per cent of the Netherlands foreign trade. After 1557 and 1566 there were some signs of decline.

Rome: for the funding of ancient Rome, see N. Morley, *Metropolis and Hinterland: The City of Rome and the Italian Economy, 200 BC–AD 200* (Cambridge University Press, 1996) and G. Rickman, *The Corn Supply of Ancient Rome* (Oxford: Clarendon Press, 1980). Rome may have had 650,000 or more inhabitants in the time of the Emperor Augustus.

Trajan: Marcus Ulpius Trajanus, Roman Emperor AD 98–117. born AD 53. Progressive social and financial policy with a large programme of public works, especially after AD 107 building increased, probably as a result of the treasure won in the Second Dacian War (five million pounds (lb) weight of gold and double of silver).

Page 84

iron: iron was widely used in sixteenth century France for a range of purposes notably for ploughshares, knives and other utensils, nails and pins. Silver from the Joachimsthal mines and America, copper, brass and tin-plate were imported from Germany; pewter and lead from England (R. J. Knecht, *op. cit.*, p. 7).

vitriol: 'sulphuric acid' (OED).

cinnabar: 'a red or crystalline form of mercuric sulphide' (OED) used both as a source of mercury and as a dyestuff.

brazil-wood: a dyestuff, giving a red dye, from which Brazil takes its name.

sugars: production of sugar was one of the principle commercial developments associated with colonial expansion in the Early Modern period. It developed rapidly in the Azores, and had spread by Bodin's time from there to the Canaries and the Cape Verde islands. The Brazilian sugar trade grew rapidly from 1575.

Page 85

Lycurgus: traditional, probably mythical, founder (c. 1100 to 600 BC) of the idiosyncratic Spartan constitution and military system. Spartan customs introduced after 600 BC but often attributed to Lycurgus, prevented *perioikoi* and foreigners being admitted as part of the citizen body.

Page 86
Muḥammad the Great: Muḥammad [Mehmet] II Fātiḥ ('the Conqueror'), (r. 1444-46) (848-50 AH) and again from 1451 to 1481 (855-86 AH), who finally captured Constantinople in 1453 (805 AH) and even captured Otranto in southern Italy from 1479. He thoroughly reorganised the Ottoman empire, in particular he gave large endowments to religious, educational and legal institutions.
Florentine murderer: Guiliano de' Médici, natural father of Pope Clement VI, joint ruler of Florence (b. 1453, r. 1469-78) with his brother, Lorenzo the Magnificent. He was stabbed at mass in Florence cathedral by conspirators from the Pazzi family of Florence in 1478, backed by nobles and papacy (Sixtus IV, 1471-84) (Ange Politien, *Pactianæ conjurationis commentariolum* (Florence, 1478)). The conspirator, Bernado Bandini, escaped to Constantinople but was sent back by Muḥammad to Florence where the conspirators, including the archbishop of Florence, were hanged in the streets by Medici partisans (M. Brian, *The Medici: a Great Florentine Family*, tr. G and H. Cremonesi, London: Ferndale, 1980, pp. 114-18). The murder only consolidated Médici power.

Page 87
Egypt: See Genesis, ch. 39-40. In Roman times, Egypt provided large supplies of corn to Rome and it was freely distributed in Trajan's time, thus its supply received special attention. Trajan constructed the inner harbour at Ostia (near the mouth of the river Tiber) to accommodate the large Egyptian grain ships.

Page 88
Emperor Domitian: Titus Flavius Domitianus, son of Emperor Vespasian, b. AD 51. Ruled Rome 69-70 when Vespasian arrived. Succeeded Titus as Emperor in AD 81; changed from firm absolutist to an increasingly cruel despot.
corn, wine, salt: Bodin contended that by exporting these and other goods to Spain, France could obtain treasure, whilst France's few imports, oil, spices, silks etc. could be reduced if Frenchmen were energetic enough.

Page 89
wool: England's exports of raw wool were, in fact, very slight by the time Bodin was writing, and was negligible by the 1580s. The export of woollen cloth was much more important.

Page 90
Strabo: 64/63 BC-AD c. 21, Greek historian and geographer, wrote *Historical Sketches* (forty-seven books, now all lost) and *Geography*, of which seventeen books survived.
Aristophanes: (c. 450-c. 385? BC), an Athenian playwright of Old Comedy, whose eleven plays survived.
Sylvius: probably Aeneus Sylvius (Pope Pius II, Énéas Sylvius Piccolomini) (1458-64), b. 1405 in Sienna, who wrote the popular *Histoire d'Eurialus et Lucrèce*.

Page 91
Cato: the austere Marcus Porcius Cato 'Censorius' (234-149 BC), initiated Roman rule in Spain c. 190 BC and wrote the *De Agri Cultura* c. 160 BC on the development of vine, olive and fruit growing and grazing for profit in Latium and Campania (Plutarch, *Cato Maior* in R. E. Smith, *Classical Quarterly* (1940)).

Page 92
Rondelet: Guillaume (1507-66), French naturalist, professor of anatomy of the university of Montpellier. His book, *Libri de Piscibus Marinis* (1554-55), describes 250 marine animals, many from the Mediterranean.
Agde: a Mediterranean port of ancient origin, it remains an unprepossessing fishing port.

Page 93
Poggio of Florence: Poggio Bracciolini, Gian Francesco (1380-1459), Italian humanist, eloquent writer, calligrapher and discoverer of forgotten classical texts. Chancellor of Florence from 1453. Appropriately, he rediscovered Ammianus Marcellus' *Res gestae*, Apicius' work on cooking.
Adrian: Adrien Boeijens, Pope Adrien VI 1522, (b. 1459), known as the Flemish Pope and Adrian of Utrecht. Dean of Louvain, Bishop of Tortosa, Grand Inquisitor of Aragón in 1516, made cardinal in 1517. He was appointed regent of Castile in 1520 by his former student, Emperor Charles V, which was resented by the Spanish nobles and led to urban rebellions in 1520-21 that threatened Charles' authority in Spain.
Beguines: Béguines, name given to orders of pious women in monastic religious order, founded 1184, without taking their vows, in the Low Countries. Adrian VI was more at home with the customs of his homeland than with those of Rome. Can be confused with *Bégards*, women heretics, by extension, bigot.
Paulus Jovius: *aka* Paolo Giovio (1483-1552), Italian historian of vivid, elegant style; author of *Turcicarum Rerum Commentarius* (Paris, 1539) and a Latin history of Florence (1494-1547), *Historiarum sui temporis libri XLV* (1550-52). Owner of famous art collection who found favour with Pope Leo X and also Pope Clement VII in the sack of Rome in 1527.
Ferdinand, King of Naples: possibly Ferdinand II (r. 1495-96).

Page 94
cast: in the fifteenth century the first experiments were made to improve coin production by mechanical means. Henry II obtained a coinage press in 1550, and it was a Frenchman, Eloy Mestrell, who organised the adaptation of English minting to this technology under Elizabeth I.
Portugueses: possibly the gold Portuguese coin *cruzado*, from 1457 (3.48 grams)
Joachimthaler: large silver thalers which appeared after 1519, called after the Joachimsthal ((Jachymov) mines in Bohemia.
Constantinople: Turkish İstanbul. Ancient Byzantium. It was founded as a Greek colony in the eighth century BC as part of the Persian empire; a free city

under the Roman Republic; In AD 324 Constantine I made it his capital and the seat of his empire (AD 330) and ecclesiastical centre for Christianity for the Byzantine empire (AD 498–1453). From the sixth to the thirteenth centuries it was besieged by Persians, Russians, Arabs and Bulgurs. Captured 1203 by crusaders, it was plundered for its gold and great wealth. In 1261 it returned to Byzantine rule until it was made capital of the Ottoman empire by Mehmed II in 1453 who defeated the last Byzantine Emperor Constantine XI. Under Mehmed II it became known popularly known as İstanbul. Byzantine coinage was based on pure gold *solidus* and dominated European trade to the thirteenth century. Small silver coins were used in the Ottoman empire until the fifteenth century when some gold coins were used, alongside Venetian ducats and other European silver coins.

Tiberius II: Constantinus (d. AD 582), Byzantine Emperor (r. AD 578–82), fought the Persians, Avars and Slavs, cf. p. 105.

King Childeric: the ambitious and brutal Merovingian ruler, Chilperic I (AD c. 539–84), cf. p. 105. The story of from Gregory of Tours (d. c. 1010), *Historia Francorum* (Paris: apud Andream Wechelum, 1567), bk. 6 (ii)

thaler: total production of silver in Europe peaked in 1530s and is shown in the stiking of very large silver coins (*guldinar, gulden groschen* or *talers*) which were produced by imperial, nobles', municipal and ecclesiastical German mints from 1486, most famous in the sixteenth century being those of Saxony and Brunswick. Origin of the word 'dollar'.

Page 95

Demosthenes: (384–22 BC), orator and assistant to official prosecutors in public trials. *Against Timocrates* (353 BC), a political law-court speech was written for Diodorus. Timocrates proposed the abolition of hereditary immunity from taxation granted to public benefactors; also that embezzlers such as Androtion, should be given an extension of time for repayment.

acid: in the third century AD, silver issues were heavily debased with copper. Before striking, the blanks were immersed in acid to leach out the surface copper to expose more silver.

Page 96

Reference should be made to Pliny the Elder, bk.s 3–37 on minerology and metallurgy and their use in the arts, *Naturalis Historia*.

Page 97

quatrin: of Florence. Four *dinari* piece of *monnaie noire*, essentially copper rather than silver.

Queen of England: Elizabeth I (b. 1533, r. 1558–1603). Her mother was Anne Boleyn and her father King Henry VIII of England. After the Catholic reign of her sister Queen Mary, she enforced Protestantism by law, despite the edict of Pope Pius V against her in 1570.

obole: half a *denier* (q.v.) equvalent to a *maille*, introduced by Charlemagne.

lead: lead decays easily and is not usually used for coins, except in the Deccan in ancient India and in pre-Roman Gaul.

bagatin: *baggatino,* pure copper coin minted from 1473 in Venice, despite no shortage of silver, cf. the copper *cavalli* struck in Naples in 1472. Venice was a major centre for the growing trade in copper from the Alps and Carpathians in the late fifteenth century.

Page 98

Philip the Fair...debased the coinage: after a century of stable coinage, the scale on which Philip IV debased it, relying on his regal rights over coinage, was dramatic. Rather than impose direct taxation and under the stress of war against England in 1295, he began ten years of debasements in which he made massive profits from his mints. The church and nobles reacted in 1303–4; attempts to return to earlier standards were followed by further debasement in 1311 when he again needed money for war against Flanders.

Dante: *Paradiso,* 19, p. 119.

Page 99

King of Bourges: as dauphin, Charles (VII) had fled to Bourges in 1418: at his accession in 1422, it was the centre of the limited area he could control ('the Kingdom of Bourges').

First Punic War: 264–41 BC, between the Roman Republic and the Carthaginian empire, for the control of Sicily and Corsica. Peace terms included the evacuation of Sicily by Carthage and the payment of an indemnity of 3,200 talents. Soon after the First Punic War (235 BC?) a change was made in Roman coinage with the standards regularised: the *didrachm* (102.5 grams) of six *scruples* and the *as* of 240 *scruples.* See also Punic wars (q.v.)

Hannibal: (247–183/2 BC), like his father, Hamilcar Barca, a great Carthaginian general, who acquired a base in Spain to renew the Punic attack on Rome; invaded Gaul, then Italy via the Alps in the Second Punic War (218–201 BC). Despite initial success, he was inadequately supported from Carthage and obliged to obtain local provisions; defeated by Scipio Africanus Major (q.v.) at the battle of Zama (202 BC), he eventually took his own life. The impact on the Hannibalic War on Rome was drastic, with only the Roman mint producing during the war. The *as* was reduced from 240 *scruples* to 144 in 217 BC and to seventy-two *scruples* in 209 BC. Silver coins were also debased.

lex Papiria: the Roman law *Lex Papiria* (191 BC) reduced the copper coin (*as*) to half an ounce, hence *asses semiunciales* equalled 100/297 *denarii,* which continued as standard even under the emperors.

Page 100

Drusus: Drusus, Marcus Livius Drusus, a tribune in 122 BC, consul in 112 BC. Died c. 109 while censor with Scaurus. His son of the same name was a senatorial leader.

Netherlands: most densely populated part of Europe, its trade centred on Antwerp, but politically connected with Spain. Trade based on credit-purchases

Response to the Paradoxes of Malestroit 161

and bill-payments, through bankers. Exchange fluctuations and commodity price variations stimulated the interest of sixteenth-century financiers from cities like Anwerp, Genoa, Lyon and Augsburg (NCMH, pp. 50-69). Netherlands was one of France's best customers for wine, whilst it produced fine linen.

coinage of iron: Greece possessed small iron-deposits and the furnaces of the ancients could not normally produce cast iron, though statues were made by chasing pure wrought iron. After 700 BC, values were expressed in a handful of iron spits, the drachma (q.v.). In the harsh environment of ancient Sparta, where the trade was in the hands of the *peroikoi* rather than with the Spartan citizens, iron coins were used only occasionally.

Page 101
Guinea: its trade was controlled by Portugal in the fifteenth century.
gold dust: apart from a little gold cast into ingots at Timbuktu, most gold crossed the Sahara in the form of gold dust. For the importance of African gold to the European medieval economy see 'European Silver and African Gold', P. Spufford, *op. cit.*, pp. 163-87).
Ethiopia: the Aksumite kings who ruled northern Ethiopia (second to ninth century AD) issued small gold coins, some bronze and a few silver, from the third to tenth century.
Alvarez: Francisco Alvarez, a Portuguese priest, landed in Massawa in 1520 and spent six years in Ethiopia. Sent by King Manoel I of Portugal, when the Ethiopian empress regent requested help from the Portuguese against Muslims on the coast. He was the first westerner to give a detailed account of Ethiopia, and the court of Emperor Lebna Dengel, in his *Truthful Information about the Countries of Prester John of the Indies* (1540).
Arcadius: possibly (AD c. 377-408), Eastern Roman Emperor who ruled with his father Theodosius I.

Page 102
Celsius: Aulus Cornelius under Tiberius (AD 14-37) wrote an encyclopaedia including information on agriculture, medicine, military science, rhetoric, and probably philosophy and jurisprudence.
George Agricola: *aka* Georgius Agricola *aka* Georg Bauer (1494-1555), German classicist and mineralogist; highly regarded by his contemporaries such as Erasmus. Regarded as the originator of the experimental approach to science. His *De re metallica,* published 1556, (tr. and ed. H. C. and L. H. Hoover (London, 1912) deals with smelting and mining, preparation of alum etc. It also surveys historical and classical allusions to metals.
mine: Greek coin equal to one hundred Athenian *drachmae*: also an ancient measure of capacity used in France for dry goods.
Louis Hutin: Louis X, *le Hutin* (the quarrelsome) (c. 1290-1316), King of France (r. 1314-6), of the Capetian dynasty, succeeded his father, Philip IV.
Peter IV: Peter the Ceremonius *aka* Pedro the Cruel (1317/19-87), King of Aragon (r. 1336-87), of Castile and León (1350-1369), son of Alfonso XI. He picked a quarrel with his cousin, James III of Majorca, and captured the

162 *Notes*

Balearics and Roussillon (1343-44) from the semi-autonomous Kingdom of Majorca. See also David Abulafia, *A Mediterranean Emporium: the Catalan Kingdom of Majorca* (Cambridge University Press, 1994).

Page 103
Pope Innocent III: Lothaire, Count of Segni, b. 1160 in Rome (r. 1198-1216), at the start of the Fourth and Fifth Crusade and the movement against the Cathars. Like Thomas Aquinas, he held that coinage belonged to the ruler.
Vermandois: province between Amiens and St-Quentin; based at Vermand, the Celtic city of the Veromandui. Jean Bodin was deputy for Vermandois in 1576.
Estates of France: *Etats-généraux,* the national representative body, with elected representatives of the three orders of clergy, nobility and the third estate. During the time Bodin wrote his book they met 1560-61, 1561 and 1576-7. Blois (q.v.).

Page 104
Archimedes: (c. 287-12 BC), the greatest mathematician of antiquity, born and died in Syracuse; determined the proportions of gold and silver in a crown made for Hieron and invented the science of hydrostatics, concerned with the specific gravity of different substances when floated in water.
King Hiero: Hieron II (c. 306-215 BC), King of Syracuse who was defeated by the Romans in the Punic Wars and thereafter paid annual tribute to them. Under Roman protection and with his commercial skills, Syracuse became wealthy and magnificent.
alloy: coins, often made of electrum, an alloy of silver and gold, first appeared 650-600 BC in West Asia Minor.

Page 106
Greece: its gold and silver currency was accepted far from its mint of origin, as in Egypt. The international diffusion of Greek coinage led to the production of local coinages by the Persians, Etruscans and others.
solde: lit. military pay (Latin *solidus*, money); tax contribution of towns to the crown, ie. infantry tax, eg. *solde des 50,000 hommes de pied* paid in 1543.
Pollux: Julius Pollux of Naucratis, second century AD Greek scholar and rhetorician, compiled *Onomasticon*, an encyclopaedic thesaurus of terms on a wide range of subjects from synonyms, subject-vocabularies to religion, law and crafts.

Page 107
Attic: Attica was a state in eastern part of central Greece. Until the sixth century BC, the country districts were largely independent. During the fifth century BC it was taken over by Athens.

Page 108
Queen of England: Elizabeth I (q.v.) continued her father's denominations and restored the purity of silver coinage. She discontinued the groat, but continued the two-pence piece.

angenine: small Lorraine currency.
Punic wars: three wars (264–41 BC; 218–201 BC; 149–6 BC) in which Rome gradually took over from Carthage as the dominant power in the western Mediterranean. The Second Punic War marked a turning-point in ancient history with far-reaching changes in economic and political life, the destruction of Carthage (146 BC) and the enslavement of its population. Thereafter no power really threatened Rome's existence for centuries, with Carthage reduced to a Roman province (Africa).
lex Papirius: in this Roman law, *semunciaria* (89 BC), presented by the tribune C. Papirius Carbo, the *as* was reduced to the weight of one twenty-fourth of a pound *(libra)* which was half an ounce *(uncia)*.

Page 109
Livy: Titus Livius (59 BC–AD 17), Roman historian, who wrote the history of Rome in 142 books, though only thirty-five books are now extant; a popular author in the Middle Ages and Renaissance.
Ætolians: a central Greek country, developed after the fifth century BC. Its loose tribal organisation gave way to a federal state in the fourth century BC, and expanded its influence over Delphi. It became Rome's first active ally in Greece proper.
pope's court: the *curia* in Rome.
Herodotus: (484?–430/20 BC), born in Halicarnassus, Greek author of the masterpiece the *History* of the Greco-Persian War; a great traveller in North Africa and the Persian empire.
Daric stater: a standard coin struck in various materials, the Daric *stater* being of gold. Daric from Darius, the name given to several Persian kings from the fifth century BC, eg. Darius I (521–486 BC) who attempted to expand the Persian empire into mainland Greece in a series of conflicts.
Nero: Nero Claudius Caesar, Roman Emperor (AD 54–68), tyrant. His devotion to art was real; he rebuilt Rome after the fire of AD 64 in grandiose style and mainly to glorify himself. The buildings included the immense *Domus aurea* (golden palace).

Page 110
East Indies: during Augustus' rule there was great demand for Indian luxuries, aided by the discovery of open-sea routes from Africa to India. Augustus received Indian envoys and 120 ships sailed for India each year. There was some anxiety about the drain of gold money to pay for these imports (Pliny the Elder, *Naturalis Historia,* bk. 6, sections 96–101; bk. 12, section 84). The principal imports to Rome were perfumes, pepper and other spices, gems, ivory, pearls and Chinese silk. The Romans exported linen, coral, glass, base metals. They also sent gold, silver and copper coin and large hoards have been found in South India.

Page 111
creutzer: *kreutzer* from the obverse type of double cross; a large German silver coin copied in Austria, Switzerland and the Tirol.
patard: silver coin from Burgundian Netherlands issued from 1433 to the sixteenth century, initially 0.48 fineness.
Salerno: in Sicily, subject to a prince who had his own mint.

Page 112
carlins: *carlin, grosso, carlino*. A large silver coin (3.34 grams) of Naples, first issued 1278 by Charles I of Anjou.
taris: *tari* is a small struck gold coin, influenced by Arab coins (such as the *rubā'i* or quarter-dinar) and commercial ties with the Fāṭimid empire, and found in southern Italy and Sicily c. 1050–1194.

Page 113
ride: possibly from the gold 'riders' introduced to Brittany in 1420s, similar to the *salut*. Philip, Duke of Burgundy struck 'riders' or *cavaliers* for the Netherlands in 1433.
Venice: known variously as *ducato d'oro, zecchino, sequin* or ducat were pure gold coin struck 1284–c. 1840 (3.56 grams), which were copied in Rome, the Middle East and India.
Genoa: pure gold coins, *genovino/genoin*, struck from 1252 (3.53 grams).
Hungary: bankrupted by corruption and incompetence, Hungary was prey to the Süleyman the Magnificent's grand campaign (*sefer-i humāyūn*). In 1526, the Turks defeated the Magyars at the battle of Mohács. Thereafter, Ferdinand of Hapsburg occupied western Hungary as a bulwark for Vienna against further Turkish expansion. By 1540s, a tripartite division of Hungary had emerged with royal (Hapsburg) Hungary, Turkish-occupied Hungary centred on Buda and Transylvania (a virtual military governate). Süleyman died in Hungary (1566).
Lucca: issued gold florins by 1275.
Bologna: issued gold coins (*bolognino d'oro*) around 1379 (3.55 grams).
Saluzzo: marquisate of. In the treaty of Cateau-Cambrésis (1559), France returned Bresse, Savoy and Piedmont to the Duke of Savoy and only retained Saluzzo and five fortified places in Piedmont, including Turin.
Sicily: the oldest Italian dominion of the crown of Aragon. In the fourteenth century there were civil wars, which were followed by a long period of comparative peace until the threat of invasion from the Turks in the mid-sixteenth century. Gold coins, *augustale*, were struck by Frederick II in 1231 (5.3 grams).
Milan: *ambrosino d'oro* gold florins issued before the end of the thirteenth century.
Ancona: only good natural harbour on the central East coast of Italy.
Ferrara: see Renée of France (q.v.).

Page 114
Farnese, Alexander: Pope Paul III, Alessandro Farnese (q.v.). The family were in service to the papacy from the twelfth century. His grandfather was Ranuccio Farnese the Elder, a *condottieri* in the 1400.
Solothurn, Lucerne and Unterval...Berne: long dominated by the Holy Roman Empire, by the fourteenth century the Swiss Confederation developed with cantons, some sees and abbacies, striking their own money. Switzerland became a country divided by religion, laws, and economic interests by the sixteenth century. Of these cantons, only Berne was Protestant; the rest Catholic, allied with Austria.
billon: an alloy of silver with a high proportion of base metals, such as copper, divided into *billon blanc* and *billon noir*. Around 1515 there were about a dozen types of billon coins circulating in France, including the *dizain* and the *sizain*.

Page 116
Moulins: the French court spent three months from December 1565 to March 1566 in Moulins. In January 1566, the Assembly of Notables was called which included princes, royal councillors and officers of state and the first presidents of six *parlements*. The ordinance of Moulins in February 1566 aimed to strengthen the monarchy, with its eighty-six articles which covered many aspects of government, law, justice, trade guilds and so on, but was largely ineffective.
florins of Germany: the imperial *gulden* or florin was issued from 1339; florins of the Rhine (*rhinegulden*) were struck from 1354–1626 by electors and other princes, but declined in weight and fineness (1354 0.98 fineness; 1419 0.79).

Page 118
Juno: the goddess associated with women, marriage, the moon and the state. One of her titles was Moneta. The temple of Juno Moneta, dedicated by Camillus in 345 BC, housed the early Roman mint after 289 BC, which at first only produced bronze bars, and later the silver and gold *denarius*; hence *moneta* came to mean 'mint'. By 269 BC there were three more mints probably at Beneventum, Tarentum and a northern mint, though they produced coins of different standards for the *as* (240, 288 and 300 *scruples*).
Marius Gratidianus: praetor c. 86 BC, devised an *ars probandi denarios* to separate good from bad money. His *ars* meant, no doubt, fixing small stamps to the *denarius* to reveal any underlying base metal. After a scrutiny (*spectatio*), a bag of money would have been labelled with a *tesserae mummulariae*.
Charlemagne: Charles I, King of the Franks (r. AD 768-814), one of the greatest figures in the Middle Ages with many legends related to him. His kingdom stretched from the North Sea to the Pyrenees and the Ebro, in Italy to the Garigliano, and from the Elbe to the Atlantic. He tried to establish order and justice and protected learning. He had mints in France, the Rhineland, the Low Countries and elsewhere.
Charles: Charles IV *le Bel* (r. 1322-8), son of Phillip IV, *le Bel*, succeeded his brother Philip V *le Long* as King of France. On his death the direct line of the Capetian dynasty came to an end.

Page 119
Villeneuve d'Auvignon: possibly Villeneuve d'Aveyron, a village near Villefranche de Rouergue on the watershed between the Célé and the Lot.
Villefranche de Rouergue: medieval mint; between Figeac and Cahors, a *bastide*, re-founded by Alphonse de Poitiers, Count of Toulouse in 1232.

Page 120
depreciation: over time the *livre* was fairly continually depreciated. Charlemagne's *libra argenti* was probably about 7,000 grains of silver. By the time of Louis IX it was less than twenty-five per cent of this (probably less than 1,750 grains). The main cause of this depreciation was probably due to the ease with which kings could raise income in an emergency by reminting the existing coinage at a lower standard or fineness.
***Conseil des Finances*:** until 1523, French revenue was adminstered by two sections: the royal lands with four treasurers under the *chargeur de trésor* and extraordinary revenue (*gabelles, aides, tailles, traites* and *impostions foraines*) by four receivers-general of finance. From 1523, the two sections were centralised and by 1554 had one controller (NCMH, pp. 448-9).

Page 123
***Philip*:** gold coin *Philippus* of Philip II of Macedon, popular in the ancient world, many of which were sent to Rome after 200 BC.
zuza: zuz, an ancient Hebrew silver coin, worth one-quarter of a shekel.
Estates of Blois: Blois was the seat of a line of counts. In 1397 it passed to the House of Orléans and to the crown in 1498 when Louis XII, who was born in Blois, succeeded to the throne. As a result of Bodin's conduct at the Estates of Blois in 1576, when he opposed the suggestion that all the king's subjects should be Catholics and upheld the rights of the third estate, he lost favour with Henry III (R. J. Knecht, *op. cit.*, pp. 462, 481-2).
Marcel: probably Claude Marcel, *prévôt des marchands* who no doubt directed the Paris militia at the time of the St-Barthélemy's Day massacre.

Page 125
treaty of Ætolia: Aetolians co-operated with Antiochus III against the Romans, which led to their defeat. They lost their influence and conquered lands and in 189 BC the Aetolians were forced to accept a treat as subject allies of Rome.

Page 127
Lydian stone: 'a black variety of jasper (basanite) used by jewellers as a touchstone for testing gold' (OED).

INDEX

accommodation, cost of 43
acid, effect on coin 95-6
acting fees 76
Adrian VI, Pope 93
Æsop 76
Ætolia 109, 125-6
Africa 56, 63-4, 76, 101, 107-108, 126
Agde 92
Agricola, G. 102, 107
Agrippa 56, 109
Alençon, Duke of 12
Alexander Severus, Emperor 67, 99, 125
Alexander the Great, King of Macedonia 71
Alexandria 66
alloy 104-5, 108, 110-1, 113-4, 116, 118, 119, 124, 126
Alps 56
Altantic Ocean 90, 92
alum 69, 84
Alvarez, F. 101
amber 70
Amiens 57
Anatolia 54
Ancona 113
Angers 11; House of Notre Dame 11
animals, values of 58, 74, 89
Anjou 62, 64; province of 58, 79
Antonin, History of 78
Antoninius Pius, Emperor 67
Antwerp 83
Apelles 71
Apicius 76, 91
Appian 77, 85, 102, 107
Aquinas, T. 17-18, 27, 30
Arabia 54, 64, 87
arable land, prices of 56
Arabs 63-4
Aragon 64, 66, 68, 102-3, 113
Arcadius, Emperor 101, 108

Archimedes 104
Aristophanes 28, 90
army pay 74
Asia 56, 75, 125-6
assaying 96-7
Asti 62
Atahualpa [Atabalira], Inca King 64
Athenæus 76, 91
Athens 86
Attica 107, 123
Augustus, Emperor 59, 71, 80, 83, 90, 110, 123
Auvergne 56, 58, 66, 67, 79
Auxerre 57
Avignon 54, 57, 114
Azoa 83

Bacon, N. 49
balance of payments, French 25
Baltic Sea 65, 87
banking, development of 25
Barbary 66, 68-9, 71, 81, 92, 112
Barbette, E. 98
Barcelona 111
barley 58
baronies, sale of 56-7
Baudrillart, H. 11, 13, 21, 27
Bayonne 92
Beguines 93
Beirut 66
bell-metal 103
Berne 106, 114
Berry, duchy of 57
Bertin, Maître D. 69
billon 114
Blondus, F. 57
blood money, rates of 57
Bodin de St Laurent, J. 11-34, 49-50, 123
Bologna 64, 113
book trade 65
Bouillon, G. de 57

Boulogne 102
Bourges, King of *see* Charles VII
Bourbonnais 58, 79
brass 97, 100
brassage, rights of 117
brazil-wood 84
Brie 56
Britain 14
Brittany 22, 92, 111
bronze 103
Brusa [Bursa] 54
Budé, G. 70, 74, 101–102, 107
Burgundy 62, 65, 87, 113

Cahors 18
Cairo 66
Caligula, Emperor 75, 91, 96
Candace, Queen of Sheba 59
capon, cost of 43, 46, 58, 79
Capua, Prior of 66
Caracalla, Emperor 70
carat 78, 94–6, 104–105, 107, 112–3, 116, 119, 120–1, 125–6
Cardan, J. 70
Carmelite Order 11
carpentry, French trade in 65
Castille 81, 113, 114
Catholic Church 11–12; League 12
Catilans 64
Cato 91
cattle 41, 63
Caesar, Julius 72, 75–7
Celsius 102, 107
Ceres, Lady of Sicily 55
Chambre des comptes 39, 53, 58–9, 117
Champagne 58, 79
charity 85
Charlemagne, King of the Franks 118
Charles, Count of Valois 61
Charles IV, King of France 118
Charles V, Holy Roman Emperor 64, 93, 113
Charles V, King of France 57, 60–2
Charles VI, King of France 61–2, 99

Charles VII, King of France 61, 78, 99, 110–1
Charles VIII, King of France 62, 113
Charles IX, King of France 39, 51, 62, 113, 115, 117, 120, 124
Châtelet 55, 79, 127
Childeric [Chilperic], Merovingian King 94, 105
Christians 62
Cicero 56, 76
cinnabar 84
civil war (Orleans-Burgundy) 65
Clagny, M^r de 71
Clenard, N. 67
Cleopatra, Queen 71
climate 13
cloth 43, 46, 54, 65, 84, 88, 89; damask 54; gold 73; half-silk 54; linen 65, 84, 88; purple & dyed 53; samite 54; satin 54; serge 69; silk 54, 69, 71–2; silver 73; velvet 22–3, 41, 43–5, 53–4
clothing 54, 84; extravagance in 72–3; Italian women's 86
coin, brass 74, 97, 101; copper 47, 49, 81, 99, 107, 119; gold 46, 47, 74, 94–5, 98, 101, 107, 108, 120; iron 100; lead 97; leather 61; rossette copper 98; silver 42, 44–7, 53, 74, 78, 81, 94–5, 97–9, 102, 107, 110, 118, 120
coin types:
  angelot 57, 81, 82, 94, 112–3
  angenine 108
  asse 74, 99, 101
  aureus 123
  bagatin 97
  bezant 61, 64; gold 61
  blanc 43, 94, 110, 112, 115, 119; pieces of three 124; pieces of six 124
  carlin 112
  carolus 94
  Cornoadis 97
  creutzer 111

demi-teston 94
denier 14–15, 42–3, 46, 58, 63, 67, 74–5, 77–82, 95, 97, 99–102, 104–16, 118–9, 120–1, 123–6; au milieu 94; common 106; current 120; fine 42, 112, 114, 120; obole 97; par le bord 94; petit 106, 110; Roman 101, 107, 123; silver 80, 97, 123; tournois 42, 79, 114, 115
dollar, silver 105
double 97, 119, 124
douzain 42, 46, 47, 57, 94, 119
drachma 74, 80, 102, 106–7, 120, 123
ducat 64, 68, 81, 83, 100, 112–3; double 81, 100
écu 15, 22–3, 41, 44–7, 54, 56–7, 60, 62, 67, 69, 71, 73, 75–7, 79–80, 82, 106–107, 113; au soleil 82; aux fleurs de lis sans nombre 41; couronne 74, 81–2, 109, 113; d'or aux fleurs de lis sans nombre 77; new 114, 127; old 77–8, 81–2, 96, 113, 127; sol 70, 82–3, 96, 105, 113; soleil 41, 53, 55, 81–2, 113, 124
ferlin 119, 121
florin 62, 111; German 116; silver 111
franc 14, 43, 58, 60, 62, 70, 81, 79, 97, 107, 124; à cheval 42, 45, 77–8, 81–2, 113; à pied 42, 45, 77–8, 81–2, 113; gold 42, 45, 57, 82–3; tournois 58
Geldern brelingue 111
gros 106–107, 111–2, 120, 123; tournois 42, 46–7, 106
Henri 81; double 81
imperial 112, 118
Iocondalle 94
Joachimthaler 94
leton 100–1
liard 43, 80, 97, 110, 119, 124; double 110

livre 41–6, 53, 55, 61–3, 66, 78–80, 82, 102, 106, 109, 111, 114–7, 120; ordinary (Scotland) 111; sterling (Scotland) 111; tournois 14–6, 42, 61, 78, 82, 110–1, 120; tournois petit 61
medin 81, 112
milrais 81
mina 107
mine 102
mouton 79; à la grand laine 81
noble 60, 79, 81; gold 60, 81; rose noble 123
obole 74, 94, 107
patard 111
penny 108
pezan 64
Philip 123
piece 112, 120, 123
pistolet 81, 113, 121
Portugueses 94, 105
pound 101, 107–109, 111–2, 125; merchant's (France) 107; Roman 107, 112; sterling 111
quatrin 97
rapesemin 111
rapin 111
real 57, 80, 81, 100, 105–106, 108, 114–5, 123; gold 81; old 100; Spain 80, 105–6, 123
Reichs grosschen 111
ride 113
schessind 111
seraph 81
shekel 123
sol [sous] 14–15, 42–7, 53, 55, 57, 58, 74–5, 77–82, 97, 99–100, 106–11, 114–16, 119, 120, 124; brass 97; de taille 112; du pays 112; gold 57; new 46; old 46, 78, 79; petit 115; silver 57, 77–9; tournois 41–2, 46, 79, 106–7, 109, 114, 120, 123; weight of 57
solidus 82, 113; gold 112, 113
stater, Attic 123; Daric 109

170 Index

talent 71, 77
tari 112
teston 73, 94, 100, 110, 114, 120
thaler 94
vache, de Bretagne 124; de Foix 124
zuza 123
coinage, base 49, 114, 110-11, 116, 119, 120, 124; abolition of 123-45; prohibition of 102, 120; cast 94-5, 98, 122; clipped 94, 98, 103, 121-2, 124; form of 121-2; hammered 97-8, 121-2; proportions gold: silver 105-7; reform 31-3, 125-7; small value 33; stamped 101, 121; values 77; weight 77-8, 105-106, 122-3
Cologne 111
colourings 84
commodities 15
commoners, rights of (1318) 57
commonwealth 49-50
Comtat Venaissin 57
Comynes, P. de 62
Conseil des Finances 120
Constantinople 94, 105
Copernicus 20-1, 30
copper 33, 49, 78, 81, 84, 95, 99-101, 103-5, 107-12, 116, 118, 121; rosette 94, 97, 98, 101, 116
copperas 84
corn prices 22-3, 26, 65, 68, 84, 87-8
corrosion 95-6
cost increases 39-50, 51, 53
counterfeit 94-5, 98, 102-4, 116, 118, 119, 121-2, 124, 127
court registers 59
craftsmanship, value of 83
Crassus, Emperor 74-5
Curio 77
currency, counterfeit 94-5; debased 22, 47, 78, 82, 98-100, 102-3, 110-11, 120; (1300) 110; (1551) 78; evaluation of 123; forged 98, 107, 118; instability of 49, 112

D'Avenel, G. 15
Damascus 54, 83
Dante 98, 102
Daric *see Persia*
David II, King of Scotland 60
dearness, cause of 59
debasement 16, 18, 22, 24, 26-7, 29, 31, 34, 53, 59, 47, 53, 59, 78, 82, 98-100, 102-3, 110-2, 115, 119, 120; government 32; illegal 32; price changes due to 31; private 32; remedies for 31-3
debt law 73-4
Demosthenes 95, 118
Denmark 65
depreciation 23, 120, 124
devaluation 16, 60, 100, 109, 113
Didius 74
Domitian, Emperor 88
dowry 61, 62
dress, form of 54
drugs 84
Drusus, Livius 100, 118
Du Prat, A. 73
dung-eaters 90
Durel [Dürer, A.] 71
dyestuffs, French trade in 65

East Indies [Indies] 87, 88, 110, 126
Eastern products 25
Edward I, King of England 61
Edward II, King of England 61
Egypt 59-60, 64, 73, 87, 121
Elizabeth I, Queen of England 97, 108, 121
ell 43-5, 53-4
England 12, 33-4, 56, 60, 64, 65, 89, 92, 99, 111, 113; mines 89
Ephesus 86
escheat, law of 87
estates 47
Etats-généraux, 103; Blois 11-12; 123; Orleans 62, 68
Ethiopia 73, 101
Europe 14

exchange 41
exchange rate equilibrium 31
exchange rates 31, 41, 44, 46-7, 58, 77, 102, 123; international 100, 110, 112, 114; (1508) 58
export duties 28; concessions 89; metals 115; prohibiting 31; restrictions 89; trade 59, 68, 84, 89
extravagance 31, 76, 84

Fail, N. de 21
family, inalienable right of 13
famine 83, 87
Farnese, A. [Pope Paul III] 70, 114
fashion demands 72-3
Fauchet, M^r 57
Faur, M^r du 51
Ferdinand II, King of Spain 66
Ferdinand II, King of Naples 93
Ferrara 113
ferrumination 122
festival food prices 74
festivities, ordinances on 75
Fez 66
fines 57
fish 65, 75-6, 86, 89-92
Flanders 68, 73, 88-9, 100, 111-2, 115; salt tariffs 88
Florence 57, 66, 69, 81, 83. 86, 93, 113-14; sale of 57
Foix, F. de 121
Fontainebleau 71
food, game 91; luxury 75-6, 84; prices 75-6, 79-80, 84, 89; prohibitions 92-3; superfluity of 73; taboos 91-3
foreign exchange markets 31
foreign trade 100
forgery 32; 96-8, 114
France 11-27, 41, 44, 55, 67, 80, 87, 92, 98, 107, 110, 113; agriculture 25, 63; customs of 58; House of 66; population growth 65; silk mills in 54; trade with 65
Franche-Comté 65, 89

Francis I, King of France 66, 69, 78, 111, 113; ordinance (1540) 104
Franconians 57
fraternities 68
fraud 116, 118-19
free enterprise 32
French crown lands 24; revenue 25
French workmen in Spain 66

Galen 75, 90
Galicia 92
Gascony, perfumes of 69
Gaul 56
generaux subsidiaires 117
Genoa 54, 64, 66, 67, 69, 83, 103, 113: house of Saint George 67
Germany 21, 56, 60, 66, 72, 94, 101, 108, 111, 113, 116, 125
gilding 109
glass, abundance of 60
gold 115-6, 117-9, 121-3, 125-7; abundance of 58-60, 66-8, 74-5, 84; devaluation of 109; gold 14, 16, 22-6, 41-2, 44-7, 49, 53-4, 57, 60-5, 68-9, 73-7, 81-4, 88, 94-5, 98, 100-12; currency 23-4; gold, export of 68; prices 125-6; standard 14; trade, profit 115-6
gold dust 101
gold-plate 103-5, 115
gold-work, adulteration of 103-5
goldsmiths 115-6
Goths 77
grain 55, 68, 87, 88, 94, 97, 100-101, 104-09, 111-16, 118, 119-21, 123,124, 126; dealers 68; regulation and storage 87
Gratidianus, Marius 118
Greece, ancient 54, 73, 75, 80, 91, 94, 101, 106-7, 113, 118, 121, 125
Greek commonwealths 109
Grenada 68
Gresham's Law 16, 28-30, 34
Grice-Hutchinson, M. 19
guaiac 84

172 Index

Guinea 101
Guyenne 64, 89, 92

Hadrian, Emperor 77, 125
hairstyles, laws on 70
Hales, J. 34
Hannibal 99
Hauser, H. 15–16, 20, 24
hay prices 58, 79
healthy eating 90–1
Hebrew law 73, 109, 121, 123
Heliogabalus, Emperor 67, 94, 105
Henry, Emperor of Luxemburg 57
Henry II, King of France 42, 62, 78, 80, 82, 106, 117. 119, 124
Henry III, King of France 39–48, 51, 66, 69, 82, 92, 111, 113
Henry VIII, King of England 70
Herodotus 109, 125
Herpin 57
Herullians 77
Hiero [Hieron], King of Syracuse 104
high prices, reasons for 66–8
Hirrius 75
Holland 14
honey 84
Hopkins, S. V. 16
horses 84
household charges 61
housing, furnishings, extravagance in 73; prices 80, 82–3
Hungary 65, 77, 113
imports 84; limitation on 68; tariffs 88–9
income tax 63
India 54, 64, 73, 125
Indies 19
inflation 33–4, 87; causes of 23–7; effects of 30–1
Innocent III, Pope 103
interest rates 67, 124
iron 84, 100, 122
Isabelle of France 61
Isle de France [Île de France] 56
Istanbul 83, 86, 92
Italian trade 25, 28

Italians, opinion on 28
Italy 54, 56–7, 62, 64, 66–7, 69–71, 73–4, 83, 86, 88–9, 97–8, 107–108, 111, 113, 118, 125
ivory 84

Jacob, W. 16
Jerusalem 60
Jevons, W. S. 23
jewellery 54, 70–1, 104; Italian 86
Jews 56, 66
John II, King of France 42, 45, 60–1, 77, 113, 118
Joinville, Seigneur de 61
Joplin, T. 32
Joseph (lord of Egypt) 87
Jovius, Paulus 93
Juno, temple of 118
Just Price 18, 26, 34
Justinian, Emperor 53, 57, 82

La Limagne d'Auvergne 56
La Marche 58, 79
labour, cost of 67
land value 16, 23, 43, 55, 56, 58–9, 79, 80; scarcity 59
Languedoc 56, 66, 68, 69
Laôn 11–12
Latin (non-perishable) merchandise 41, 53, 55
Latin America, discovery of 63–4
law, sacred 126
lawsuits, reduction of 126
Le Cointe 95
lead 84, 86, 95, 97, 103; Italian 86
leather 84, 61
Leo of Africa 83
Levant 54, 63, 66, 69, 71
Levasseur, M^r 16
lex Aternia-Trapeia 74
lex Fannia 74
lex Papiria 99, 101
lex Papirius 108
Liège 97
Limoges 83
Limousin 66, 67

Lionel, Duke of Clarence 62
Livres, M^r de 78
Livy 109, 125
Loire 56, 75
Lombard, P. 70
Lombards (bills of exchange) 63
Lombardy 57
London 83
Lorraine 97, 108
Louis of France, Duke of Orleans 62
Louis IX, King of France [Saint Louis] 42–3, 46, 57, 60, 77–8, 106
Louis X, King of France [Hutin] 102
Louis XI, King of France 62
Louis XII, King of France 80
Low Countries 12, 111
loy 126
Lucca 66, 113; sale of 57
Lucerne 114
Lucullus 76
luxuries, analysis of 24, 26
Lybian desert 83
Lycurgus 85,100
Lydian stone 127
Lyon(s) 54, 83; Bank of 66

Macedonia 59
MacLeod, H. D. 28
Mahommadans 60
maître des comptes 54
Majorca 90, 103, 111; King of 103
Malestroi(c)t, C. J. de 15, 21–3, 25–7, 39–51, 53–6, 58, 77, 78, 82–4, 89, 127; paradoxes 21–3, 39–48, 51; first 41–3, 46, 47; second 44–8; third 47
Malynes, G. de 34
Mantua 113
manufactured goods, trade 65
marc [mark] 14–15, 46, 62, 77–9, 82, 94, 100, 102, 104–12, 114–17, 119–21, 123, 125; *d'emirance* 94; gold 94, 112, 115–17, 120, 125; silver 46, 62, 78–9, 107–08, 111, 115–17, 120; mark, wrought 78, 94, 110

marcasite 69
Marcel, C. 123
Marius 76
Mark Antony, Emperor 77, 100, 118
Mauretania 101
Maximilian I, Holy Roman Emperor 62
Maximilian II, Holy Roman Emperor 66
McCulloch, J. R. 27
McIver, R. M. 12
meat consumption 92; diseases of 91; prices 90
medallion 91, 121; gold 118, 123; Vespasian 125
Medici, Guiliano de' 86
Mediterranean Sea 63, 90–2
Menil, M^r du 51
Messina 112
metals 103; proportions of 121
Method for the Easy Comprehension of History 13, 77
Michaelangelo 71
Middle East, retail trade in 64, 66
Milan 62, 73, 83, 113
Mincion, Messire 63
mineral imports 88
mines, gold 122; silver 122, 126
Minorca 90, 103; King of 103
mint officers, salaries of 117
Mint Par 28–9
mint-masters 111–18, 124
mints, allocation of 116; profit from 120; revenues 116
Moluccas 64
monetary background 13–15
money 39–40; adulteration of 103; sacred 126; stability of 39–48, 93–4; standardisation of 77, 94; base 33; value of commodity 30; demand for 17, 30; supply 17, 18; value of 19; velocity of circulation of 30; value of 39–40, 49, 52
money-changers 115, 124, 127
monopoly 24, 31, 59, 68, 84, 87
Monroe, A. E. 21, 34

174 Index

Moors 72, 73
Morocco 66
mortgages 106
Moulin, Mr C. du 82
Moulins 116
Muḥammad the Great [Mehmet II], Sultan 86
Naples 65, 93, 112
Navarre 66
Navarro, M. de Azpilcueta 18
Navarrus 18-20, 29
Near East 27
Negus (Prester John) 71
Nero 109
Netherlands 100
New World 14-15, 25, 60, 63-4, 71, 92, 111
Normandy 64, 92, 111, 117
northern countries 88, 109-10, 126
Norway 65
Nuremburg 83, 111

oats, value of 58
oil 69, 84
oppression 62
ordinance (1294) 53; (1540) 82, 106; (1561) 78; Henry II 82; on value & circulation of money 44; Saint Louis for the Peaceful State of the Kingdom 54
ore, value of 58
Oresme, N. 18, 28
Orient 107
Orkneys 92
Orleans 65, 87
Ottoman empire 66
ounce 99, 101-2, 106-9, 111-12, 120, 123; common 112
overtipping 73

paintings, value of 71
Palermo 112
paper trade 65, 84
parchment, Italian 86
Paris 11, 16, 25, 57, 61-2, 67, 69, 73, 79-80, 83, 102, 105, 111, 117; uprising in 1306 98
Paris Standard of rental wheat (1522, 1524) 55
parity 112
Parker, M. 49
Parthians 77
pastel 84, 88-9
Paul III *see Farnese, Alessandro*
Paulus, Æmilius 59, 76
Paulus, Lucius Æmilius 77
peace treaty (France-England) 61
pearl trade 60, 70-1
perfume, Italian 69, 86
perishable commodities 22
Perseus, King of Macedon 59
Persia 64, 71, 109, 118, 121, 123
Persian Gulf 64
Peru 25, 64
Peter IV, King of Aragon 102-103
Petty, Sir W. 22
Phelps-Brown, E. H. 16
Philip I, King of France 57
Philip III, King of France 61
Philip IV, King of France [the Fair] 53, 63, 78, 98-9, 110, 118; debased coinage (1306) 98, 102; ordinance (1294) 53
Philip V, King of France [the Tall] 57, 61, 63; ordinances of 57
Philip VI, King of France [de Valois] 41, 44, 53, 61, 77-8
Picard, Dr 92
pillage, English 65
Pinatel, J. 97, 119
piracy, policy of 14
pitch 84
Piurians [Pyurres] 64
Plato 69, 85, 120
Pliny 59, 60, 71, 75, 96, 102, 107, 108, 110, 122, 125-6
Plutarch 59, 74, 77, 91
Poggio, B. 93

Poitiers, battle of 60
Poitou 79
Poland 65, 89, 117
Pollux, J. 106, 109
Polybius 74, 80
Pompey 76-7
pope's court 109
Portugal 25, 64, 68, 81, 113, 121
Poyet, G. 68
precious metals 14, 16-17, 19, 22, 25, 27, 28, 31; coined 17
precious stones 70
Prevost, M^r 51
price, commonly accepted 81; fixing by royalty 68, 126; rises 41, 43, 58, 59, 83-4; inflation 15-17; level 18, 30; rises 22; stable 47; stabilisation 31; world 28-9
Procureur Général 12
produce, cost of 55
profiteering 89, 94
Protestant 11
Protogenes 71
Provence 52, 62, 68, 69, 92, 102
Punic Wars 108; First 99, 101
Purchasing Power Parity 19
Puys, J. du 49
Pyrenees 56, 69

Quantity Theory, emergence of 20-2, 29-30
quarters (weight) 104
quicksilver 84, 122

rabbit consumption 90; plague of 90
Raphael 71
rate fixing 123
Red Sea 64
regulation of rate and standard of money 126-7
regulation of value of goods 127
relative scarcity theory of value 19, 24-6, 29-30, 34
relativism 12
Renée of France 62
rent 22, 46, 47, 79, 127; secured 127

Republic 13
Responses by Bodin to Malestroit's paradoxes 21, 30, 33, 53-127
retail price control 127
revenue, landed/settled 45-7, 80, 106; loss of 44-6; secured 127
Rhine 56, 88
Ripuarians, laws of 57
Robert II, King of Scotland 60
Romagna 50
Roman empire 56, 59, 73-7, 80, 83, 85, 91, 93, 99, 101, 103, 106-7, 109, 112-13, 118, 121, 123, 126
Roman law 73
Rome, Capitol 109; foundation of 74; Pantheon 109
Rondelet, G. 92
Roover, R. De 34
Roscius, Q. 76
royalty, example of 84, 93; pleasure of 59; personal income of 61; influence of 68, 83; pleasure of princes 69; role of 127; speculation by 107, 124
rye, value of 58, 87

Sabine, G. H. 13
saffron 84
Saintonge 56
Saladin 60
Salamanca, School of 19
salaries 47
Salerno 111
salt 25, 65, 84, 88-9, 101
Saluzzo 113
Saracens 63
Saxons 57
scarcity 59, 68
Scholastics 18, 21; analysis of demand 25-8, 30, 34
Schumpeter, J. A. 17, 34
Scipo family 76
Scotland 60, 65, 89, 111
Scottish-French alliance (1371) 60
services, cost of 67; extravagance in 73
Servius, King of Rome 74

Seville 83
Sforza, Bianca 62; Lodovico (the Moor) 62
sheep, value of 58
shoes, cost of 43
Sicily 56, 92, 113
Sienna 81, 113
silver 14, 16, 24–6; 41–3, 45–7, 49, 53, 54, 58–60, 62, 64, 65–9, 73–9, 80–4, 88, 91, 94–112, 114–19, 121–7; abundance of 58–60, 66–8, 74–5, 84, 109; alloy 96–7; cheapness of 62; silver, currency 23–4; export of 68; fine 46–7, 108, 114; for grain (1531) 55; prices 125–6; purchasing power of 15; scarcity of 61, 63; standard 14
silver coinage 22, 24, 42; aduleration of (1300) 78
silver-plate 115
slavery 63, 74
Slavonia 76
social justice 13
solde 106
Solon 74
Solothurn 114, 115
sovereignty 13
Spain 14, 17–19, 25, 55, 60, 64–9, 72, 73, 89–90, 94, 97–8, 100, 106–8, 111, 113, 121, 123, 125
Spanish-Flanders war 68
Sparta 100
spice trade 54, 64, 65, 69, 84
Spiegel, H. W. 20–1
Spooner, F. C. 15
St-Barthélemy's Day Massacre 11
state 13; absolute power of 13
steel 84
Strabo 90
Strasburg 111
Suetonius 59, 67, 107
sugar 84
Sulla 75, 76
sulphur 84
Sweden 65
Swift, J. 22

Swiss 66, 114
Sylvius [Pope Pius II] 90
Syria 54, 64

Tacitus 80, 103, 106
tax, assessment 81; exemption 59; salt 63
taxation 61, 67, 88; proportional 13
Tiberius, Emperor 60, 75, 105
Tiberius II, Emperor 94
Timocrates 118
tin 84, 95, 97, 103, 122
Toledo 111
touchstone 104
Toulouse 11, 14, 17, 18, 20, 54, 55, 92; property register 55
tournois 114
Tourraine 102
Tours 54
trade 13, 26–8, 31, 67, 84–5, 89, 127; agreements 89; benefits of 27–8; loans 67; terms 25
Trajan, Emperor 83, 87
Tripoli 66
Trouillard, N. 12
Troyes 58; measure 58
Turks 72, 81, 86
Tuscany 68

unit of account 14–15
universalism 12
Unterval 114
Urbino 71
usury 59, 124

vair 54
Valencia 66, 113
Valois, House of 61
Varro, M. 75, 88
Venice 57, 64, 66, 81, 83, 97, 102, 107, 112–14
Venus 72
Vermandois 123
Vespasian, Emperor 69, 109, 118, 125
Villefranche de Rouergue 119
Villemor, Sieur de 122

Villeneuve d'Auvignon 119
vineyards 56, 88
Visconti, Bernabo 62; Galeazzo II 62; Gian Galeazzo 62; Valentina 62
vitriol 84

wage, daily 43, 45-7, 58, 80-1, 123
wages, building 16
waste 59, 68
water, displacement of 104
wax 84
West Indies 64, 71
wheat prices 16, 41-2, 53, 55, 58, 79, 88

wine prices 22, 41-3, 45, 53, 55, 64, 65, 68, 79, 84, 88-9
woad trade 65
woman's labour, cost of 58
wood, Brazil 84
wool trade 89
world market 28-9
Wurzburg 111

Yimocates 95

Zarate, Augustin de 64

PRIMARY SOURCES IN POLITICAL THOUGHT

This series makes available a number of the important but, until now, inaccessible texts in the history of political thought. Many of these have been overshadowed by longer or more famous works by the same authors, lost in the obscurity of periodical publication, never translated into English, or simply overlooked or neglected by modern scholars. The series presents the definitive editions of these texts, prepared to the highest standards of contemporary scholarship. These stand as permanent works of reference not only for professional scholars but also for researchers and the general reader.

Already Available

Liberalism, Democracy, and the State in Britain: Five Essays, 1862–1891
Edited and introduced by Julia Stapleton
ISBN 1 85506 534 7 : 168pp : Hb : £25.00 $40.00
ISBN 1 85506 535 5 : 168pp : Pb : £9.95 $15.95

Response to the Paradoxes of Malestroit
Jean Bodin
Translated by Henry Tudor and R. W. Dyson
Introduced by D. P. O'Brien
Notes by J. C. M. Starkey
ISBN 1 85506 532 0 : 177pp : Hb : £32.00 $48.00
ISBN 1 85506 533 9 : 177pp : Pb : £11.95 $19.95

Forthcoming Titles

On the Power of Emperors and Popes
William of Ockham
Translated and introduced by Annabelle Brett
August 1998
ISBN 1 85506 552 5 : Hb
ISBN 1 85506 553 3 : Pb

Forthcoming Titles

The Political Writings of John Wesley
Edited and introduced by Graham Maddox
August 1998
ISBN 1 85506 554 1 : Hb
ISBN 1 85506 555 X : Pb

Founder Editor

Henry Tudor

Editorial Board

R. W. Dyson, **Julia Stapleton** and **Peter Stirk**, all of the University of Durham.
The editors gratefully acknowledge the financial support of the **Publications Board of the University of Durham** in the preparation of this series.

Thoemmes Press

UK Office
11 Great George Street, Bristol, BS1 5RR, UK

USA Office
22883 Quicksilver Drive, Dulles, Virginia 20166, USA